SHOOTING UP

SHOOTING UP

COUNTERINSURGENCY AND THE WAR ON DRUGS

VANDA FELBAB-BROWN

BROOKINGS INSTITUTION PRESS

Washington, D.C.

Copyright © 2010
THE BROOKINGS INSTITUTION
1775 Massachusetts Avenue, N.W., Washington, D.C. 20036
www.brookings.edu

Library of Congress Cataloging-in-Publication data

Felbab-Brown, Vanda.
    Shooting up : counterinsurgency and the war on drugs / Vanda Felbab-Brown.
        p. cm.
    Includes bibliographical references and index.
    ISBN 978-0-8157-0328-0 (alk. paper)
    1. Drug traffic—Developing countries. 2. Drug control—Developing countries.
I. Title.
    HV5840.D44F45 2010
    363.4509172'4—dc22   2009040259

9 8 7 6 5 4 3 2 1

Printed on acid-free paper

Typeset in Sabon

Composition by Cynthia Stock
Silver Spring, Maryland

Printed by R. R. Donnelley
Harrisonburg, Virginia

To Jelena, Josef, and Seyom

CONTENTS

FOREWORD

America's single most acute military and diplomatic challenge has come to be known by a geographical neologism: "Afpak." The vocabulary of that conflict features another, more familiar term that has acquired totemic significance: "counterinsurgency." And defining *that* word requires another: "counternarcotics." That is the subject of Vanda Felbab-Brown's deeply knowledgeable, powerfully argued, and timely book.

In Vanda's cutting-edge work at Brookings, she has been influential in deepening the understanding in policy circles of the nexus between illicit narcotics and insurgency. In the summer of 2009, as casualties and controversy associated with Afpak mounted, her analysis and recommendations helped shaped a new shift in policy that emphasized not eradication of poppy crops, as before, but interdiction of drug traffickers, destruction of opium-processing facilities, and promotion of alternative agricultural development. Providing alternative livelihoods for those whose subsistence depends on poppy farming will continue to be key to the "hearts and minds" component of U.S. and NATO strategy.

The Taliban's exploitation of Afghanistan's drug economy is only one of many examples of the relationship between insurgency and illicit commerce, and Vanda knows many of those cases firsthand from fieldwork and interviews in Colombia, Peru, Burma, and India. She draws further on the cases of Northern Ireland, Turkey, and Mexico. She knows the reality on troubled ground well enough to take account of a factor too often ignored in the midst of polarized politics and the heat of battle: human security. If the innocent bystanders—those caught between insurgency and counterinsurgency—feel themselves victimized by the latter, they are more likely to be tools of the former. She makes a pragmatic as well as compassionate case for tending to the interests of the marginalized people who are the initial producers of the illegal goods and who become caught up in the military struggle.

Brookings prides itself on fact-based research that leads to sound judgments and fresh ideas of use to policymakers—and those who are charged with carrying out policy. It's hard to imagine a better example of those values put to work in an urgent and important cause than this book.

STROBE TALBOTT
President
Brookings Institution

Washington, D.C.
October 2009

ACKNOWLEDGMENTS

No strategies for countering the pernicious relationship between illicit economies and large-scale violence can succeed unless they are based on a valid understanding of the sources of that relationship and what sustains it. Valid answers depend ultimately on the appropriateness of the questions. It is especially for their insistence on the latter and for their guidance on designing well-targeted research that I am forever indebted to my mentors at MIT—to Kenneth Oye for emphasizing the structure of the incentives of the actors involved and the often-surprising nature of the coalitions to which such incentives give rise; to Barry Posen for stressing the analytical focus on the distribution of material power and its inescapable effects; to Chappell Lawson for insisting that close attention be paid to local socioeconomic structures and cultural and institutional settings; and to Roger Petersen for stressing the complex, including the psychological, motivations of insurgents, their opponents, and the wider population—and also for his counsel on the tricks of the trade of fieldwork.

My fellow students in the Ph.D. program at MIT also deserve special thanks for vigorously debating the issues with me during the dissertation-writing phase, as do the directors and scholars at Harvard's Belfer Center for Science and International Relations, where rigorous exchanges on the logic of anyone's inquiry (including mine) made me more intellectually conscious of what I was doing.

The transformation of what was initially an academic study into a continuing policy-oriented project, of which this book is an installment, has benefitted from highly informative consultations not only with scholars in the two centers of research with which I have been affiliated since locating in Washington—the Brookings Institution and Georgetown University's Security Studies Program—but also with the wide range of distinguished experts, policymakers, and informed laypersons who have generously shared their insights with me. They are too numerous to list here, but I do want to single out some of the individuals with whom I have had invaluable discussions of counternarcotics policies and dynamics in specific regions and some of whom also have facilitated my fieldwork: David Mansfield, Marvin Weinbaum, Ronald Neumann, Peter Reuter, Mauricio Romero, Pierre-Arnaud Chouvy, Kevin Healy, Francisco Thoumi, Mark Schneider, Michael Shifter, Coletta Youngers, Adam Isacson, Bruce Riedel, Michael O'Hanlon, Carol Graham, Cynthia McClintock, David Scott Palmer, John Bailey, Bruce Hoffman, and María Clemencia Ramírez.

And then there are my bosses at Brookings—each a distinguished scholar-statesman—who have been essential to my work. Carlos Pascual, Brookings vice president and director of Foreign Policy until taking up his post as U.S. ambassador to Mexico in August 2009, with his knowledge of how the local rubs up against the global and how they can mutually enhance each other, inspired me to see the possibility of progress on seemingly intractable issues and showed me how to create the procedural mechanisms for moving policy in the right direction. His exchanges with me on which constraints of reality can be bent, how power can be responsibly harnessed, and the possibilities for symbiotically melding global affairs with attention to people's basic, everyday needs have strongly reinforced my determination to persist in working on issues that have an impact on both the international realm and peoples' personal lives. I also appreciate the help of Martin Indyk, Carlos's successor as Brookings vice president and director of Foreign Policy, who facilitated the publication process for this book and has encouraged my subsequent research and writing on those issues. And it has been especially gratifying to work on important public policy issues at a prestigious institution whose president, Strobe Talbott, a former deputy secretary of the Department of State and an exemplary scholar and writer, has a substantive and detailed interest in one's work and is very supportive of it.

I also want to recognize the importance of certain members of Brookings's professional staff: Charlotte Baldwin—the hidden power in the Foreign Policy program—for making sure that the things that needed to happen did in fact take place; Peggy Knudson and Kristina Server for tireless and crucial support, along with the rest of the Brookings administrative staff; and Gail Chalef for helping to bring attention to the ideas in the book and spinoff writings.

Special thanks go to Laura Cardona Blanco, my former student at Georgetown University, for highly skilled and multifaceted help as a research assistant.

The resulting book also owes a great deal to the professionals at the Brookings Press: to Mary Kwak for the surgical precision and wherewithal to cut more than a third of the manuscript and still not lose either its essence or its detail; to Eileen Hughes for fine-tuning the narrative with a skilled ear; to Inge Lockwood for meticulous proofreading; to Susan Woollen and her team of designers for helping to generate the striking cover, which recalls David Hockney and Paul Outerbridge; and to Susan Soldavin, Robert Faherty, and the rest of Brookings Press team for helping to promote the ideas.

In an effort like this, there are various behind-the-scenes facilitators. They include Miriam Villegas and the intrepid people at Tropical Birding: Keith, Christian, Richard, Renzo, Rob, Peter, and Yvonne, who often were indispensible in mobilizing local contacts and networks deep in the jungles and mountains of the world and getting me into remote and marginalized areas infused with illegality and violence. To avoid compromising their safety, I cannot reveal the names of many other local fixers and enablers in crime-ridden ghettoes and illicit crop fields, but I am no less grateful for their critical assistance.

My deep thanks go too to the many people around the world whom I interviewed for this project. They include committed government officials and representatives of international organizations as well as nongovernmental experts. But they also include people caught up in terrible circumstances—in violence, poverty, and illegality—who, though they have few opportunities to escape, are nevertheless determined to be agents, not simply victims of their lives. Many talked to me at great risk to themselves and to those that they care for. What I can offer in return is this book, whose purpose is to find ways to mitigate conflict, reduce illegality, and enhance U.S. and local security in a way that also addresses their needs and strengthens their human security.

I am also grateful to Vera Regulova and Amy Wagenfeld and Jeff and David for varied and unwavering support over many years.

My mom, Jelena, deserves very special affection and admiration for being willing, despite her anxious concerns, to put up with her daughter's runs in the wild. I wish that my father, Josef, were alive to take pride in this product of his daughter's adventures, for he instilled in me from my youngest years a passionate love for the wild in its many forms and a sympathetic eye toward all of its creatures but also taught me how to defend myself in times of danger.

Finally, my deepest thanks go to my husband, Seyom Brown. He has been with me from the inception of this project and his support has covered all its possible (and sometimes impossible) facets. Not only has he been my most valued interlocutor and critic, he also has been called upon frequently to take on the role of courageous bodyguard, impromptu doctor of tropical diseases, and driver of various vehicular and animal forms of transport—and to be himself a hardy beast of burden, carrying supplies into the wild. His commitment to me has been so strong that even at times when he could not accompany me, the risks to me were high, and the costs to him substantial, he never stood in the way of my doing what he knew was my passion. The bond between us has always carried me through the toughest moments and immeasurably enriches my life.

I and Brookings are grateful to the Belfer Center for Science and International Affairs; the Carroll Wilson Program at MIT; the Royal Ministry of Foreign Affairs, Norway; and the Liberty Mutual Group for their generous support for this project.

The views expressed in this book are mine solely and should not be ascribed to any of the persons or organizations acknowledged above or to the trustees, officers, or other staff members of the Brookings Institution.

ONE

ILLICIT ECONOMIES AND BELLIGERENTS

A story from Afghanistan's rural south, the region that has been at the core of the Taliban's effort to regain control of the country, suggests the complexity of the relationship between illicit economic activity and military conflict. Taliban insurgents had hammered up posters offering to protect farmers' opium poppy fields against government attempts at eradication, with a cell phone number to call if the eradicators appeared. In one village near Kandahar, the villagers caught on to a counternarcotics sting operation in which an agent posed as an opium trader.[1] After his visits to the village to buy opium were followed with raids on the villagers' crops, the villagers phoned the Taliban. The Taliban instructed them to invite the suspected informant back, captured him, and forced him to call in the police. When the police arrived in the village, the Taliban ambushed them, killing several policemen, including the police chief. The Taliban scored a success against the government and limited its presence in the area. Equally important, this episode fortified the relationship between the local population and the Taliban, even though the village residents had previously shown no pro-Taliban feelings.

The Kandahar story is just one example of how many belligerent groups—whether terrorists, insurgents, paramilitaries, or local warlords—have penetrated the international drug trade and other illicit economies. Realizing that belligerent groups derive large financial resources from such activities, governments have increasingly turned to suppressing illicit economies, not only as a way to curtail criminal activity but also as a strategy to defeat belligerents. Yet often those efforts not only fail to eliminate

1

or significantly weaken belligerent groups but also impede government counterinsurgency/counterterrorism efforts.

Much of U.S. anti-narcotics policy abroad is based on the premise that the suppression of drug production will promote both anti-drug and counterterrorist goals. This book challenges this "narcoguerrilla" premise. I show that, far from being complementary, U.S. anti-narcotics and counterinsurgency policies are frequently at odds. Crop eradication—the linchpin of U.S. anti-narcotics strategy—often fails to significantly diminish the physical capabilities of belligerents. Worse, it frequently enhances their legitimacy and popular support.

DEALING WITH ILLICIT ECONOMIES:
A PERVASIVE PROBLEM

Illegal drugs, the predominant focus of this book, are one example of a larger class of illicit goods, services, and economic activities. Other illegal or semi-legal commodities include conflict diamonds, special minerals, weapons, alcohol, wildlife, human beings, human organs, toxic and industrial waste, and components of nuclear, chemical, or biological weapons.[2] Illegal or semi-legal activities include gambling, prostitution, illicit trading in legal goods, document forging, piracy, and maritime fraud. Illicit economies thus encompass economic commodities, services, and transactions the production or provision of which is either completely prohibited by governments or international regimes (or both) or partially proscribed unless their production or provision complies with economic or political regulations, including requirements for special licenses, certification, payment of taxes, and so forth. Such activities tend to be highly lucrative, in substantial part because of their illicitness.

Illicit economies exist in some form virtually everywhere. For example, some part of the illegal drug economy—whether production, trafficking, or distribution—is present in almost every country. The principal drug-growing and drug-refining countries and regions are the Andean countries of Peru, Bolivia, and Colombia; Mexico; Afghanistan, Pakistan, and Central Asia in the Golden Crescent; Myanmar and Laos in the Golden Triangle; and Morocco. Turkey and Hong Kong are crucial refining and transshipment locales. The United States and Canada are major producers of marijuana and methamphetamines. At various times in history,

China, Thailand, Lebanon, and Jamaica have also been major producers of illicit drugs.

The book specifically focuses on *illicit* markets, not markets and resources in general. As distinct from licit markets, illicit markets have several crucial characteristics: they offer very high profits, and because governments and legitimate businesses cannot openly participate in them, outside-the-law actors, such as insurgent groups, can capture a significant share of the market. Crucially, governments frequently feel obliged to destroy the illicit economy, thus allowing belligerents to offer themselves as its protectors and obtain the support of the local population that depends on the illicit economy.

In this book, I discuss a broad range of illicit activities, including illegal logging (Peru, Afghanistan, and Burma); extortion (Colombia); and illegal traffic in legal goods (Afghanistan). However, my primary focus is the interaction between the illicit drug economy and military conflict. Drugs are the main focus because they best epitomize the nexus between crime and insurgency, because drugs are by far the most lucrative of all illicit economies, and because narcoterrorism—rather than "wildlife terrorism," for example—dominates the attention of policymakers. Former attorney general John Ashcroft gave words to a common view when he said that "terrorism and drugs go together like rats and the bubonic plague. They thrive in the same conditions, support each other, and feed off each other."[3]

The Organization for Economic Cooperation and Development calculates that as much as $122 billion is spent every year in Europe and the United States on heroin, cocaine, and marijuana.[4] Conservative estimates of the retail value of the global trade in illicit narcotics reach around $300 billion to $500 billion annually.[5] The drug trade is where the money is—both for belligerent groups that exploit the trade and for governments that devote billions of dollars annually to fight the trade, reduce drug consumption at home, and deprive belligerents of drug profits.

The existence of an illicit economy, while almost always closely associated with a criminal organization or syndicate, does not by itself give rise to terrorists, warlords, or insurgents. Yet when belligerent groups penetrate existing illicit economies (or set up new ones), the resulting interaction profoundly affects their means and strategies and even, under some circumstances, their goals and identities. Examples of belligerent groups that have exploited the drug trade include the Taliban and the Northern Alliance in Afghanistan; the FARC (Revolutionary Armed Forces of Colombia), AUC (United Self-Defense Forces of Colombia), and ELN (National Liberation Army) in Colombia; the Shining Path and the MRTA (Tupac Amaru Revolutionary Movement) in Peru; the Real IRA (Real Irish Republican Army) in Great Britain; the KLA (Kosovo Liberation Army) in Yugoslavia; Hezbollah in Lebanon; the PKK (Kurdistan's Workers Party) in Turkey; and ETA (Basque Homeland and Freedom) in Spain. Appendix A provides a more complete listing of groups.

THE NARCOTICS TRADE AND INSURGENCY: THE CONVENTIONAL VIEW

U.S. government thinking has been dominated by the conventional view of the nexus between illicit economies and military conflict, which starts with the premise that belligerent groups derive large financial profits from illegal activities.[6] Those profits fund increases in the military capabilities of terrorists, warlords, and insurgents and a corresponding decrease in the relative capability of government forces. Consequently, governments should focus on eliminating belligerents' physical resources by eliminating the illicit economies on which they rely. For example, President Álvaro Uribe of Colombia has argued that "if Colombia would not have drugs, it would not have terrorists."[7] Or as one World Bank official told me, "If we destroy the coca, there won't be any more war in Colombia."[8]

The conventional view frequently maintains that whether or not the belligerent groups ever had any ideological goals, once they interact with the illicit economy, they lose all but pecuniary motivations and become indistinguishable from ordinary criminals. In many cases, they partner or merge with drug trafficking organizations. Profiting immensely from the illicit economy, they have no incentive to achieve a negotiated settlement with the government.[9] Aggressive law enforcement—principally through eradication of the illicit economy—thus becomes the government's only option.

Advocates argue that as an added benefit, eradication will reduce drug consumption in market destination countries, such as the United States. For example, the 2003 *International Narcotics Control Strategy Report,* issued by the Department of State, states that the closer we can attack to the source, the greater the likelihood of halting the flow of drugs altogether. Crop control is by far the most cost-effective means of cutting supply. If we destroy crops or force them to remain unharvested, no drugs will enter the system. . . . Theoretically, with no drug crops to harvest, no cocaine or heroin could enter the distribution chain; nor would there be any need for costly enforcement and interdiction operations.[10]

In short, the conventional government view is based on three key premises: belligerents make money from illicit economies; the destruction of the illicit economy is both necessary and optimal for defeating belligerents because it will eliminate their critical resources; and belligerents who participate in the illicit economy should be treated as no different from criminals who participate in the illicit economy. While this approach is especially prevalent in government circles, it is rooted in academic work on narcoterrorism, exemplified by Rachel Ehrenfeld's book *How Terrorism Is Financed and How to Stop It.*[11] The conventional view is also informed by the "greed" literature on civil wars, which focuses on how belligerents profit from conflict;[12] the emerging literature on the crime-terror nexus, which argues that the war against terrorism can no longer be separated from the fight against transnational crime;[13] and the cost-benefit analysis of counterinsurgency, which puts stopping the flow of resources to insurgents ahead of winning hearts and minds.[14]

THE POLITICAL CAPITAL OF ILLICIT ECONOMIES

I argue that the conventional narcoguerrilla view is strikingly incomplete and leads to ineffective and even counterproductive policy recommendations. It fails to recognize that belligerents derive much more than just large financial profits from their sponsorship of illicit economies. They also obtain freedom of action and, crucially, legitimacy and support from the local population—what I call *political capital*. By supporting the illicit economy, belligerents both increase their military capability and build political support, whereas belligerents who attempt to destroy the illicit economy suffer on both accounts. That insight lies at the heart of my political capital model of illicit economies in the context of violent conflict, which is illustrated and supported by the case studies presented in this volume.

Four factors largely determine the extent to which belligerents can benefit from their involvement with the illicit economy: the state of the overall economy; the character of the illicit economy; the presence or absence of thuggish traffickers; and the government response to the illicit economy.

—The state of the overall economy—whether it is poor or rich—determines the availability of alternative sources of income and the number of people in a region who depend on the illicit economy for their livelihood.

—The character of the illicit economy—whether it is labor intensive or not—determines the extent to which the illicit economy provides employment for the local population.

—The presence or absence of thuggish traffickers and the government response to the illicit economy—which can range from suppression to a laissez-faire approach to legalization—determines the extent to which the population depends on the belligerents to preserve and regulate the illicit economy.

In a nutshell, supporting the illicit economy will generate the most political capital for belligerents when the state of the overall economy is poor, the illicit economy is labor intensive, thuggish traffickers are active in the illicit economy, and the government has adopted a harsh strategy, such as eradication.

The political capital approach is inspired in part by academic critiques of the war on drugs. Like many critics of current anti-narcotics efforts, I believe that the war on drugs is failing both at home and abroad. Aggressive supply-side campaigns have failed to stem the flow of drugs into consuming nations and are impoverishing and radicalizing rural populations in producing nations.[15] However, I extend my critique by focusing on the multiple ways in which the war on drugs can allow belligerents to obtain political capital. In addition, I identify the critical factors that shape the size of their gains.

The political capital model builds on the hearts-and-minds approach to counterinsurgency, which emphasizes the importance of the "legitimacy game" for both insurgents and the government.[16] It is informed by the large and sophisticated literature on peasant rebellions,[17] and it draws on academic studies of the relationship among terrorism, legitimacy, and power. As Conor Cruise O'Brien puts it, "the power of terrorism is through political legitimacy, winning acceptance in the eyes of a significant population and discrediting the government's legitimacy."[18] Richard Rubenstein similarly argues, "It is a myth that terrorist groups can be 'crushed in the egg' by cutting off their external sources of supply. It is the local political base that makes the terrorist organization or breaks it. Politically isolated groups turn to banditry or disappear because of political weakness, not from a shortage of materiel."[19] In order to win the war on terror, governments must respond with policies that deprive belligerents of their legitimacy and consolidate the government's popular support. The same is true, I argue, of counterinsurgency in the context of an illicit economy.

This model has direct implications for the policy options facing governments. It suggests not only that *eradication* of illicit crops is unlikely to weaken belligerents severely but also that this strategy frequently is counterproductive, particularly under the conditions outlined above. Eradication alienates farmers from the government and reduces their willingness to provide intelligence on belligerents. Thus, eradication increases the political capital of belligerents without accomplishing its promised goal of significantly reducing their military capabilities. *Laissez-faire,* on the other hand—tolerating the cultivation of illicit crops during conflict— leaves belligerents' resources unaffected but may decrease their political capital. *Interdiction*—interception of illicit shipments, destruction of labs, and capture of traffickers—may be even more effective: it can decrease belligerents' financial resources without increasing their political capital because it does not directly and visibly threaten the population's livelihood. But because interdiction, like eradication, is extremely resource intensive and difficult to carry out effectively, it is unlikely to bankrupt belligerents to the point of defeating them. Finally, when feasible, *licensing* the illicit economy—for example, India and Turkey license opium poppy cultivation for the production of medical opiates—can reduce belligerents' financial resources and political capital while increasing the government's.

THE CASE STUDIES

In this book, I examine the relationship among illicit economies, military conflict, and political capital through detailed case studies of three countries: Peru, Colombia, and Afghanistan. I also more briefly explore the cases of Northern Ireland and Burma and bring in illustrations from India, Mexico, and Turkey. (Case selection is explained in detail in appendix C.) For each of the principal case studies as well as for Burma and India, I conducted months of field research in each country, interviewing government officials, military officers, the population involved in illicit economies, and, as much as possible, belligerents and drug traffickers. (Some had been captured; some were still at large.) Although the book draws heavily on those interviews, the citations are kept vague to safeguard the interviewees. Even when the physical security of those I interviewed was not in question, as in the case of government officials and representatives of international organizations, I agreed to quote them without attribution due to the politically sensitive nature of the topic. In each of the main case studies, I ask the following questions:

—*How does access* to illicit economies affect the strength of belligerent groups?

—*What conditions* influence the size and scope of the benefits that belligerent groups derive from their interaction with illicit economies?

—*How do government policies toward the illicit economy* affect the strength of belligerents and ultimately limit, contain, or exacerbate military conflicts?

The three main cases—each containing poor regions wracked by violent conflict—represent the most significant examples of global efforts over the past three decades to combat narcotics production. They also represent some of the most significant violent conflicts of the past thirty years. Governments in these three countries have faced an especially stark trade-off between their desire to limit belligerents' resources and the need to win the hearts and minds of the population.

In Peru—the world's largest producer of coca leaf until the mid-1990s—two leftist guerrilla groups, the Shining Path and the MRTA, became deeply involved in the illicit narcotics economy in the 1980s. Involvement brought the Shining Path financial and political gains and helped it become one of the most formidable leftist guerrilla movements in Latin America, one that nearly toppled the government in the early 1990s. Throughout that period, shifts in counternarcotics policy, which alternated among eradication, interdiction, and laissez-faire, had a critical impact on the success of the government's efforts to combat the insurgency.

Colombia, the world's largest producer of cocaine, is frequently presented as the poster child for the conventional government view of drugs and insurgency, as illustrated by the earlier quote from President Álvaro Uribe. The country has seen various belligerent groups, notably the leftist group FARC, expand dramatically as a result of their participation in the drug trade. Colombia has also been the scene of the most intense and prolonged aerial spraying campaign in history—an effort that is often credited for bringing about the decline of the FARC. However, a detailed examination challenges the conventional view. Eradication of coca cultivation did little to weaken the FARC; the success of the counterinsurgency campaign can be traced instead to direct military pressure.

Afghanistan has been the largest producer of opiates in the world since the mid-1990s. Since the mid-2000s, production of opium there has reached levels unprecedented in the modern history of the drug trade. Over the same period, Afghanistan has become one of the most important locations in the U.S. struggle against terrorism and, along with Iraq, its main theater of counterinsurgency operations against the resurgent Taliban, which has been deeply involved in the drug trade despite first proscribing it as un-Islamic. Thus, for the United States, Afghanistan has come to epitomize the nexus of drugs and insurgency. It illustrates the extreme difficulty of state-building in a country where an illicit economy constitutes the dominant economic sector and where a multitude of actors across all segments of society (insurgents, terrorists, tribes, government officials and representatives, and the rural population) participate in the illicit economy.

Much of the internal dynamics of the nexus of drugs and insurgency in Afghanistan is identical or analogous to the dynamics in Peru and Colombia. But Afghanistan greatly surpasses the two Latin American countries when it comes to the size of the illicit economy—its economic significance in terms of the number of people that it employs and as a percentage of the country's GDP—and the region's geostrategic significance for U.S. vital national interests.

During the 1980s, U.S. officials saw Peru as one of the most important fronts in the fight against communism in Latin America, but the outcome of the confrontation between the Shining Path and the government did not threaten U.S. security. Since the mid-1990s, Colombia has been one of Washington's staunchest allies in the Southern Hemisphere, and the United States has a strong interest in reducing and hopefully ending the violent conflict there. Because Colombia is the principal supplier of drugs to the United States, combating its drug economy also is an important U.S. goal. But once again, the primary geostrategic and security interests of the United States (including the prevention of attacks on the U.S. homeland and critical assets abroad) are not greatly affected by the outcome of the Colombian struggle.

In Afghanistan, however, the drug-conflict nexus impinges directly on U.S. vital geostrategic and security interests. Al Qaeda conducted the 9-11 attacks from Afghanistan with the acquiescence of the Taliban; subsequently, along with NATO partners, the United States deployed tens of thousands of troops to Afghanistan to defeat the Taliban regime and support a domestically and internationally accountable Afghan state. The failure of the U.S. effort to defeat the resurgent Taliban in Afghanistan would embolden not only al Qaeda, but anti-American jihadists throughout the world. It would make it very hard to stabilize nuclear-armed Pakistan, which faces its own form of the Taliban and other jihadi insurgents. It would pose a significant threat to the viability of NATO, thus generating pressure in the United States to reassess its alliances. And finally, developments in Afghanistan will have great repercussions for relations among Pakistan, India, China, Russia, Iran, Saudi Arabia, and the United States.

BEYOND MILITARY CONFLICT

This study is concerned primarily with the effect of illicit economies on military conflict. However, it is important to recognize that illicit economic activities, such as the burgeoning production of drugs, have other profound consequences for states. A large-scale illicit economy threatens the state by giving criminal organizations the means to enter politics and to corrupt and undermine the democratic process. Thanks to the financial resources and political capital generated by the illicit economy, leading drug traffickers frequently experience great success in politics. They are able to secure official positions of power as well as wield influence from behind the scenes. Moreover, as politicians bankrolled with illicit money achieve greater success, established political actors are tempted to participate in the illicit economy, leading to endemic corruption. Afghanistan, Guatemala, and El Salvador serve as examples of that dynamic.

Large illicit economies dominated by powerful traffickers also have pernicious effects on the quality of law enforcement and the judicial system. As the illicit economy grows, the government's investigative capacity diminishes. Traffickers increasingly appear to be above the law. Frequently they turn to violence to deter and avoid prosecution, killing or bribing prosecutors, judges, and witnesses.[20] Inevitably the credibility of law enforcement and the courts and, more broadly, the government's authority decline. Colombia in the late 1980s and Mexico today provide powerful reminders of how extensive criminal networks can corrupt and paralyze law enforcement and how high levels of violent criminality can devastate the judicial system.

In addition, illicit economies have important negative economic effects. On the one hand, drug cultivation and processing generate employment for the poor rural population, which frequently numbers in the hundreds of thousands; such activities may even facilitate upward mobility. But a burgeoning drug economy also contributes to inflation and undermines the stability of a nation's currency, thereby harming legitimate, export-oriented industries. It also encourages real estate speculation and displaces production of legitimate goods and services. Since the drug economy is more profitable than legitimate production and requires less infrastructure and investment, frequently the local population is uninterested in participating—or unable to participate profitably—in legal forms of economic activity. The illicit economy can thus lead to a form of "Dutch disease"—the name given to the situation in which a boom in an isolated sector of the economy pushes up land and labor costs and thereby causes stagnation in other core sectors. Finally, it appears that the small share of the final profits captured by drug-producing countries is used mainly for unproductive consumption by the traffickers rather than productive economic investment.[21]

This economic effect is not a universal rule. In Peru, for example, I encountered a village in the La Convención–Lares area where the population was able to invest illegal coca profits into a local school, medical facilities, an electricity generator, and an ecotourist lodge.[22]

PUBLIC POLICY IMPLICATIONS

Most government and many academic analyses emphasize that the drug trade and other illicit activities help finance terrorism, insurgencies, and civil wars. Either the desire for financial resources is seen as the cause of military conflict or the financial resources are viewed as a means of prolonging the military conflict. The major policy recommendation derived from such analyses is to suppress illicit economies in order to deprive belligerents of resources. To the extent that belligerents' political gains are mentioned at all, they appear in country-specific critiques of the war on drugs, with little or no effort to offer a systematic model of the political gains that belligerent groups derive from their participation in illicit economies.

This book seeks to fill that analytical void by showing how belligerents reap not only financial gains but also freedom of action—an important component of military capabilities—and, crucially, political capital from their role in the illicit economy. The belligerents obtain political capital by fulfilling several functions. They protect a reliable and lucrative source of income for the local population against government efforts to suppress the illicit economy. They protect the population from brutal and unreliable traffickers. And with the financial profits from the illicit economy, they provide otherwise absent social services to the local population.

More broadly, this book contributes to the growing understanding of the dynamics of counterinsurgency and counterterrorism. It joins the debate about how best to defeat insurgencies and terrorist groups: whether by attempting to limit belligerents' physical resources or by focusing on winning the hearts and minds of the population. The book reveals the extraordinary difficulties and low rates of success associated with efforts to deprive belligerents of resources by suppressing illicit economies and underscores the host of adaptations available to belligerents, producers of illicit commodities, and traffickers. Instead of bankrupting belligerents, suppression efforts typically fail to make a significant difference in their physical capabilities while antagonizing the population that depends on the illicit economy. That is true in particular of harsher suppression methods and under certain theoretically specified conditions, as the following chapters show.

TWO

THE POLITICAL CAPITAL MODEL OF ILLICIT ECONOMIES

As a corrective to the conventional narcoterrorism view of the nexus between illicit economies and military conflict, I present a richer, more complex framework—the political capital model—that explains how belligerents' involvement in the illicit economy affects their strength and how government policies toward the illicit economy affect the conduct and outcome of conflict. This model describes the strategic interactions among belligerents, traffickers, the population, and the government in the context of illicit economies. It also specifies a set of factors that affect the size and scope of the gains that belligerents derive from the illicit economy.

The conventional narcoterrorism view focuses narrowly on the financial and thereby military benefits that belligerents gain from participating in illegal economic activities. The political capital model moves beyond that view to argue that a belligerent group's involvement in the illicit economy affects both components of belligerent strength: *military capability* and *political capital*. Military capability includes physical resources (money, weapons, and number of fighters) and freedom of action. Political capital consists of perceived legitimacy (the population's belief that the belligerents' actions are justified) and popular support (the population's voluntary provision of supplies, shelter, and intelligence to the belligerents).

The relationship between a belligerent group's involvement in the illicit economy and its strength is mediated by four conditions, both structural and actor-determined: the state of the overall economy, the character of the illicit economy, the presence or absence of thuggish traffickers, and the

FIGURE 2-1. *The Political Capital Model of Illicit Economies and Violent Conflict*

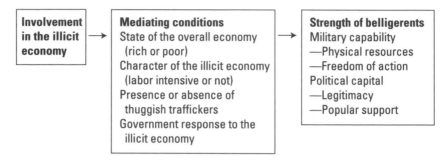

government response to the illicit economy (see figure 2-1). This chapter examines each of those variables and relationships in depth.

I argue on the basis of my analysis that eradication of illicit crops has dubious effects on the capabilities of belligerents and that it is extremely unlikely to weaken them severely. However, eradication does alienate the local population from the government and hinders the government's intelligence-gathering efforts. In short, eradication increases the political capital of the belligerents without significantly weakening their military capability.

BELLIGERENTS' INVOLVEMENT IN THE ILLICIT ECONOMY

The belligerents that are the subject of this analysis include any nongovernment armed group—including insurgents, terrorists, paramilitaries, and warlords—regardless of political orientation. As used here, the term does not include nonpolitical criminal gangs or syndicates. I do not assume any particular motivation on their part, beyond the desire to avoid defeat. Similarly, I assume only that the government seeks to suppress violent opposition and that traffickers seek to profit from the illicit economy.

Belligerents' involvement in the illicit economy can be positive or negative, or there can be no involvement. *Positive involvement* means that the belligerents sponsor the illicit economy.[1] It includes protection of the illicit economy against other actors, as well as direct forms of participation, such as trafficking. *Negative involvement* means that the belligerents seek to destroy the illicit economy through such policies as prohibition or eradication. *Non-involvement,* or neutrality, means that the belligerents have a laissez-faire policy toward the illicit economy; they seek neither to protect nor to destroy it.

Positive involvement in the illicit economy increases both aspects of belligerent strength: military capability and political capital. Negative involvement in the illicit economy decreases the strength of belligerents along those dimensions. Non-involvement leaves their strength unaffected.

Involvement in the Illicit Economy and Military Capability

The relationship between a belligerent group's involvement in the illicit economy and its military capability is relatively straightforward, although sometimes underappreciated. The following discussion briefly examines how such involvement affects belligerents' physical resources, freedom of action, and political capital and highlights the influence of the four conditions noted above.

PHYSICAL RESOURCES

The financial profits that belligerents reap from involvement in the illicit economy can range from tens of millions to hundreds of millions of dollars a year. The magnitude depends on the extent of a group's involvement in the illicit economy, the existence of competing "sponsors" of the illicit economy, and international market prices for the illicit commodities produced. Profits typically increase as belligerents become more deeply involved in various aspects of the illicit economy—for example, as they move from simply taxing the growers of illegal crops to providing protection and safe airstrips to drug traffickers, taxing precursor agents, and getting involved in money exchange and laundering. Profits also increase as the number of other actors capable of fulfilling such functions declines.

Profits can be used both to expand the range of weapons and to increase the numbers of fighters that a belligerent group has its disposal. For example, as shown in the chapter on Peru, before the communist guerrilla group the Shining Path managed to tap into the drug trade, it had to rely on attacking police outposts and commercial mining operations to obtain handguns and dynamite, its only weapons. Once the guerrilla group began to profit from drugs, it was able to procure more sophisticated weapons such as machine guns, G-3 and FAL automatic rifles, and U.S.-made hand grenades and mortars.[2] Moreover, it could afford to pay its fighters a salary and hire a far greater number of combatants.

FREEDOM OF ACTION

By allowing belligerent groups to procure weapons and other materials through the market, involvement in the illicit economy enables the groups to optimize their tactics and strategies in pursuit of their larger goals. That freedom of action is a crucial component of belligerent strength that is ignored by the conventional view. Belligerents without ready access to cash typically devote great effort to attacking isolated military outposts and police stations to obtain basic small arms and ammunition and to robbing banks and farms to obtain money and food. Such activities, though they have little overall impact, consume valuable time, deplete the groups' energy, divert them from attacking more strategic targets with greater political and military impact, and expose them to the dangers of being detected, having their weapons confiscated, and being captured or killed by law enforcement agents or private security guards.

Once belligerent groups solve their procurement and logistics problems by tapping into the drug trade or other illicit economies, they can take on larger military units or attack high-impact, high-visibility civilian targets that do not bring them immediate material benefits. Or they can continue with hit-and-run operations against small military units, but choose their targets with larger strategic goals in mind. Access to illicit markets can therefore greatly accelerate the process of transforming a ragtag band of insurgents that hides in caves trying to make Molotov cocktails into a formidable strategic force.

Participation in the illicit economy can also limit belligerents' freedom of action by making it necessary for them to defend the illicit economy against government action. A belligerent group's freedom to retreat from drug cultivation territory, for example, can be compromised by its perceived need to defend coca fields. However, that constraint is a matter of choice, not a matter of necessity. If the belligerent group does not retreat in order to protect the fields, it does so because it chooses such a strategy, not because it lacks the capacity to adopt another strategy. To return to the example of the Shining Path, before tapping into the drug trade, it dissipated tremendous amounts of time and energy attacking police outposts, mines, and farms. As a result, it was unable to mount any large-scale operations against government and military targets. Once its procurement and logistics problems were solved through positive involvement in the drug trade, it could concentrate on military operations of real value and take on actual military combat units.

Involvement in the Illicit Economy and Political Capital

Belligerents can gain substantial political capital as well as military resources by becoming positively involved in illicit economies. By political capital I mean principally two things: legitimacy—the belief among local residents that the belligerents' actions are beneficial and justified; and popular support—residents' willingness to provide supplies, shelter, and intelligence for the belligerent group. Among the components of popular support, willingness to withhold intelligence on the belligerents from the government—or to supply intelligence on government forces to the belligerents—is perhaps the most critical. But in extreme cases, the population may go even further, engaging in riots and military actions on behalf of the belligerents and against the government.

As are physical resources and freedom of action, legitimacy and popular support are closely linked, but they are not identical. The population may see a belligerent group as legitimate, for example, but hesitate to provide it with support due to the risk of government reprisal or the belief that the belligerents will ultimately be defeated.[3]

HOW DO BELLIGERENTS GAIN POLITICAL CAPITAL?

Many factors shape a belligerent group's ability to win legitimacy and popular support, including its ideology, ethnicity, relative brutality, and strength relative to that of the government. But another crucial building block is its ability to feed, protect, and serve the local population. In poor rural areas, sponsorship of the illicit economy often allows belligerents to quickly demonstrate their power and expose the government's unwillingness or inability to provide for the population's needs. By protecting the illicit economy, belligerents can protect the local population's livelihood from government efforts to suppress it. They also can protect farmers from brutal and unreliable traffickers, who frequently pay the local population for their illicit products on one corner but then rob them on another and kill farmers who fail to deliver their promised quotas, even if the failure resulted from government eradication efforts. Moreover, belligerents can bargain with traffickers for better prices on the farmers' behalf. Similarly, if several belligerent groups are involved in the illicit economy, belligerents from one group can protect the illicit economy against another group if it seeks to destroy the illicit economy or is less protective of the peasants' interests and more closely aligned with the traffickers.

TABLE 2-1. *Benefits That Belligerents and the Local Population Obtain from Each Other*

Benefits that belligerents provide to the local population
Reliable source of livelihood
Better prices from traffickers
Protection from the government
Protection from traffickers
Protection from other belligerent groups
Otherwise absent social services

Benefits that the local population provides to belligerents
Denial of intelligence on belligerents to government units
Provision of intelligence on government units to belligerents
Denial of intelligence on belligerents to opposing belligerent groups
Provision of intelligence on opposing belligerent groups to belligerents
Provision of shelter, supplies, and safe houses
Riots and military action on behalf of belligerents and against the government
Military action against opposing belligerent groups

In addition, with profits from the illicit economy, belligerent groups can cease to extort food and supplies from the local population and instead provide otherwise absent social services, such as health clinics and transportation infrastructure. They also can get credit for being nationalists by serving as protectors and sponsors of the illicit economy in cases in which it is threatened by a foreign power. In short, belligerents function as security providers and economic and political regulators. Successful positive involvement in the illicit economy thus allows belligerents to act as protostates. Table 2-1 summarizes how belligerent groups derive political capital from illicit economies and shows the benefits that they deliver to the population and the payoffs that they obtain.

How many of the security and regulatory functions belligerents actually provide is determined both by factors that are partially outside the control of the belligerents, such as the presence or absence of traffickers (discussed in detail below), and by the belligerents' own choices and policies. For example, groups motivated primarily by the desire for economic profit may provide fewer social services than politically motivated groups. As shown in chapter 4, in the early 1980s Colombian paramilitary groups, which functioned essentially as bodyguards for the major drug cartels, did not court the population. They had no political objectives and participated in the illicit economy for profit only; hence they provided no regulatory or protective benefits to the population. In fact, they behaved very thuggishly and capriciously toward the *cocaleros,* the coca farmers. In contrast, the leftist guerrilla group FARC, which had defined political goals and sought to mobilize the population on its behalf, chose to provide a variety of protective and regulatory services to the population.

Compared with other potential sources of political capital, sponsorship of an illicit economy has distinct advantages for belligerent groups. Unlike ideology, which typically promises hard-to-deliver benefits sometime in the future, sponsorship of the illicit economy allows belligerents to deliver immediate benefits to the population. In most cases, the belligerents do not need to create an illicit economy; they simply need to embrace and regulate the illicit economy that already exists. Moreover, participation in the illicit economy can be a more reliable source of legitimacy and popular support than ideology. Over time, the appeal of a group's ideology may decline or growing brutality may erode its popularity. Nonetheless, by continuing to provide vital services to the local economy, belligerents often can count on continued support from the population.

This argument flies in the face of the conventional government view on narcoterrorism, which mistakenly assumes that once a population becomes disenchanted with the belligerents' ideology, the belligerents become completely illegitimate and forfeit their popular support. That is often said to occur when belligerent groups involved in the illicit economy allegedly become motivated solely by financial profit. The conventional view maintains that past that point, belligerents' legitimacy and popular support are unaffected by government efforts to destroy the illicit economy.

In contrast, the political capital model argues that positive involvement in illicit economies may generate political capital for belligerents even when the group's ideology is unappealing to the population. My analysis here is informed by work in criminology, which has found that even purely criminal organizations can create political capital as long as they provide more effective economic support, order and dispute resolution, or physical security to the population than do alternative claimants to power.[4] A leading work in this literature is Diego Gambetta's classic study of the Sicilian mafia. Gambetta asks two questions: what do the mafiosi offer, and what must they do to remain successful?[5] He argues that the key to the mafia's success lies not in the provision of illegal goods, such as drugs, which constitute only a peripheral activity, but in their provision of security. In poorly administered Sicily, there was an acute need for protection from untrustworthy and dangerous business competitors, corrupt government officials, and ordinary thieves and robbers. The mafia has thrived and even acquired a certain legitimacy by filling that need.[6] Many residents consider the mafia's services, even if they involve the use of violence, "extralegal" rather than illegal.

Similarly, Gianluca Fiorentini and Sam Peltzman show that once a criminal organization has acquired a monopoly on coercion in its area, it can perform activities typically performed by the state, such as levying taxes; providing public goods, such as a stable system for establishing property rights and arbitrating disputes; and regulating private agents, such as by introducing entry restrictions on participants in economic markets in order to limit excessive competition.[7] Such services are analogous to the functions that belligerents often fulfill by protecting and regulating illicit economies.

HOW MUCH POLITICAL CAPITAL CAN BELLIGERENTS ACQUIRE?
Four conditions help shape the degree to which belligerents can use their involvement in the illicit economy as a source of political capital: the state of the overall economy, the character of the illicit economy, the presence or absence of thuggish traffickers; and the government response to the illicit economy. Those factors determine how useful and necessary the belligerents are to the local population and hence how much support they receive from the population in return for their management of the illicit economy.

THE STATE OF THE OVERALL ECONOMY. The state of the economy affects the amount of political capital that can be built or destroyed by a belligerent group's involvement in the illicit economy. If the economy is poor and much of the population depends on the illicit economy, belligerents' support for the illicit economy can generate large amounts of political capital. If the economy is rich and the population has many other economic options, belligerent groups derive only a small amount of political capital, if any at all, from positive involvement in the illicit economy. Conversely, if the overall economy is poor and belligerents attempt to destroy the illicit economy, they lose significant political capital. As the following chapters show, when many, if not most, belligerent groups first encounter illicit economies, such as drug cultivation, they seek to eliminate them for ideological reasons. But when they do so in poor countries where the population depends on such economies for survival, be it qat smuggling in Somalia or poppy cultivation in Afghanistan, they greatly antagonize the population. Conversely, when the Basque separatist group ETA (Euskadi Ta Askatasuna [Basque Homeland and Freedom]) became involved in drug smuggling in comparatively rich Spain, where the population had plentiful access to legal livelihoods, it not only did not augment its political capital, but in fact antagonized the population to some extent.

THE CHARACTER OF THE ILLICIT ECONOMY. Illicit economies vary greatly in their labor intensiveness. Some activities, such as coca or opium poppy cultivation, generate large-scale employment. Others, such as the refining of coca and opium, the production of synthetic drugs, or trafficking in illicit substances, require little labor. All else being equal, the more labor intensive the illicit economy, the more political capital a belligerent group can generate through positive involvement. If the illicit economy is not labor intensive, it employs only a small segment of the population and hence generates only a small amount of political capital for the belligerents. Conversely, if belligerents attempt to destroy a labor-intensive illicit economy, they will suffer large losses of political capital.

Belligerents therefore gain more political capital by protecting the cultivation of illicit crops than by participating in or providing protection for trafficking. But that said, the political capital that belligerents derive from both simple trafficking in illicit commodities and the production of synthetic drugs may not be negligible, especially in poor countries. Even illicit economies that are not labor intensive create important local powerbrokers, whose support can deliver significant political benefits to belligerents. Moreover, a vibrant, non–labor-intensive illicit economy often gives a boost to the local economy as a result of spillover effects, such as the emergence of rest houses and restaurants for traffickers and increased sales of consumer goods. Consequently, belligerents still obtain some political capital from positive involvement in non–labor-intensive illicit economies, albeit a considerably smaller amount than in the case of labor-intensive ones.

THE PRESENCE OR ABSENCE OF THUGGISH TRAFFICKERS. Traffickers include a variety of entities. They can be criminals or criminal cartels, but they also can be corrupt government officials or even rival belligerent groups that

TABLE 2-2. Benefits That Belligerents and Traffickers Provide to Each Other

---

Benefits that belligerents provide to traffickers
Protection from government
Protection of transport systems and routes
Protection from belligerents themselves
Protection from other criminal organizations or belligerent groups
Guarantee of reliable production from peasants

Benefits that traffickers provide to belligerents
Financial payoffs
Denial of intelligence on belligerents to government units
Provision of intelligence on government units
Denial of intelligence on one belligerent group to another
Provision of intelligence on one belligerent group to another

---

have taken on the trafficking role. While the conventional narcoterrorism view sees belligerents and traffickers as largely indistinguishable, the reality is that the two groups typically exist in an uneasy alliance.[8] Belligerents provide traffickers with protection from the government, from other criminal organizations, and from belligerent groups, including themselves. Moreover, they make sure that producers deliver promised raw materials, they protect producers from the government, and they make sure that farmers do not cheat (by keeping some of the illicit products for themselves or selling them to rival groups) or abscond from the region. In return, the traffickers provide the belligerents with financial benefits and intelligence on the government's military movements. (See table 2-2 for a summary of the benefits that each group provides.)

However, the interests of belligerents and traffickers conflict when it comes to determining the price of their services, with belligerents wanting to extract fees that are as high as possible and traffickers wanting to pay as little as possible. In addition, when traffickers are thuggish, belligerents can generate political capital by protecting the population against abusive practices. For example, they can prohibit traffickers from killing farmers who fail to produce promised quantities of coca. They also can act as agents for the local population—for example, by bargaining on producers' behalf for better prices from the traffickers and preventing the traffickers from establishing a monopoly in a region—once again clashing with the interests of traffickers, who do not want such outside regulation.

Belligerents cannot perform those functions if local traffickers are not thuggish—that is, if they care about the producers' well-being, do not abuse them, and pay reasonable prices—or if there are no independent traffickers in the region because the belligerents and the traffickers are the same entity. Belligerents therefore face a strategic choice: whether or not to eliminate traffickers from a region's illicit economy. That choice involves a potential trade-off between the belligerents' desire for political capital and desire for financial profits. By eliminating thuggish traffickers, the belligerents lose some political capital but may reap greater financial gains by taking over the traffickers' role. However, such gains are not guaranteed; they depend on how well the belligerents perform as traffickers. If they do poorly—a distinct possibility given the complexity of the international drug trade—the entire sector could suffer. As described in chapter 4, when the FARC eliminated independent drug traffickers from the territories that it controlled in the mid-to-late 1990s, it stopped providing the population with many protective and regulatory services. Instead it became an increasingly brutal monopolist, and its political capital among the *cocaleros* declined precipitously. At the same time, the FARC's financial gains were limited by its failure to take over international smuggling and distribution routes.

GOVERNMENT RESPONSE TO THE ILLICIT ECONOMY. A government's policies toward the illicit economy can vary from repressive policies designed to eliminate the illicit economy to a laissez-faire approach to partial or full legalization. In the case of narcotics, such policies include eradication (compensated or not), interdiction, laissez-faire, alternative development (what has recently evolved into the concept of alternative livelihoods),[9] partial or full licensing of production, demand reduction (treatment of drug users and prevention of drug use), decriminalization, and legalization. The various policies can also be adopted in combination; in fact, the current mantra of supply-side counternarcotics policies is a so-called "holistic approach" that at least nominally combines the eradication, interdiction, and alternative livelihood approaches. Eradication and interdiction, however, frequently dwarf alternative livelihood efforts.

Each of these approaches has a different effect on the amount of political capital that belligerents can gain from involvement in the illicit economy. Broadly speaking, the more punitive the policy, the more belligerents have to gain, because more punitive policies translate into greater local dependence on the belligerents for protection.

Eradication. Contrary to the conventional government view and the narcoterrorism literature, eradication has dubious effects on the financial resources of belligerents. Even when carried out in a way that results in large-scale and lasting suppression of cultivation—a rare occurrence—eradication might not bring great, if any, financial losses to belligerents. One reason is that effective suppression of the production of the illicit commodity may actually increase the international market price for the commodity to such an extent that the final revenues may be even greater (at least temporarily), assuming that the illicit economy was not permanently and completely eliminated.[10]

Moreover, the extent of financial losses also depends on the adaptability of the belligerents, traffickers, and producers involved. Do they have the ability to store drugs and if so, to what extent? Do the belligerents have money saved? Do the farmers have the ability to replant after eradication? Can they increase the number of plants per acre to offset their losses from eradication? Do the farmers, traffickers, and belligerents have the ability to shift production to areas that are not being eradicated, such as deeper into jungles under tree cover or into higher elevations under cloud cover? Can they avoid detection by planting illicit crops between licit crops? Do they have access to genetically altered high-yield, high-resistance crops that do not die after being sprayed with herbicides?

Furthermore, even if counternarcotics policies succeeded in permanently wiping out illicit crop cultivation in particular regions, belligerents always have the possibility of switching to other illicit economies, such as extortion, illegal logging, and illegal traffic in goods like cigarettes, wildlife, gems, and human beings—and, most easily and conveniently, they can switch to cooking synthetic drugs, such as methamphetamines. In other words, do they have other sources of income? Can they generate other sources of income?

Yet, although the desired result of eradication—a decrease in belligerents' financial resources—is far from assured and is likely to take place only under the most favorable circumstances, eradication definitely increases the political benefits of the belligerents. As the government destroys the local population's livelihood, the population will support the belligerents all the more and will not provide the government with intelligence. Good local human intelligence is a crucial factor in defeating terrorist and insurgent groups, and unless the local population is willing to provide it to government units, counterterrorism and counterinsurgency missions will be seriously compromised. Eradication may even motivate the rural population to support the belligerents more actively, such as by providing them with intelligence as well as food, shelter, and safe houses or even by fighting alongside the belligerents against the government.

Moreover, even if eradication were complete and permanently successful, it is far from clear that the local population could adapt by participating in the legal economy. The local legal economy may not be extensive and accessible enough to generate a sufficient livelihood for the population, which may be forced to leave the region or join the belligerents. Thus, even in the case of total and permanent eradication, the link between the population and the belligerents may not be severed. In short, eradication loses the battle for hearts and minds without fulfilling the promise of its siren song—cutting the belligerents off from resources.

Interdiction. Interdiction, the second major policy option, involves disrupting the flow of illicit goods, destroying processing facilities and labs, and arresting traffickers. Like eradication, this policy seeks to reduce the size of the illicit economy through law enforcement; unlike eradication, it does not directly and visibly target the rural producer population. Instead, it targets drug traffickers and the much smaller portion of the population that is involved in processing. Interdiction typically results in considerably less alienation of the population from the government than eradication and creates fewer opportunities for belligerents to build political capital by coming to the illicit economy's defense. Consequently, the population may be more willing to provide information to the military on belligerents, all other factors being equal. In addition, interdiction can enhance government intelligence gathering by allowing drug shipments to be traced back not only to the traffickers but also to the belligerent groups that protect them.

If carried out effectively, interdiction can reduce the belligerents' financial income and hence their overall military capability. The destruction of processing labs and means of transportation (assuming that those facilities could not easily be replaced) would decrease traffickers' demand for illegal crops in the area involved and the prices for the crops would fall. Belligerents would see their ability to collect taxes from both farmers and traffickers decline. Similarly, policies that combat money laundering can decrease the flow of profits back to traffickers and thus the amount that they can pay belligerents. Combining interdiction and anti–money laundering efforts could theoretically drive traffickers' profits down to a level that would force them to pull up stakes and move. In the absence of alternative sources of revenue, belligerents would then suffer a significant loss of capability.

In the extreme case, if interdiction were effective to such an extent that it made illicit traffic in a certain locale impossible, its effects on the local population would approximate that of eradication. The population's livelihood would be fundamentally threatened, the number of affected people would be very large, and consequently the number of people alienated from the government would also substantially increase. Thus, the level of political capital that belligerents would derive from the illicit economy would increase, approaching the level obtained from eradication.

However, it is extraordinarily difficult to carry out interdiction effectively—to really shut down or bankrupt the illicit economy or even just substantially increase the costs for traffickers. Interdiction is believed to capture about 25 percent to 40 percent of cocaine shipments and only about 10 percent of heroin shipments, since heroin is more compact and hence easier to hide.[11] The price structure of the drug trade allows traffickers to pass many of the costs of eluding interdiction efforts on to either producers or consumers. They also can increase production capacity by the amount that they anticipate being seized in transit or alter their smuggling routes and methods. The latest adaptation, for example, is smuggling cocaine from Colombia in semi-submersible vessels. The adaptability and inventiveness of traffickers is very high, as is their ability to elude detection and apprehension. Therefore, despite the enormous resources that the United States and Colombia have dedicated to interdiction and claims of ever-increasing success rates in Colombia over the past seven years, current cocaine prices in the United States are among the lowest ever, indicating that the supply has not been reduced.[12]

Combating money laundering is even more difficult than interdiction since the targets can choose from a long menu of options, including cash smuggling, currency exchange bureaus, front companies, real estate investments, securities, trusts, casinos, and wire transfers, to name a few. In the case of Islamic groups, the problem is further complicated by the availability of informal funds transfer systems, such as *hawala,* that easily escape monitoring.[13] Moreover, initiatives that target money laundering typically require intensive international cooperation, which often is lacking.

Nonetheless, while high levels of effectiveness are exceptionally hard to achieve and therefore are unlikely to greatly reduce belligerents' financial gains, the advantage of interdiction is that is does not threaten farmers directly and visibly. Unlike eradication, it thus reduces belligerents' political capital and also introduces new points of vulnerability and opportunities for intelligence gathering.

Laissez-faire. A third government policy option is to take a hands-off approach similar to "decriminalization" of production.[14] The government does not legalize the production of illicit substances and commodities, but it does not try to enforce its prohibition against the illicit economy either. Such a policy reduces the political gains of the belligerents. Since the government is not threatening the population's livelihood, the positive relationship between the belligerents and the population is weakened. All other factors being equal, the population is more willing to provide intelligence on the belligerents to the government and otherwise support the government against the belligerents.

Similarly, traffickers' dependence on belligerent groups for business protection is greatly reduced. Consequently, the traffickers may well attempt to displace the belligerents from the illicit economy by providing intelligence on the belligerents to the government or physically fighting the belligerents in order to avoid paying for protection.

The real downside of this policy is, of course, that it is unlikely to affect belligerents' financial gains. Moreover, if the international demand for the particular illicit commodity involved—an exogenous variable—is not satiated or is growing, laissez-faire is likely to result in expansion of the illicit economy in that particular locale and hence may increase belligerents' financial benefits. The only way to reduce belligerents' financial resources under a laissez-faire policy is to displace the belligerents from the illicit economy. They could be displaced by traffickers if they no longer need the belligerents' protection or by the government if it obtains better intelligence from the population and the traffickers.

Licensing of Production. Licensing of production allows the government to deprive belligerents of political gains since the government no longer threatens the livelihood of the population. Consequently, the population is much more motivated to provide the government with intelligence on the belligerents, if not to support the government more actively.

Licensing of production, especially if carried out in a way that makes diversion of production into illicit uses and illicit traffic very difficult, also substantially decreases the financial profits of belligerents. Moreover, since the government now captures at least a part of the revenues from the economy, its own financial resources are increased.

The difficulty with this policy, especially in the case of illegal drugs, is the limited size of legal markets for derivates from illicit crops. Although opium resin derivates are widely used in medicine for anesthetics such as morphine and codeine, heavy legal and political regulation makes it very difficult for new entrants to participate in the medical market.[15] The legal outlets for coca derivates are even more limited, again consisting of a very limited market for pharmaceutical products, such as specialty anesthetics, and at various periods in the past for items such as coca wine, coca toothpaste, and coca soap. However, licensing of production that complies with certain regulations has been adopted in the case of diamonds, for example. In that case, certificates are issued to indicate that the diamonds do not come from mines belonging to belligerent groups (blood diamonds) and that consequently they are legal and legitimate.[16] Such licensing schemes have been applied to other commodities, such as ivory and timber.

Legalization. Full legalization entails not only the legalization of production of a certain commodity, but also its legal consumption. Unlike licensing for special limited purposes or with certain regulatory constraints, this approach entails the broad legalization of the previously illicit product. In the case of drugs, for example, poppy cultivation would be allowed not only for the production of morphine and codeine but also for the production of opium and heroin. Processing, trade, retail sale, and consumption of the previously illegal commodities would also become legal. Since in this case the government would once again not destroy the livelihood of the population, belligerents' political gains from sponsorship of the illicit economy would be greatly reduced, if not virtually eliminated, and the population would be willing to provide the government with information on the belligerents. Moreover, the financial benefits of the belligerents would also be greatly reduced. Instead, the government would capture the financial gains in the form of taxes. Expansion of the economy and of consumption of the commodity would be likely to follow as well.

However, although both the political capital and physical resources of the belligerents would be greatly reduced, they may not be altogether eliminated because without effective government preventive measures, the belligerents could set up a parallel informal, illegal economy alongside the legal one. They could tax the producers considerably less than the government and hence attract a portion of the producers to their parallel economy. The emergence of the parallel economy would be analogous to the existence of an illegal market for stolen cars in the context of the legal car market.

In the case of illicit drugs, full legalization remains politically infeasible in most countries. However, certain pariah governments that may not be significantly concerned about their international legitimacy (such as North Korea and, at times in the past, Panama and Afghanistan) and may be less sensitive to additional sanctions (for example, by the United States for failure to cooperate with U.S. counternarcotics policies[17]) could adopt at least veiled legalization. Under veiled legalization, illicit crop cultivation and drug production would remain de jure illegal but would be de facto permitted and the government would tax and regulate the illicit economy and participate in its marketing.[18] Thus, unlike in the case of laissez-faire, the government would not only tolerate the illicit economy but also actively manage it, even if not officially declare it legal.

Full open legalization, however, remains a definite possibility in the case of other illicit economies and commodities, such as illicit logging. A government can easily remove the prohibition on logging in national parks and tax the industry. While environmental groups may oppose such a move, the international pressure to amend such a policy would likely be considerably smaller than in the case of legalization of illicit narcotics.

THE GOVERNMENT'S DILEMMA

To recap, government policies toward the illicit economy seemingly face a trade-off between winning the hearts and minds of the population and decreasing belligerents' military capability. In fact, repressive government policies toward the illicit economy, such as eradication of illicit crops, increase the political capital of belligerents most likely without fulfilling their promise of reducing the belligerents' physical resources. Laissez-faire government policies toward the illicit economy decrease belligerents' political capital and, all other factors being equal, increase the government's political capital in terms of legitimacy and the population's cooperation with the government. However, such policies leave belligerents' financial profits unaffected or even increased. Licensing or legalization policies greatly decrease both the political capital and the military capability of belligerents.

The posited effects are relative to each other. The political capital model makes no statements regarding what policies toward the illicit economy are necessary or sufficient to defeat belligerent groups. Other factors, such as the size of government forces relative to that of belligerent forces and the relative levels of government and belligerent brutality obviously also play a vital role. My theory simply explains why and how government policies toward the illicit economy hamper or enhance government military efforts against belligerents.

Of the four factors that have a significant effect on belligerents' strength as a result of their involvement in the illicit economy, the most important is the state of the overall economy. The second-most-important factor is the character of the illicit economy. The third and fourth are, respectively, government response and the presence of thuggish traffickers.

The state of the overall economy is the most important factor because it determines how many people depend on the illicit economy for their basic livelihood and hence how they view the government response to the illicit economy. Similarly, the second-most-important factor—the character of the illicit economy—determines the extent of the population's positive or negative views of government policies. Those views have a crucial influence on the level of belligerents' political capital and the level of popular support for the government. Both are structural conditions outside the immediate control of the government or the belligerents.

Although government policy toward the illicit economy ranks below the state of the overall economy and the character of the illicit economy, it nonetheless is a critical variable and the only one over which the government has direct and ready control. In a poor country with a labor-intensive illicit economy—by far the most prevalent combination of factors in the context of drugs and military conflict—government policy toward the illicit economy has a major impact on belligerents' political capital. However, even in poor countries, that impact is considerably weakened when the illicit economy is not labor intensive. Government destruction of methamphetamine labs in poor countries, for example, affects a relatively small number of people. In a non–labor-intensive economy in a rich country, the impact of government policies on belligerents' political capital is very small. The presence or absence of traffickers has the weakest effect on belligerents' political capital because it affects the profits and work conditions of the producers (farmers) but not the overall importance of the illicit economy to the population.

EMPIRICAL IMPLICATIONS

The political capital model of illicit economies has several empirical implications that run counter to the predictions or assumptions of the conventional narcoterrorism model.

Belligerents' Popularity and Legitimacy

According to the conventional view, a belligerent group engaged in the drug economy is no more popular in drug-producing areas than in areas where drugs are not produced. Sponsorship of the illicit economy does not bring any political support to the belligerents; instead, their legitimacy is based wholly on their ideology and their use or nonuse of violence toward the population. Similarly, they are equally popular or unpopular in areas of illicit crop cultivation as in areas of drug trafficking without cultivation or areas of synthetic drug manufacturing without cultivation.

In contrast, the political capital model predicts that support for a belligerent group active in the drug economy will be stronger in drug-producing regions, especially in regions where illicit crops are cultivated. The population will approve the sponsorship of the illicit economy by the belligerents. Moreover, support for belligerents will be strongest in drug-producing regions even when the ideology of the belligerents is no longer appealing, the belligerents have become more brutal, or their overall popular support has declined and under any combination of those conditions. Support for the belligerents will be weaker in periods or areas of trafficking only—that is, in periods when and areas where there is no cultivation of illicit crops—or in periods when and areas where the belligerents are engaged only in the manufacture of synthetic drugs or other non–labor-intensive illicit economies.

Belligerents as Bargaining Agents

The conventional government view does not conceive of belligerent groups as bargaining on behalf of the producers for better prices from the traffickers, since such activity does not increase the belligerents' financial profits. The political capital model predicts that belligerent groups may well take on such a role because their ability to obtain better prices from traffickers for illicit products will increase the population's cooperation with the belligerents.

The Relationship between Belligerents and Traffickers

The conventional government view holds that violence between belligerent groups and traffickers is rare and implies that very close collaboration between drug traffickers and belligerents, amounting at times even to organizational fusion, is pervasive. It also predicts that alliances between the traffickers and the belligerents will be weakest when government attempts to destroy the illicit economy are most aggressive. My theory projects a very different outcome: narcotraffickers and belligerents will be in conflict frequently, physically fighting and trying to displace one another from the illicit economy. Traffickers may even conspire with the government in order to get rid of the belligerents; therefore, trafficker cooperation with the government will increase when the government does not attempt to interdict flows of illicit drugs or bust labs.

The Impact of Eradication Policies

The conventional government view implies that government policies toward the illicit economy do not affect the degree to which the population cooperates with a counterinsurgency effort. The conventional view does, however, assume that eradication severely weakens belligerent groups and deprives them of physical resources, thereby making them incapable of carrying out effective antigovernment operations. Deprived of earnings from their particular illicit economy, they are unable to obtain weapons, finance their operations, and pay their soldiers. Moreover, the expectation is that government success against belligerents will be greatest when and where a government carries out the most extensive and repressive eradication.

The political capital model leads to starkly different expectations concerning the effects on belligerent strength of government policies toward the illicit economy. First, the population's willingness to supply the government with intelligence and otherwise cooperate will be much less if not altogether absent during periods when the government carries out strong suppression of the illicit economy, especially eradication. Indeed, the population engaged in the affected illicit economy will condemn government suppression efforts and praise the belligerents for protecting the illicit economy. At the same time, however, if the belligerents neglect to protect the illicit economy, they will alienate the population and lose political capital. My theory predicts that eradication will not severely weaken belligerents, who will either continue to find ways to derive large profits from the illicit drug economy or switch to other forms of illicit economic activity. During periods when and in regions where the government has adopted a laissez-faire approach to the illicit economy or has fully legalized it, the population will cooperate with the government to a much greater degree and provide it with intelligence. All of these predictions and the two larger models behind them are tested in the case studies that make up the heart of this volume.

COLOMBIA

Quito ★

Manta

ECUADOR

Ambato

Guayaquil

Cuenca

Tumbes

TUMBES

Loja

Iquitos

Amazon

Leticia

Benjamin Constant

Talara

PIURA

Sullana

Piura

Paita

Rio Marañón

AMAZONAS

Yurimaguas

Chachapoyas

Moyobamba

Tarapoto

LAMBAYEQUE

SAN
MARTIN

Chiclayo

CAJAMARCA

Cajamarca

Upper Huallaga Valley

Cruzeiro
do Sul

BRAZIL

LA LIBERTAD

Trujillo

Salaverry

Santa
Lucia

Pucallpa

Chimbote

ANCASH

Huaraz

HUANUCO

UCAYALI

Rio Branco

SOUTH
PACIFIC
OCEAN

Huanuco

PASCO

Goyllarisquizga

Cerro de Pasco

Cobija

Huacho

JUNIN

MADRE DE DIOS

Rio Madre de Dios

Pan American Highway

Lima

Huancayo

Apurimac
Ene

Callao

LIMA

CUSCO

Puerto Maldonado

Huancavelica

HUANCAVELICA

Quillabamba

Ayacucho

Cusco

Pisco

Abancay

APURIMAC

PUNO

BOLIVIA

Ica

ICA

AYACUCHO

PERU

Nazca

Juliaca

Pan American Highway

AREQUIPA

Puno

Desaguadero

Guaqui

La Paz

Arequipa

Matarani

MOQUEGUA

Moquegua

TACNA

Oruro

Ilo

Tacna

Arica

CHILE

Peru

—·—·— International Boundary

—·—·— Department Boundary

★ National Capital

◉ Department Capital

——— Road

——— Rivers

0   100   200 Kilometers

0   100   200 Miles

THREE

PERU

The Coca Path

From the 1980s through the mid-1990s, Peru was the world's largest supplier of coca leaf and coca paste, the raw ingredients for cocaine.[1] The illicit narcotics economy in Peru employed up to 500,000 people, generated large inflows of hard currency at a time of acute economic crisis, and represented at least 4 percent to 5 percent of Peru's GDP (during some years, perhaps even more).[2] The United States devoted a large amount of resources to combat the drug trade in Peru and put a great deal of pressure on the Peruvian government to do so as well.

At the same time, Peru experienced the emergence and growth of one of the world's most brutal and effective communist guerrilla movements, Sendero Luminoso (Shining Path). The insurgency gained strength steadily throughout the 1980s, and by the early 1990s, many Peruvian and foreign analysts believed that it would topple the government. Over the first ten years of the conflict between the government and the insurgents, 20,000 Peruvians were killed and 500,000 people fled their homes, while $10 billion in infrastructure was destroyed.[3] The Peruvian government finally succeeded in defeating the Shining Path in 1995, but remnants of the movement continue to operate in the countryside.

This chapter analyzes the interaction between the illicit narcotics economy and insurgency in Peru. It focuses on the activities of Sendero Luminoso (also referred to here by its initials, SL) from the 1980s until its defeat in the early 1990s but also briefly examines the involvement of a second potent insurgency in Peru, the MRTA (Movimiento Revolucionario Túpac Amaru [Túpac Amaru Revolutionary Movement]).

35

According to the conventional narcoguerrilla view, the government defeated the Shining Path by treating and combating the guerrillas and the drug traffickers as a single entity.[4] I show, however, that the evidence fundamentally contradicts that assertion. In fact, the government defeated the Shining Path by tacitly acquiescing in the rural narcotics economy and by undertaking an urban intelligence operation, unrelated to the counternarcotics effort, that resulted in the capture of the group's leader. When Sendero was defeated, the drug economy was at its peak. Only several years after the defeat of Sendero was there a substantial decline in the size of the illicit economy.

ORIGINS OF THE SHINING PATH

The Shining Path (or, to give its full name, the Communist Party of Peru on the Shining Path of José Carlos Mariátegui) emerged in the rural Andean province of Ayacucho in the early 1960s when Dr. Abimael Guzmán began the long process of recruiting and organizing a system of cadres to seize political and military power in Peru and establish a radical Marxist society.[5] In 1970, the group split from the more traditional Peruvian Communist Party and began to use the name Sendero Luminoso. Under Guzmán's leadership, the Shining Path embraced a variant of Maoist ideology that called for waging a protracted guerrilla war in the countryside that would culminate in the capture of urban centers and the destruction of markets in any form, including small local markets. Guzmán combined his Maoist strategy with the radical *indigenismo* of José Carlos Mariátegui, a Peruvian communist theoretician of the 1920s who called for an agrarian communist system based on the indigenous peasant community.[6]

In 1979, Guzmán and the Shining Path central committee made the decision to undertake an armed struggle. On May 17, 1980, the day before Peru's first free presidential election since the military coup of 1968, four masked students from the University of Ayacucho (where Guzmán had been a professor of philosophy), armed with nonfunctioning pistols, entered the town hall in the city of Chuschi in Ayacucho region, tied up the registrar, and burned the registration book and ballot boxes.[7] The long revolution thus was launched with a purely symbolic act.

Over the next year, the armed struggle remained limited in scale. In 1980, Shining Path activity—mostly bombings of police stations and government installations in the Andean region and in Lima—resulted in seven deaths. In 1981, the number of terrorist attacks grew to 685, but only thirteen people were killed.[8] As Richard Clutterbuck observes, "the SL spent 1980 and 1981 building up their support organizations in the villages in Lima, training their 'People's Guerrilla Army' and, perhaps more important, raising funds by bank robberies and extortion."[9] Sendero militants carried out more than fifty bank robberies in Lima in 1981. But those efforts brought in only limited funds, making it impossible for Sendero to pay its soldiers or buy many weapons.

Despite its limited resources, Sendero tried to win popular support by providing regular paramedical services, agricultural advice, and at least limited food handouts to rural villagers. The Senderistas also killed, pushed out, and robbed well-to-do landowners and shopkeepers, distributing the spoils among the peasants.[10] But such time-consuming activities generated only limited gains and hence limited popular support for Sendero. Nonetheless, Guzmán pressed forward. The number of people killed by the Shining Path, in both executions and attacks, rose into the hundreds in 1982, and the group mustered sufficient resources to field three company-size units of one hundred fighters or more.[11] The resulting violence was sufficient to scare President Fernando Belaúnde Terry into overcoming his unwillingness to use the military to suppress the insurgency.

THE COCA ECONOMY

In 1983, the Peruvian military was deployed to the region of Ayacucho to suppress the insurgency. The military campaign rapidly pushed the Shining Path out of its strongholds in the highlands of Ayacucho and made considerable inroads into its logistical channels. Seriously weakened and on the run, the Shining Path was forced to open a new front in the Upper Huallaga Valley (UHV), a remote and inaccessible region that was ideally suited for guerrilla warfare. That area also happened to be the main coca production region in Peru. Around 300,000 families were growing coca on more than 100,000 hectares in the region,[12] and 95 percent of economic activity in the UHV was coca-based.[13]

By the mid-1980s, the Peruvian drug trade was believed to generate global revenues of more than $24 billion, of which several billion dollars went to coca paste producers and local traffickers in Peru and about $240 million, or less than 1 percent of the total value of the Peruvian illicit drug trade, went to peasant producers.[14] Nonetheless, coca growing provided a much better livelihood for highland farmers than other economic activities. Even with only two full harvests of coca leaves per year (typically there were more), the mean annual income of a *cocalero* (coca farmer) in the Upper Huallaga Valley was estimated to be $3,630—three-and-a-half times Peru's per capita annual income of $1,000 and many times the income of a peasant in non-coca regions.[15] Other estimates put the average annual revenue of a *cocalero* as high as $12,350, some 60 percent of which was profit. The net per-hectare revenues of coca farmers were estimated to be ten times higher than those of cacao farmers and ninety-one times higher than those of rice farmers.[16] Traffickers paid farmers two to eight times as much per hectare for coca leaves as farmers received for cacao pods, four times as much as they received for rubber, and more than forty times as much as they received for corn.[17]

Even the seasonal workers hired to collect coca leaves earned twice the average rate in the licit agricultural sector, while *pisadores* (peasants who stamp on coca leaves to make coca paste) made several times the wages of coca leaf pickers. In the mid-1980s, *pisadores* earned up to $40 a day while a schoolteacher earned $23 a month—less than a dollar a day.[18] In fact, some parents' associations in the UHV provided teachers with a hectare or more of land for growing coca to supplement their earnings.[19] Typically, local peasants cultivated the plot and arranged for the processing of coca on the teacher's behalf.

In addition to its profitability, several other factors contributed to farmers' preference for coca. The plant (*erythoxylum coca*) grows in acidic tropical soil in regions characterized by rugged terrain, high humidity, and heavy rainfall—conditions that are unsuitable for many legal crops. Native to the region, it requires little care, thus minimizing expenses on fertilizers and pesticides. With a lifespan of thirty years, coca is also very durable, and it supports three to six harvests a year. Compared with the remarkably hardy coca plants, legal crops tend to have fewer harvests per year, they tend to be less sturdy, and their market prices are subject to greater fluctuation. Moreover, farmers often had to go into debt to acquire the seeds, fertilizers, and other supplies needed to grow legal crops. In contrast, traffickers would advance financing, fertilizers (not necessary for cultivation of coca but helpful), seeds, and even technical assistance to the *cocaleros*.

The weakness of the infrastructure in the Upper Huallaga Valley and many other parts of rural Peru also favored coca cultivation. The lack of ready transport for such agricultural commodities as bananas, citrus, and pineapples not only substantially raised transaction costs for the peasants but also frequently resulted in products spoiling before they arrived in local markets. Coca leaves and paste, on the other hand, were frequently picked up by traffickers right at the farm, eliminating transport costs. Even when farmers took coca products to the local market themselves, the shipments weighed less than equivalent-value shipments of licit products and were less subject to spoilage.[20] Moreover, coca served as a means of exchange. Wages, for example, were often paid in coca, and coca was bartered for potatoes, corn, and other crops.[21]

Not all coca in the UHV and other areas of Peru was illegal; a legal traditional market for coca remained. At least since the days of the Incas, the highland people of the Andes have chewed coca as a mild stimulant, pain reliever, hunger suppressor, and treatment for altitude sickness.[22] A 1970 survey revealed that about 15 percent of Peru's population chewed coca daily.[23] In addition, there was a legal industrial market for cocaine produced for specialty pharmaceutical purposes, as well as a small market for a Coca-Cola extract. Production for the traditional and licit markets was regulated by Peru's national wholesale agency, ENACO (Empresa Nacional de la Coca [National Coca Enterprise]). However, the price of coca in the illicit economy was three to fifteen times as high as the price in the licit economy. Moreover, cultivation for legal personal and industrial purposes absorbed only a small percentage of overall production. In 1986, for example, of the estimated 100,000 tons of coca leaf produced, ENACO purchased only 4,000 tons.[24]

THE GOVERNMENT RESPONSE TO THE COCA ECONOMY: ERADICATION AND ALTERNATIVE DEVELOPMENT

In 1978, under mounting pressure from the United States, the government of President Francisco Morales Bermúdez launched an effort to eradicate the coca economy in the UHV. It placed coca-growing regions in the departments of Huánuco, San Martín, and Loreto under a state of emergency and ordered government forces to destroy coca crops, confiscate land, and incarcerate resisting farmers. Operation Mar Verde (Operation

Green Sea), as the effort was dubbed, resulted in the eradication of only sixty of the estimated 12,000 hectares of coca in the UHV in 1978. At the same time, increasing prices for coca attracted more migrants into the region, and coca cultivation increased.[25]

Five years later, the government undertook a second wave of eradication under the name CORAH (Control y Reducción de los Cultivos de Coca en el Alto Huallaga [Special Project for the Control and Eradication of Coca in the Upper Huallaga Area]). Under the program, funded with $1.3 million a year from the U.S. Bureau for International Narcotics Matters, 450 men were hired to dig up coca plants. In addition, the government paid farmers a nominal fee—$300 per hectare—for their losses.[26] At its peak in 1985, CORAH eradicated 5,000 hectares of coca.

Alternative development—an effort to provide coca farmers with legal livelihoods while eradicating their illicit crops—fared little better. Funded with $3 million in annual support from the U.S. Agency for International Development (USAID), PEAH (Programma Especial del Alto Huallaga [Upper Huallaga Area Development Project]) was intended to promote crop substitution and general economic development in the Upper Huallaga Valley.[27] In order for farmers to participate in PEAH, CORAH had to certify that they were not cultivating any coca, but obtaining certification turned out to be a bureaucratic headache, partially stemming from the lack of a land registry and legal titles and compounded by the fact that it was unclear who was cultivating coca legally for ENACO. Moreover, the farmers who participated in PEAH's projects were unable to earn enough money to support their families and repay the debts that they had to incur in order to cultivate legal crops. Legal crops took too long to become productive, generating income only after several years, and crop failures and declining market prices impoverished many farmers. Thus, PEAH largely failed, souring the peasants on the concept of alternative development—a distrust that persists today.

Eradication and the failure of alternative development generated widespread resentment among highland peasants and resulted in the early 1980s in the formation of local defense committees to negotiate with the central government. One leading body was FEDIP (Frente de Defensa de los Intereses del Pueblo [Front for the Defense of the People's Interests]) of Tocache province, which was formed by *cocaleros* in the northern part of the UHV. At the peak of FEDIP's activity in 1986, its membership included tens of thousands of *cocaleros*. Their agenda included legalization of coca cultivation, expansion of markets for legal uses of coca for medicines and food, and protection against the abuses of UMOPAR (Unidad Móvil de Patrullaje Rural [Rural Mobile Patrol Unit]), a government-backed paramilitary force that protected eradication units and was widely accused of gross human rights violations. In addition, FEDIP called for the agricultural and industrial development of the region and the development of social services and infrastructure.

SHINING PATH'S ABOUT-FACE ON DRUGS

When the Shining Path was pushed into the Upper Huallaga Valley in the early 1980s, it found a large-scale drug economy flourishing amid grinding poverty. It also encountered a peasantry that was premobilized and in many cases organized in opposition to the government; however, the Shining Path did not immediately take advantage of that windfall. In fact, Sendero's first reaction was to prohibit drugs as anti-Marxist, just as it had prohibited prostitution, tried to limit the consumption of alcohol, and attacked markets elsewhere. The group sought to win popular support through the same methods that it had used in the central highlands—criticizing the government and denouncing capitalism, including by prohibiting the illicit economy.[28] That message did not resonate with the *cocaleros* of the UHV. Their main grievance was not destitution, for they were considerably better off than peasants elsewhere in Peru, nor was the main target of their anger capitalism or even exploitation by drug traffickers. Their main grievance was the government threat to the coca economy. Sendero's anti-drug policies and its prohibition of cultivation alienated the farmers, and the group was unable to build political capital and increase its strength.[29]

Within two years, Sendero's leaders realized that their initial policy was a mistake. By 1985, Sendero had begun to offer coca growers its protection, initially by infiltrating the Tocache FEDIP and other peasant defense groups. Political support for the guerrillas quickly began to grow. Clyde B. Taylor, deputy assistant secretary for narcotics matters with the State Department, explained in testimony before the Senate in 1985:

Many [*cocaleros*] see coca eradication efforts as a threat to their survival. When [Sendero] recruiters announce that they have come to protect the livelihood of growers against government interference, they find ready listeners. Paradoxically, the U.S.-funded eradication efforts may be making the remaining growers more desperate and more susceptible to the blandishments of terrorist recruiters.[30]

Sendero was aided in its efforts to win the allegiance of the *cocaleros* by the ineffectiveness of other political actors. Politicians from traditional parties representing the region in the Peruvian congress, such as Senator Andrés Quintana Gurt of the Huánuco region or the mayors in Tocache and Tingo María, were critical of the government's counternarcotics policies but unable to bring about meaningful policy change. For their part, the *cocalero* defense groups organized strikes and shut down roads, paralyzing economic activity in the valley, and they captured and beat up UMOPAR members to prevent them from carrying out counternarcotics activities.[31] Most important, they forced the federal government into negotiations. But they failed to achieve any meaningful and lasting concessions or to win any real improvements in the lives of the rural population. By the mid-1980s, they were largely defunct.[32]

Sendero had two crucial advantages over those groups. First, as a military force, it could use violence on a far greater scale to repel eradication teams. Second, unlike the establishment politicians and the *cocaleros'* defense organizations, Sendero was under less pressure to deliver immediate results. Every failure of the peasant organizations' negotiations with the government exposed their weakness. But Sendero was offering to solve the farmers' problems by overthrowing the system, which pushed its deadline far into the future. At the same time, through the use of force, it was able to repel eradication teams in the present.

By 1986, the Shining Path had consolidated its control of the Upper Huallaga Valley, where coca cultivation reached 107,500 hectares that year.[33] It also had learned how to exploit coca production for its own ends. Sendero's first step was to levy a 5 percent tax on sales of coca paste to traffickers who exported it to Colombia, thereby generating around $30 million a year.[34] Later Sendero began to charge traffickers a fee to protect their coca processing facilities and cocaine labs and a facilitation fee of $5,000 to $15,000 for each plane taking off from an airstrip that it controlled, raising another $75 million a year.[35] Over time, Sendero also sought to limit direct interaction between the *cocaleros* and the traffickers. It established a system of delegations, charging groups of Senderistas with responsibility for dealing with traffickers. To gain access to coca leaf, a trafficking organization or individual trafficker had to register with

Sendero and pay a $15,000 fee. Reportedly 50 percent of that fee went to Sendero's central accounts, 40 percent was used to purchase supplies for local units, and 10 percent was left with the delegation.[36]

Finally, Sendero branched out into other phases of cocaine production and distribution, including currency exchange. Colombian traffickers would arrive in Peru with U.S. dollars, which they needed to exchange for Peruvian currency in order to carry out local transactions. Initially, they exchanged money in banks. However, once the Shining Path diversified its operations, it insisted on handling all currency exchanges. Sendero fixed the exchange rate and thus earned large profits on hard currency at a time when the Peruvian government's hard currency reserves were depleted.[37]

As the conventional narcoguerrilla view would predict, Sendero's positive involvement in the illicit economy led to a substantial increase in its military capability. However, that view captures only part of the story. Equally important, the Shining Path's sponsorship of the coca trade gave rise to significant political capital—a critical effect that the conventional view overlooks. As the political capital model suggests, those gains were particularly sizable because coca cultivation in Peru was (and remains) highly labor-intensive and dominated by often-thuggish traffickers. In addition, the parlous state of the Peruvian economy offered farmers in the UHV few alternative sources of livelihood. During the 1970s, per capita economic growth was only 0.9 percent a year, but during the 1980s, the economy declined, on average, by 3.2 percent a year.[38] Annual inflation hovered at three-digit levels, peaking at 7,650 percent in 1990, and unemployment and underemployment were high.[39]

Against that backdrop, the following discussion details the ways in which Sendero benefited from its involvement in the illicit economy, focusing first on the impact of involvement on Sendero's military capability and the spread of the insurgency. It next examines Sendero's efforts to build political capital and the impact that different counternarcotics policies—the fourth variable identified by the political capital model—had on those efforts.

SPONSORSHIP OF THE ILLICIT ECONOMY AND THE SHINING PATH'S MILITARY CAPABILITY

Estimates of Sendero's annual profits from the drug trade varied between $20 million and $550 million.[40] Even at the lower end of the range, funds of that scale allowed Sendero to significantly increase its physical capabilities in the UHV. While elsewhere in the country—including in its traditional stronghold, Ayacucho—Sendero could operate only in small columns of ten to fifteen soldiers, in the UHV it was able to field companies of 60 to 120 individuals. In addition, drug money gave Sendero access to more powerful weapons. Although dynamite stolen from mines continued to be used more often than any other weapon, after 1986 the guerrillas also procured weapons such as M-60 machine guns, G-3 and FAL automatic rifles, U.S.-made hand grenades, grenade launchers, and 81-millimeter mortars.[41] After gaining access to drug money, Sendero was also able to pay salaries to its soldiers—in fact, very large ones by Latin American standards—as well as provide its members and sympathizers with food, housing, and livestock.[42] The common salary range was $20 to $500 per month;[43] in coca-producing regions, salaries may have been as high as $1,000 a month.[44] Thus, as much as $5 million a year was spent on salaries for an estimated 10,000 guerrillas. At the same time, the salary of top military generals in Peru was less than $200 a month, and enlisted personnel earned about $10 a month.[45]

Access to drug money also gave the Shining Path greater freedom of action. Early in its history, the group was forced to devote a great deal of time and energy to raiding police and army outposts in order to seize weapons.[46] After 1986, it was able to focus on attacking regular military units and continuing its campaign of terror. In addition, Sendero's drug funds eliminated any need for foreign sponsors. The group was therefore able to develop its struggle on its own terms, without outside interference.[47] Unlike other Marxist guerrillas, the Shining Path was not financially hit by the collapse of the Soviet Union or the economic crisis in Cuba and the subsequent drying up of resources from those two countries.

Finally, its participation in the drug economy helped Sendero become a more effective fighting force. For example, Sendero units assigned to protect coca fields from eradication engaged in combat with Peruvian and U.S. counternarcotics forces. Because the anti-narcotics squads typically had better equipment and training—often provided by the United States—than the government's counterinsurgency forces, the Senderistas were forced to improve both their tactics and strategy in order to prevail. As a top Peruvian military official put it, "Providing security for the drug lords is good training."[48]

The increase in the Shining Path's military capability fueled an increase in the number of attacks after 1986, from under 2,000 a year in 1983, when the group entered the Upper Huallaga Valley, to more than 3,500 by the end of the decade. Equally important, the scope and intensity of the violence grew. While very small-scale Sendero attacks, such as robberies of farms, were common earlier in the period, the post-1986 attacks were considerably larger and more deadly.[49] For example, the level of casualties that the Shining Path was able to inflict on the police and military forces rose from thirty-one policemen and one soldier in 1982 to 229 policemen and 109 soldiers in 1989.[50]

Over the same period, the Shining Path expanded its theater of operations. By 1991, it controlled not only Ayacucho and neighboring Huancavelica and Apurímac, but also parts of the regions of San Martín, Huánuco, Pasco, Junín, and Cusco. It also was able to extend attacks into more prosperous regions far from its base, such as Arequipa and Ica. An estimated 25 to 40 percent of Peruvian territory was brought under effective Sendero control or shadow Sendero administration, and more than half of the population lived under a state of emergency.[51]

SPONSORSHIP OF THE ILLICIT ECONOMY AND THE SHINING PATH'S POLITICAL CAPITAL

The Shining Path owed its success to more than just the increased resources provided by the drug trade. It also was aided critically by the increase in political capital that resulted from its positive involvement with the illicit economy. From that perspective, its single most important policy was probably the simple decision to protect coca fields from eradication. Protecting the fields took a variety of forms. In August 1987, for example, Sendero led the *cocaleros* to shut down the jungle highway between Tingo María and Tocache. They destroyed bridges, erected barriers, and dug trenches, preventing the passage of eradication teams. A year later, to prevent eradication and limit the presence of the state, Sendero helped the *cocaleros* organize a general strike that shut down business and paralyzed traffic in the UHV for five days. Sendero also routinely engaged counternarcotics units and fired on CORAH, UMOPAR, and PEAH workers. Over time, Sendero managed to place entire zones of the UHV off limits to CORAH eradicators and immobilized PEAH's programs.[52] In a further blow to the government's efforts at alternative development, shortly after the Palmas de Espina palm oil plantation and processing plant began operations in the UHV, the Shining Path attacked it and inflicted 1.5 million dollars' worth of damage.[53]

To further boost its legitimacy, the Shining Path adopted language and imagery that stressed the state's threat to people's subsistence. As Cynthia McClintock recounts, Sendero described the Peruvian state as *hambreador* (making people hungry) and genocidal, intentionally killing people through starvation.[54] It adopted such slogans as "Against genocide and against eradication." Simon Strong quotes a Senderista commander in Lima, Félix Cóndor, arguing in a eulogy for a boy: "They say that we are terrorists [but] the terrorists are those who kill us with hunger every day."[55]

The Shining Path's Nationalist Appeal

Sendero developed further political capital by turning widespread resentment against the U.S.–sponsored coca eradication program into a nationalist campaign. As an experienced U.S. Drug Enforcement Administration (DEA) agent put it, "You'll have imperialists cutting down coca trees in front of a crying peasant woman. Mao could not have thought of anything better."[56] Sendero welcomed any increase in U.S. participation in counternarcotics efforts as an opportunity to build its strength, reasoning that if it could turn the insurgency into "a war of national resistance," then "90 percent of the population would follow us."[57] In the late 1980s, as DEA agents and private contractors stepped up their participation in efforts to interdict the drug trade, Sendero representatives predicted a war of national liberation between "the U.S. interventionist forces" and the Peruvians whom Sendero would lead.[58] In an interview with the Peruvian daily *El Diaro,* a Senderista commander commented: "Here are the American advisers, their mercenary pilots, veterans of the counterrevolutionary Vietnam war, who were defeated by that small nation—here they will be defeated by the masses together with their Army of Popular Liberation [the Shining Path]."[59] Both U.S. and Peruvian journalists started reporting on the eerie Vietnam-like image that U.S. agents in fatigues and Huey helicopters brought to the area. The Sendero Luminoso encouraged that comparison, playing the nationalist card.[60]

The Shining Path as Rural Service Provider

Sendero also built both legitimacy and popular support by protecting *cocaleros* against abusive drug traffickers. Prior to the intervention of the Shining Path, farmers risked being killed by drug traffickers if they failed to deliver a certain amount of coca leaves, even if the failure was due to government eradication efforts.[61] Sendero put an end to that practice. More broadly, as a coca plantation employee commented to a Lima journalist: "From [the day the SL came] our salaries went up, and there aren't so many abuses. The Senderistas come every week and ask the townspeople how they are being treated by the traffickers, if there have been abuses, what problems we have."[62] Over time, Sendero moved to regulate all sorts of aspects of the illicit coca economy. After *cocaleros* complained repeatedly about the traffickers' use of altered weights in weighing coca leaves, Sendero established rules about how to weigh coca. Similarly, Sendero negotiated better prices for the farmers from the traffickers. When U.S.-Peruvian interdiction efforts disrupted coca processing and traffic in 1985, Sendero protected *cocaleros* against the resulting 50 percent decline in the price of coca leaf by forcing traffickers to pay above the market price.[63] Five years later, Sendero attempted to concentrate coca leaf dealing in its own local committees and bases, allowing it to set the prices paid to *cocaleros* at above-market rates.

In addition, Sendero acquired political capital by using drug profits to provide social services. The Upper Huallaga Valley, like most of rural Peru, lacked such basic services as a sewage system, roads, schools, and hospitals. The financial resources obtained from coca production allowed the Shining Path to deliver the social services that were lacking and to improve existing ones. Whenever it took over a village, Sendero established water and sewage systems and provided for street cleanup.[64] It also built better transportation systems and invested in hospitals and medicines.[65] The Shining Path supplemented the provision of social services by providing a previously missing system of law and order, albeit a brutal one.[66] Through its positive involvement in the illicit economy, the Shining Path was thus able to fill, at least in a rudimentary way, the role of the state in the areas that it controlled. As a result, the number of Sendero's *committed* supporters—those who actively promoted the group—grew to between 50,000 and 100,000, while its passive support was even larger.[67]

The importance of that support is highlighted in the following discussion of the interaction between the Peruvian government's counternarcotics policies and its counterinsurgency efforts. But it can also be seen in the Shining Path's struggle with the MRTA, a rival communist guerrilla movement, in the late 1980s.[68] A relative latecomer to the drug scene, the MRTA, which had originally focused on urban areas, gradually began to emulate the Shining Path's policies of coca sponsorship and consolidated its support in parts of the coca-growing regions, such as Medio Huallaga. After a major shootout in 1987, Sendero pushed the MRTA out of the UHV and out of the drug business. Farmers' support for Sendero against the MRTA was important in Sendero's victory because the *cocaleros* provided intelligence and material support to the Senderistas. The Shining Path obtained their support by persuading villagers that the MRTA had betrayed them by conspiring with traffickers to lower coca prices,[69] but ironically, the traffickers themselves also helped Sendero push out the MRTA by providing Sendero with soldiers, arms, and intelligence.[70] The drug dealers apparently resented the MRTA's effort to control cocaine processing as well as coca cultivation.[71]

Belligerents and Traffickers: An Uneasy Alliance

The rivalry among the MRTA, Sendero, and the traffickers illustrates the uneasy relationship between belligerent groups and drug traffickers and the fallacy of the conventional belief that they should be treated as a monolithic enemy of the state. The traffickers welcomed Sendero's efforts to protect coca fields from eradication and cocaine labs and airstrips from destruction by counternarcotics forces. They also welcomed Sendero's help in ensuring that farmers delivered the promised amounts of coca leaf. But in other ways, the belligerents' intervention undermined the traffickers' interests. Sendero limited the traffickers' control of the peasant population by reducing their ability to cheat and abuse coca cultivators. First, Sendero insisted that the traffickers disband the gangs that they had hired to prevent the farmers from organizing themselves against the traffickers; if the traffickers refused, Sendero would simply kill the gang members one by one.[72] Second, the insurgents reduced the traffickers' profit margins by forcing them to pay more to the *cocaleros*. Third, they charged high and increasing fees to protect airstrips and labs. Fourth, they sought to displace the traffickers from aspects of the trade. Ironically, once the MRTA was out of the picture and Sendero had no competitors, it also tried to get involved in the cocaine-processing part of the illicit economy. In response, Colombian drug syndicates sent 300 heavily armed guards to the UHV to protect their Peruvian intermediaries and cocaine shipments from Sendero's attacks and extortion.[73] In sum, the narcos and the belligerent groups in no way morphed into one actor, nor did they even have identical goals. Their relationship was one of tension, competition, and at times violent hostility.

Coercion and Popular Support

The Peruvian case also reveals the weakness of a second tenet of the conventional narcoguerrilla view: the assumption that increases in popular support for belligerents are due primarily to coercion. The evidence in Peru clearly contradicts that belief. Sendero was an extremely brutal movement that routinely mounted public executions in which victims' throats were cut or their heads smashed with stones. But that brutality turned out to be counterproductive, alienating both the uncommitted population and previous supporters. Instead of scaring the population into compliance, brutality encouraged dissent and turned the population against Sendero.

The relationship between Sendero and the population followed a pattern. The rural population initially accepted—or at least tolerated—Sendero. The level of acceptance was considerably higher in drug-producing regions. But as Sendero progressively increased its brutality—for example, by forcibly recruiting children to serve the movement—its political capital eroded.[74] To overcome the population's dissatisfaction and lack of compliance, Sendero resorted to more indiscriminate violence. But as its brutality increased, it started losing support among the rural population to such an extent that the farmers were willing to organize self-defense units. Drawing on interviews with the population under Sendero's control, Carlos Degregori argues that while the peasants welcomed some degree of order, which Sendero established, they abhorred the brutality with which the group tried to enforce its rules.[75] Similarly, Cynthia McClintock maintains that "in various areas where the Sendero was unable to make inroads or where it gradually lost support, the explanation given was excessive violence: 'The Senderistas have killed too many innocent people.'"[76]

If coercion were the predominant explanation for its support, then the areas where Sendero used more violence against the population would also be the areas where it had the greatest support. But the opposite is the case. Sendero's support was strongest in the Upper Huallaga Valley, where its sponsorship of the illicit economy allowed the movement to acquire farmers' allegiance without resorting to excessive violence. The region remained Sendero's stronghold even after the group's popularity waned elsewhere. Coercion thus does not appear to be a valid explanation for Sendero's political capital. In fact, coercion directly undermined the political capital that the group had obtained by distributing benefits to the population.

THE IMPACT OF COUNTERNARCOTICS POLICIES ON COUNTERINSURGENCY OBJECTIVES

Throughout the preceding discussion, one critical variable has been largely absent—the counternarcotics policies pursued by the government. Yet the case of Peru is especially apt for illustrating their significance. Government policy varied significantly during the period of the Shining Path insurgency, and the success of the insurgency varied along with it. The following analysis examines the relationship between the government's drug policy and the success or failure of its counterinsurgency policy, focusing on how counternarcotics policies affected the group's ability to build political capital. In a nutshell, when the Peruvian government did not attempt to eradicate coca, Shining Path's political capital was relatively low and the counterinsurgency effort was relatively effective. When the government undertook aggressive eradication, the efficacy of its counterinsurgency policy was greatly reduced.

The shifts of direction were not necessarily due to changes of heart at the top. Counternarcotics policy was largely shaped by competition between the Peruvian national police force, which was charged with eradication, and the Peruvian military, which was charged with counterinsurgency operations. The military resisted getting involved in eradication and occasionally even sought to prevent the police from conducting large-scale eradication efforts. As the relative power of the two agencies changed, changes in counternarcotics policy often took place.

Initial Laissez-Faire, 1984–85

When placed in charge of the emergency zone in 1984, Julio Carbajal D'Angelo, a general in the army, did not consider drug trafficking to be a real problem. Although eradication conducted by the Peruvian police had been in full swing for several years, Carbajal maintained that the coca business was beneficial to the Peruvian economy since it provided thousands of farmers with their livelihood and generated large foreign exchange revenues. Cocaine, he argued, was the gringos' problem.[77] He also maintained that involving the military in the fight against drugs could expose his officers and soldiers to potentially corrupting temptations.[78]

In 1984 and 1985, Carbajal and his successor actively paralyzed the counternarcotics efforts of CORAH and UMOPAR by refusing to protect the police and counternarcotics units against attacks or to provide them with intelligence on the location of fields and labs. In June 1985, for example, Peruvian soldiers stood by as the *cocaleros* organized strikes and attacked UMOPAR and CORAH, despite police demands that the military break up the strike. The military also severely restrained the movement of the counternarcotics units, de facto confining UMOPAR to their barracks for five months from August 1984 to January 1985.[79] When the military authorized UMOPAR and CORAH to operate, it allowed them to do so only in areas where Sendero was not present or was weak. As a result, the counternarcotics teams were not able to eradicate even one single hectare of coca in 1985, although they destroyed forty-four labs.[80]

Carbajal made sure that the military's attitude toward counternarcotics was known among the population. In the Monzón district, for example, he publicly reassured the gathered *cocaleros,* "We guarantee that you will be able to continue with your normal economic activities." His policy of keeping the anti-drug squads from operating earned him significant support from local farmers as well as drug traffickers. In the six months of his tenure, Carbajal managed to develop a rather positive relationship with the local population, and both farmers and traffickers provided him with intelligence that allowed him to drop platoons of soldiers along Sendero's escape routes and throughout the region of its operations.[81] Consequently, Carbajal was able to disperse the guerrillas' columns in 1984 and push them out of the UHV.[82]

The success of the laissez-faire policy in motivating coca farmers to cooperate with the counterinsurgency effort is underscored by the fact that this period was also a period of the military's greatest brutality. The military routinely brutalized farmers merely suspected of sympathizing with the guerrillas, and its so-called "dirty war" alienated the rural population tremendously. The fact that the farmers were willing to provide the military with intelligence when eradication was halted, despite the brutality, reveals the crucial impact that the government's anti-narcotics policy had on the effectiveness of its counterinsurgency efforts. It also highlights the difficulty that the Shining Path faced as it attempted to build political capital in that environment.

Return to Eradication, 1985–89

Later in 1985, Alan García, the new president, under pressure from the United States and seeking to capitalize on a popular anticorruption drive, adopted stringent anti-drug operations. As a result of both its success against Sendero and the new emphasis on counternarcotics at the highest levels of Peru's new government, the army was ordered to pull out of the UHV and the state of emergency was lifted. The withdrawal was greeted in the UHV with dismay; local politicians lobbied the government to reinstitute the state of emergency, and the population signed petitions to bring the army back. Nonetheless, the army was ordered to scale down its operations in the area, and the police resumed coca crop eradication. Thus, 355 hectares of coca were eradicated in 1987, 5,130 hectares in 1988, and 1,285 hectares in 1989. The total area under cultivation during those years was 109,500, 115,630, and 115, 630 hectares respectively.[83]

Despite the end of the dirty war, the animosity of the local population toward the police and its alienation from the government grew dramatically. The farmers stopped providing intelligence on Sendero. The belligerents were able to reestablish their presence in the region rapidly, infiltrating first those regions that were hardest hit by CORAH's eradication. The police frequently found itself outgunned and outmanned by the insurgency.[84] Sendero also began controlling entire towns, such as Uchiza and Tocache. At the same time, the Peruvian and U.S. governments sought to beef up interdiction operations and to separate the guerrillas from the drug traffickers by targeting the traffickers intensively. The effort to provoke a split between the two groups did not pan out. In fact, the more aggressively the government and the U.S. Drug Enforcement Agency went after the traffickers, the more the traffickers sought protection from Sendero and the closer the cooperation between the narcos and Sendero grew.

The aggressive eradication effort culminated in the Spike fiasco. In March 1989, tebuthiuron, a controversial new herbicide spray known by the trade name Spike, was tested in the UHV. The coca growers were profoundly disturbed by the new threat, fearing potentially vast damage to their livelihoods and health as well as the environment.[85] Sendero denounced the use of Spike, claiming that "the Yankee monopolies themselves say [Spike] is like a series of small atomic bombs."[86] The Shining Path capitalized on the outrage of the *cocaleros* and with their support launched a military attack against the Uchiza police post that resulted in one of the Peruvian government's worst defeats in the UHV.[87] In that case, the farmers not only applauded Sendero but actively joined the guerrillas (as did the narcos) in defeating the police. Significantly, that was one of the rare instances in which the peasants actively fought alongside Sendero. The group's activity peaked, and entire swaths of the countryside came under its control. In this, its second phase, the government's anti-narcotics campaign was clearly counterproductive with respect to the anti-guerrilla campaign.

The countryside was in such turmoil that Guzmán finally came to believe that the Shining Path was gaining the upper hand militarily. Many exposed army and police outposts were destroyed or overrun; others were abandoned because of growing material shortages, high desertion rates, and inaccessibility as Sendero cut off access routes. In 1988, in an infamous interview in *El Diario*, a Lima newspaper that served as Sendero's mouthpiece, Guzmán analyzed the ideology, organization, strategy, and tactics of his movement and declared that his original estimate of a fifty-year war was too pessimistic and that it was time to carry the war into the cities. The guerrilla campaign thus expanded from the rural to the urban theater, including Lima—or, in classic Maoist terms, from the first phase, protracted defense, to the second phase, equilibrium.

Guzmán's decision to focus on Lima was highly controversial among Sendero's other leaders. A faction led by Guzmán's wife argued that Guzmán's sudden change of heart contradicted Maoism and was premature.[88] Both she and his top lieutenant, Osmán Morote, warned that support for Sendero in the countryside was insufficient and that the risk of defeat in Lima was too great.[89] Analyst Enrique Obando argues that Guzmán decided to escalate simply because he became impatient;[90] similarly, Carlos Iván Degregori maintains that over time Sendero's leadership succumbed to unjustified overconfidence.[91] It is very likely that Guzmán's impatience and false optimism were stimulated by the vast gains that Sendero obtained from its positive involvement in the illicit narcotics economy and the subsequent and unanticipated increase in its power.

What Guzmán failed to realize, however, was that to a large extent, Sendero's political capital with the *cocaleros* was a function of the government's counternarcotics policies. When the government stopped eradicating, Sendero lost much of its political capital.

Laissez-Faire Redux, 1989–90

That is precisely what happened in the third phase of the government's effort. The UHV once again was placed under a state of emergency with the military in charge, and the military once again adopted a laissez-faire approach toward drug cultivation. In April 1989, an army brigadier general, Alberto Arciniega, assumed control of the emergency zone. From the outset, he made it clear that he would concentrate on defeating the guerrillas and not on combating drug trafficking. He believed that gaining the cooperation of the local populace was crucial for winning the counterinsurgency campaign:

> It is necessary to consider that any rebel group seeks to gain the people's support, and in the Huallaga Valley these are primarily cultivators of coca and are repressed. How can we win their support? By taking them out of their present precarious situation, that's how. The *cocalero* peasants were harassed by the police and by any other official organization that happened by because they were considered to be criminals. CORAH harassed them by eradicating their crops, the police by considering that they were engaged in criminal activities. . . . We are talking about 80 percent of the population! What we do then is to change the situation to keep the coca growers, the group which Sendero supports in order to accomplish its goals, from being subject to harassment. If we can persuade the people to join us, the war is won.[92]

To demonstrate his commitment to not interfering with coca production, Arciniega refused to cooperate with the police, whom the farmers resented for their coca suppression practices and human rights violations, and he did not allow police units to stay at his military base. Arciniega also promised large-scale economic aid to the region to promote alternative development. Although the farmers' previous experience with alternative development policies had been poor, they nonetheless preferred alternative development to eradication. The general's acquiescence in coca cultivation was applauded by the populace and won him an unprecedented level of popular support. When he asserted in the city of Uchiza, in the UHV, that the fight was against Sendero, not against the growing of coca, 30,000 *campesinos* cheered.[93] With intelligence provided by both farmers and drug traffickers, Arciniega was able to mount successive attacks against Sendero. The laissez-faire policy toward coca cultivation thus greatly facilitated the counterinsurgency effort.

The bad experience with Spike and other counternarcotics efforts also led civilians in Lima to question the wisdom of the anti-drug operations. Eradication came to be seen as counterproductive not only by the Peruvian military but also by politicians and technocrats in the government. They feared that repressive enforcement measures would only lose the hearts and minds of the Peruvian *cocaleros* to the Shining Path. Hector Vargas Haya, a congressman from Peru's dominant center-left party, APRA (Alianza Popular Revolucionaria Americana [American Revolutionary Popular Alliance]), declared, "What we need in this country are greenbacks, not Green Berets."[94] Primarily as a result of such concerns, in 1989 outgoing President Garcia rejected the U.S. government's offer of $35.9 million in anti-drug aid aimed at eradication and interdiction. The new president, Alberto Fujimori, also refused the offer in 1990.

Sendero reacted to its losses in the countryside by subjecting the farmers to increased violence. Since the military's laissez-faire attitude toward narcotics deprived Sendero of the opportunity to build political capital by protecting the illicit economy, the guerrilla group tried to obtain the farmers' cooperation though coercion. But Sendero's brutality toward the *cocaleros* only further antagonized them. Peasant self-defense units called *rondas campesinas*, promoted by the government, expanded throughout the countryside. By 1993, more than 4,200 self-defense organizations had sprung up across the country, with a total of almost 236,000 members.[95]

The premise of *rondas* was that local farmers would be both more motivated to protect themselves against Sendero and better able to do so because they would know who the Senderistas were. The military forces, who were unfamiliar with the territory, often were unable to tell Senderistas from the local population. *Rondas* interacted with a variety of local organizations, such as parent-teacher associations, women's clubs, and irrigation committees.[96] In the coca-growing regions, *rondas* frequently overlapped with the *cocaleros'* defense organizations. Since the UMOPAR was no longer harassing the organizations, they could actively mobilize and recapture the farmers' trust. Moreover, because of their profits from the drug trade, the *cocalero* defense groups, now overlapping with the *rondas,* often were well equipped with weapons and did not have to depend on the military's unreliable supplies.[97] Two such organizations in particular, FEDECAH (Frente de Defensa de la Hoja de Coca del Alto Huallaga [Defense Front against Coca Eradication in the Upper Huallaga Area]) and FASMA (Federación Agraria de la Selva Maestra [Agrarian Federation of the Selva Maestra]), expanded greatly.[98] Sendero thus was trapped in fighting not only the military but also the farmers themselves—a fight that not only depleted Sendero's energy and momentum but also severed the link between the population and the guerrillas.

Sendero's losses in the countryside coincided with its move into the cities and the launching of its urban campaign. As mentioned, the decision to move to the cities took place in 1988, fueled by Sendero's optimism about how well the campaign in the countryside had been proceeding. By 1990, because the situation in the countryside was becoming more and more unfavorable, the urban campaign became all the more vital for the success of Sendero's insurgency.

Growing Reliance on Interdiction, 1990–95

Although the tolerant approach of the Peruvian military toward the drug trade was effective in terms of the overall counterinsurgency effort, it soon came under threat. As a result of information provided to the U.S. government by the Peruvian police, who strongly disliked the general, Arciniega was accused of receiving bribes from the narcos.[99] Arciniega vehemently denied the charges. A bitter public fight between the general and Melvyn Levitsky, assistant secretary for international narcotics matters with the U.S. State Department, ensued in the newspapers. Fujimori, the new Peruvian president, exploited the drug corruption charges to take control of the military and purge it of officers who were not his staunch supporters. Arciniega was thus removed from his post after having directed the counterinsurgency for seven months.[100]

Following Arciniega's removal and the subsequent investigations into military corruption—which were manipulated by Fujimori and his chief of intelligence, Vladimiro Montesinos, to eliminate opposition—the generals in charge of the Upper Huallaga Valley became careful to avoid exposing themselves to drug corruption charges. The military, moving closer to the position of the police and the U.S. government, ceased to interfere with drug suppression efforts, which now focused on interdiction, not eradication.

Although interdiction efforts had been a part of counternarcotics operations since the beginning, their intensity varied greatly over time. With Fujimori in charge, they were given special priority. Under the name Operation Condor, the U.S. and Peruvian governments sought to destroy processing labs, traffickers' airstrips, and the traffickers themselves. The United States provided Peruvian forces with Twin Bell 214 helicopters, piloted by employees of a private security company, and built an anti-drug air base at Santa Lucía in the heart of the Upper Huallaga Valley.[101] After the Santa Lucía base became fully operational in the late 1980s and the Peruvian military stopped interfering with interdiction operations, the DEA and Peruvian police severely disrupted drug traffic. Because the traffickers were not able to transport coca and cocaine out of the UHV, their demand for coca leaf dropped, resulting in a large overproduction of coca leaf in the valley. Prices for coca leaf fell dramatically, from $2 per kilo in mid-1989 to $0.30 in mid-1990, well below the cost of production.[102] The farmers saw a precipitous decline in their income.

Once again, public sentiment turned against the military. A coca grower from UHV characterized the mood: "We are very disappointed, because we thought we had governmental and military support, but now we are thinking it was only Arniciega who understood us and had the courage to live among us."[103] Disillusioned with the government, the *cocaleros* stopped providing intelligence on the guerrillas to the military. An Interior Ministry official noted that "with growing popular discontent, Sendero could recover as a major force in the valley, especially when the local growers continue not to receive the economic assistance that Arciniega promised."[104] Or, as a coca grower in the Uchiza area put it:

> We really want to move out of coca production because we know that it is harmful and because of all the problems it causes us. We are harassed and persecuted because we grow coca, and we are victims of corruption and abuse as well. But if we can't count on help from our own government or from foreign aid, then our only recourse may be to get Sendero's support.[105]

Effective interdiction renewed the population's demand for Sendero's positive involvement in the illicit economy. The Shining Path stepped in and made the drug traffickers pay higher prices to the farmers for coca leaves. Grateful, the *cocaleros* again embraced Sendero. Thus, enhanced counternarcotics suppression measures once again hampered the success of the government's counterinsurgency policy.

Fujimori recognized the political cost of aggressive counternarcotics measures and opposed eradication on those grounds. As he explained in a major speech in October 1990:

> In no way are we opposed to an effective program to eradicate illegal coca crops. . . . But we wish to address repression in a larger context. . . . An effective program of repression that leaves the peasants without other alternatives would sharply increase the number of those in extreme poverty and could unchain a civil war of unsuspected proportions. . . . We will not repeat the errors of President Ngo Dinh Diem of Vietnam, who, during the 1950s, pitted himself against the informal, common law order of the peasants. . . . We will not push peasants and their families into the arms of terrorists and drug traffickers.[106]

Similarly, during a counterdrug summit meeting among Latin American governments and the United States in San Antonio in February 1992, Fujimori rejected counternarcotics efforts unless more was done to help the farmers. During a meeting with President George H. W. Bush, in what a U.S. diplomat characterized as "an in-your-face outburst," Fujimori argued that "no government may fight against an entire population."[107] The eradication of all mature coca was thus suspended in Peru until 1996. Eradication of coca seedbeds continued; however, despite U.S. pressure, only minimal efforts were made, creating only a small dent in cultivation. In 1994, Peru avoided U.S. economic sanctions stemming from failure to obtain the annual State Department certification of compliance with U.S. counternarcotics policy only because Peru was given a national security waiver. However, in order to placate the United States, Fujimori continued to step up the interdiction effort. His intelligence chief and closest confidante, Vladimiro Montesinos, in collaboration with the CIA, began setting up the infrastructure for an expanded air interdiction program. The CIA and the U.S. Department of Defense's Southern Command (SOUTHCOM) installed radar stations to facilitate the efforts of the Peruvian air force to track drug traffickers' aircraft. In 1991, ten traffickers' airplanes were seized, seven in 1992, and thirteen in 1993.[108]

However, those efforts were seriously undermined by corruption among the military and the police. The 1994 arrest of one of Peru's most prominent traffickers, Demetrio Chávez Peñaherrera (known as El Vaticano), revealed that in the Campanilla region, where he operated an airstrip for shipping cocaine to Colombia, he had paid both Vladimiro Montesinos and the local military leadership for protection.[109] In addition, Chávez claimed, his men had cooperated with the military in keeping Sendero out of the region. Sendero was, in fact, never able to establish a significant presence in Campanilla.

In conjunction with its support of interdiction, the Peruvian military—at least in specific areas, such as the Ucayali region—adopted an explicit hearts-and-minds approach, extending the state's presence and distributing material benefits to the population, including road repair, medicines, and school supplies. To some extent, that approach helped reduce the counterproductive effects of interdiction; moreover, interdiction had less impact on farmers than eradication. Although interdiction did lead to lower prices for coca and to lower incomes, it did not altogether eliminate the farmers' livelihood. Thus Sendero had fewer opportunities to gain popular support. Instead, beginning in 1990, the provision of intelligence to the military improved and Sendero's influence weakened, resulting in significant losses of territory.

As conditions in the countryside continued to turn against Sendero, the importance of the urban theater grew. The expansion of the insurgency to Lima and the increased number of attacks and casualties created a real sense both in Peru and abroad that Sendero could topple the government. As Cynthia McClintock argues, one of Sendero's greatest strategic achievements was to create the impression in the minds of many Peruvians that its march to power was inexorable.[110]

Sendero's strategy was to bring down the government by creating a popular urban uprising to reinforce its own military effort. By creating chaos in Lima, Sendero planned to force an exodus of Peru's economic and political elite, followed by most of the foreign capital invested in the country. The resulting drain on the economy would bring the country to a standstill, causing the collapse of all social and public services and major economic deprivation for the masses, which would resort to looting and strikes. The military then would be dispatched to crush them, a move that Sendero believed would cause a schism in the military that Sendero could exploit to take over the government.

By the end of 1990, Sendero had taken control of many shantytowns on the outskirts of Lima. Economic crisis had forced the state to curtail even the most basic services among the urban poor, increasing their economic hardship, radicalizing them, and discrediting non-Sendero neighborhood organizers.[111] Meanwhile, Sendero was distributing public services, such as free haircuts and health clinics, providing roofing for schools, running soup kitchens, and organizing street trash cleanup.[112] Sendero also began detonating car and truck bombs inside the city, including in very affluent neighborhoods such as Miraflores. Between 1990 and 1992, Sendero attacked police stations, factories, businesses, and schools at an unrelenting rate and paralyzed the capital's roads to the interior. Political assassinations by Sendero became commonplace. Businessmen, doctors, and other professionals were leaving the country, and the military was experiencing high desertion rates. The police were rapidly losing credibility due to their inability to control crime.[113] Sendero's predictions appeared to be materializing. According to Enrique Obando, a prominent Peruvian defense expert and former official with the Ministry of Defense, "Sendero came very close to succeeding in its plan."[114]

Sendero's assault on the capital greatly intensified interest among the country's elite in eliminating Guzmán. In 1990, with the support of the CIA, the government created a new unit, GEIN (Grupo Especial de Inteligencia [Special Intelligence Group]), within the antiterrorism police, DINCOTE (Dirección Nacional Contra El Terrorismo [National Directorate against Terrorism]). GEIN's sole purpose was to capture Guzmán, and it finally succeeded in doing so in 1992. Guzmán's capture dealt a critical blow to the insurgency. It shattered Guzmán's image as an invincible leader and decapitated Sendero, which was a strict hierarchy organized around Guzmán. In addition, the capture provided vital intelligence on the remaining top echelons of the Shining Path.

To escape the death penalty, Guzmán struck a deal with the government and ordered his troops to surrender. Taking advantage of Guzmán's call to end the conflict, the government announced a "repentance law" in 1993, promising modest penalties or amnesty and reintegration into society for guerrillas who turned themselves in and provided intelligence. By 1995, Sendero ceased to pose a threat to the Peruvian state.

In sum, Sendero Luminoso was ultimately defeated without the elimination of coca production and trafficking in Peru—in fact, without any eradication taking place at all. Sendero was defeated instead through the combined efforts of an urban intelligence operation that led to the capture of Guzmán, independent of the counternarcotics efforts, and a rural counterinsurgency campaign that won the hearts and minds of the population by tolerating coca cultivation. In short, as predicted by the political capital model of illicit economies and military conflict, eradication hampered counterinsurgency efforts and the government's laissez-faire policy toward coca production was instrumental in defeating the insurgency in the countryside.

AFTERMATH OF THE SHINING PATH INSURGENCY

The Peruvian government accomplished its major goal with the capture of Guzmán and the defeat of the Shining Path in the early 1990s. But the United States remained focused on the war on drugs. Facing growing pressure to act more aggressively against traffickers, the Fujimori government reached agreement with the United States in 1995 on a joint aerial interdiction program called Air Bridge Denial. The United States had previously demurred from taking an active role in aerial interdiction due to policymakers' fear that civilians would be shot down by mistake, exposing the government to lawsuits. But in 1994, Congress passed new legislation authorizing the U.S. president to identify countries that posed an extraordinary threat to the United States through drug trafficking and exempted the United States from liability for civilian deaths during shootdowns of suspected trafficker aircraft. The legislation was intended to circumvent the Montreal Protocol, which made the downing of civilian aircraft a criminal offense. Nonetheless, U.S. soldiers were not to fly the interdiction airplanes; the Peruvians would. For their part, U.S. agents at the Santa Lucía center would provide the Peruvians with intelligence. As the program expanded through 2001, various U.S. government agencies—the CIA, the Department of Defense, the Drug Enforcement Administration, the National Security Agency, and Customs—provided technical assistance, trained the Peruvian counternarcotics officers, and provided intelligence.

In 1995, twenty-two aircraft were downed under the interdiction program. The fee demanded by pilots for flying drug trafficking planes increased from $30,000 per flight in 1994 to $180,000 in 1997.[115] The same period saw the spread of a fungus that devastated the coca crops and a major drop in coca leaf prices and consequently a sharp reduction in the area under coca cultivation.[116] Although production was suppressed, so was demand for coca leaf produced in Peru, and prices greatly decreased. The price of a kilo of coca leaf fell from $2.50 at the beginning of 1995 to $0.60 at the end of the year and remained under $1 per kilogram, the breakeven point for most producers, until May 1998.[117] The area under cultivation decreased from 115,300 hectares in 1995 to 43,400 in 2000 and then rose slightly, to 46,700, in 2002.[118] Manual eradication started up again in 1996 but played only a small part in driving the downward trend. The government eradicated 1,259 hectares of coca in 1996, 7,825 in 1998, and 13,800 in 1999.[119] In 1999, the area under coca cultivation in Peru, 38,700 hectares, hit a twenty-five-year low.

Air Bridge Denial also had the advantage of making it difficult for the remnants of the Shining Path to regroup, and those who did not surrender formed various loosely affiliated offshoots. After the insurgents' defeat, support for Sendero remained strongest in the coca-growing regions, notably the UHV. Those areas became home to one offshoot, Sendero Rojo (Red Path), a group of about 500 guerrillas formed by Alberto Ramírez Durand ("Feliciano"), a hardcore member of the Shining Path's top leadership, in the wake of what he saw as Guzman's betrayal. Like its predecessor, Sendero Rojo remained active in the drug trade, collecting an estimated $200 million from drug trafficking by 1994.[120]

But the government's interdiction policy made it difficult for Sendero Rojo to generate political capital from its involvement in the coca economy, and the group was too weak to pose a real threat to Air Bridge Denial. Its activities, therefore, were limited to protecting drug traffickers on land, although the group also became involved in the illicit logging of mahogany, cedar, oak, and other specialty hardwoods along Peru's northern border.

Illicit logging and the cultivation of coca are intimately linked. Before coca can be planted, the land must be stripped of trees, and in highly acidic tropical soils, deforestation frequently causes such soil degradation that few plants other than coca can be planted in cleared areas. Because illicit logging is highly lucrative and labor intensive, positive involvement in the illicit logging economy could have generated substantial political capital for the remnants of the Shining Path. But the Senderistas were handicapped by the absence of an enemy. Lacking both the means and the motivation to crack down on illicit logging, the government did little to interfere with the trade.[121] Consequently, the loggers did not need Sendero protection and showed little affinity for the group.

Suspension of Air Bridge Denial and the Rebound of Coca in Peru

Operation Air Bridge Denial came to an end after the Peruvian air force shot down a plane belonging to the Association of Baptists for World Evangelization, causing the death of a U.S. missionary and her daughter, in April 2001. Despite the 1994 legislation exempting the U.S. government from liability under the Montreal Protocol, the Baptist Church sued for $50 million and ultimately received $8 million. The United States suspended its financial and material support for aerial interdiction abroad. Washington has instituted new procedures for monitoring anti-narcotics activities and has placed additional restrictions on the "deadly force phase" of aerial interceptions, but aerial interdiction has not been reinstituted in Peru. The Peruvian government does not have the means to carry out interdiction on its own, and even giving U.S. financial aid to Peru to conduct missions could make the United States liable for interdiction mishaps.

The suspension of Air Bridge Denial in 2002 and the subsequent increase in coca eradication led to a rebound in coca cultivation and growing resentment among *cocaleros* facing the threat of eradication. Between 1999 and 2007, the area under coca cultivation in Peru increased by 40 percent, from 38,700 hectares to 53,700 hectares.[122] Coca cultivation has spread out of the Huallaga Valley to the Apurímac-Ene valleys, La Convención y Lares, San Gabán, Inambari Tambopata, Marañon, and other areas. Coca cultivation also appears to be increasing along the Napo River near the border with Colombia. Moreover, cultivation of opium poppies is emerging in the northern jungle areas. Today, according to the UN Office on Drugs and Crime, about 50,000 families are involved in coca cultivation in Peru.[123] Peruvian experts believe that that number underestimates the scale of the problem and put the number of people directly involved in the coca economy at as much as 500,000.[124]

Prices in Peru have climbed steadily since 1998, partly in response to stepped up aerial spraying in Colombia, which has fueled the spread of coca cultivation. The price of a kilo of sun-dried coca leaf rose from $0.80 in 1997 to $2.90 in 2005, then fell slightly to $2.50 and stabilized there.[125] At the same time, the scope and reach of the Peruvian drug industry has grown. Increasingly, the bulk of processing takes place in Peru. Mexican cartels have displaced Colombian traffickers as the dominant trading partners for Peruvian producers and traffickers, who also are dealing with emerging drug syndicates in Brazil.

That growth has taken place despite an increase in manual eradication. Government agents uprooted 12,072 hectares of coca in 2007, about twice the amount (6,206 hectares) eradicated in 2000.[126] Farmers have adapted in a variety of ways, such as by increasing the number of plants per hectare. While the average number of plants per hectare in the Apurímac Valley is 30,000 to 40,000, up to 300,000 per hectare have been observed.[127] The government has tried to soften the impact of eradication by investing in alternative development, but with little effect. Between 1995 and 2000, the United States spent about $15 million on alternative livelihood programs in Peru.[128] With those funds, about 600 kilometers of roads and seventeen bridges were repaired and credit was extended to several thousand families to allow them to cultivate legal crops. Some alternative development funds have also been allocated to improvements in health and education services.[129] Nonetheless, most farmers found it difficult to obtain funds or otherwise benefit from the programs. Credit and technical assistance remain scarce, critical infrastructure is still lacking, and most farmers were poorer in the early 2000s than in the previous decade. As Diego García-Sayan put it, "They were promised alternative development, and instead they got alternative poverty."[130]

Consequently, eradication has generated widespread resistance. Repeated negotiations with the government have failed to satisfy the *cocaleros,* who are demanding the suspension of forced eradication, the withdrawal of NGOs from the coca regions, and direct payments to farmers to promote rural development. Under pressure from the *cocaleros,* the Peruvian government temporarily adopted a policy of "gradual and negotiated self-eradication," allowing coca growers to destroy their own crops in exchange for a payment of $100 per hectare eradicated and $300 for every hectare reforested, plus food aid, emergency loans, and rural development.[131] However, the United States was dissatisfied with the pace of self-eradication and demanded a return to forced eradication.

Unable to achieve their demands through negotiation, coca farmers have turned again to direct action. Since 2001, violent roadblocks and protests organized by coca growers' associations have taken place throughout the coca-growing regions of Peru, and traffickers have increasingly targeted law enforcement officials and judges. In 2007, after protests in Tocache, UHV, Huánaco, and Uyacali, President Alan García ordered fighter jets to bomb the maceration pits where coca leaves are converted to coca paste.[132] The same year, the political atmosphere was so tense in Apurímac-Ene, the second-largest coca-cultivating region in Peru, that the government did not dare undertake any eradication, even though some interdiction operations continued. Nor was there any eradication in Monzón, another prominent coca-ridden region.

Opposition to the government is likely to grow as the coca farmers become better organized.[133] Although they lack the cohesion, party organization, and leadership of their Bolivian counterparts, who are represented by President Evo Morales's Movimiento al Socialismo (Movement toward Socialism),[134] Peruvian *cocaleros* have banded together in such groups as CONPACCP (Confederación Nacional de Productores Agropecuarios de las Cuencas Cocaleras del Perú [National Confederation of Agricultural Producers in Peru's Coca-Growing Valleys]). The *cocalero* movement has also sought to form alliances with a variety of other protest groups, such as anti-mining groups, environmental groups, those who oppose free trade with the United States, and even those who oppose increases in mandatory car insurance. Most important, the *cocalero* movement has good ties to many of the peasant self-defense groups that fought the Shining Path, which are still armed today. Some of these self-defense groups directly overlap with the *cocalero* groups; others are simply sympathetic to their cause.

Meanwhile, extremist parties in Peru are vying to represent the *cocalero* movement. The Humala brothers' Etno-Caceristas, an ultranationalist, fascist-like group, openly defends coca cultivation and has tried to co-opt the movement.[135] In the June 2006 presidential elections, populist Ollanta Humala came close to defeating ex-president Alan García, capturing most of the vote in rural areas. Another competitor for the *cocaleros'* allegiance is Peru's far-left Patria Roja. Smaller pro-coca political parties that emphasize their indigenous roots, such as the Qatun Tarpuy, also are emerging. Moreover, foreign leaders, such as Evo Morales and Hugo Chávez, have tried to exploit the Peruvian *cocalero* movement as part of their efforts to forge a movement of coca farmers and Andean indigenous people throughout Latin America.

Sendero's New Mobilization of the Cocaleros

Ominously, the remaining Shining Path activists are among the aspirants to leadership of the coca peasants, exploiting the social disquiet produced by eradication to reinvigorate their social base. As of 2008, at least two armed factions of Sendero have been operating in the coca-growing regions. One group of 300 guerrillas, led by "Artemio," professes loyalty to Guzmán and operates primarily in the Upper Huallaga Valley. The other faction, Proseguir, numbers between 100 and 150 insurgents; it is led by "Alipio" and is located primarily in the Apurímac-Ene area.[136] A possible third faction appears to be led by two brothers, Victor Quispe Palomino and Jorge Quispe Palomino, but overall little is known about the leaders. Some estimates put the number of its full-time combatants at as high as 700.[137] All three groups are providing protection to drug trafficking groups.

The Senderistas have begun to pledge to defend the *cocaleros* against eradication and counternarcotics agents.[138] Shining Path has apparently established a working relationship with two growers' groups, the Federación de Cocaleros del Apurímac (Apurímac Valley Coca Growers Federation) and Frente de Defensa de Ayacucho (Ayacucho Defense Front).[139] They also have participated in *cocalero* strikes and are increasingly being tolerated by coca-growing communities.[140] A prominent expert on the Shining Path, David Scott Palmer, has commented that "the Shining Path folks are working right alongside the local growers, and are helping them hoe, and helping them with [community work], and would pay for what they buy. They're seen, if not as a positive force, at least as worthy of being accepted—not embraced, but at least accepted."[141] Meanwhile, the military's efforts to destroy maceration pits and cocaine labs, increasingly small and interspersed in coca-growing hamlets, have placed the military in direct confrontation not just with the Senderistas but also with the *cocaleros*.[142]

In addition to working with coca farmers, Senderistas have found new opportunities to benefit from the drug trade by collaborating with traffickers. In response to aerial interdiction, Peruvian traffickers shifted first from air to river transport and then, once law enforcement caught up with them, to land transportation. Increasingly, smugglers carry coca paste and cocaine from the Peruvian jungle down to the coast. The drugs are then smuggled by sea to Mexico and onward to the United States.

Although hard to detect, these drug caravans are very vulnerable to capture once detected. The Shining Path appears to be protecting at least some of the trafficking routes in return for a fee.[143]

Finally, Sendero has stepped up its military challenge to the government, targeting counternarcotics teams and the Peruvian military, even if on a small scale. In 2008, the various remnants and offshoots of the Shining Path killed twenty-six people, including twenty-two soldiers and police officers. Twenty-two of those deaths took place in October, making it the bloodiest month for Sendero since the 1990s. In response to a stepped-up pressure from the Peruvian military in August and September 2009 to capture Jorge Quispe Palomino, the Senderistas shot down an MI-17 Peruvian air force helicopter and initiated several attacks against the Peruvian military in Apurímac-Ene. While the numbers of attacks and casualties are still small, they suggest a level of Sendero activity that has not been seen for almost fifteen years.

Today Sendero does not pose a strategic threat to the Peruvian state. Far from all *cocalero* groups have embraced Sendero, and the memory of Sendero's brutality still persists. However, successful recapture of the *cocalero* movement would give the guerrillas substantial political capital as well as increase their capabilities. The remnants of the Shining Path already are seeking to rebuild their political capital by offering themselves as protectors to *cocaleros* threatened by eradication. They also are reaping financial benefits from protecting the drug trade. Instead of bankrupting the remnants of the belligerents, the government's increased eradication effort, without effective alternative livelihood programs in place, has played into Sendero's hands.

Colombia

- ·—··— International Boundary
- -·-·-· Parish Boundary
- ★ National Capital
- ⊚ Parish Capital
- —— Road

0   100   200 Kilometers
0   100   200 Miles

FOUR

COLOMBIA

The Narco Wars

Colombia has had one of the world's largest illicit narcotics economies for almost thirty years. The country produces roughly 80 percent of the world's supply of cocaine and 90 percent of the cocaine sold in the United States.[1] It is also the Western Hemisphere's largest producer of heroin, supplying 50 percent of U.S. heroin. Returns from illicit drugs as a percentage of Colombia's GDP have hovered between 0.5 percent and 3 percent since the mid-1990s.[2]

Over the same period, Colombia has been torn by a civil war pitting leftist guerrillas, rightist paramilitaries, and the Colombian state against one other. The conflict has resulted in more than 47,000 casualties over the past fifteen years.[3] In addition, it has caused the internal displacement of almost 2 million people and contributed to one of the highest homicide and kidnapping rates in the world, although since 2005, those rates have decreased.

Colombia is the poster case for the conventional narcoguerrilla view. In fact, the concepts of the narcoguerrilla and narcoterrorism were developed in reference to Colombia.[4] A former Colombian ambassador to the United States, Luis Alberto Moreno, once characterized the conflict in Colombia as follows: "Drugs are the root of almost all violence in Colombia. . . . While they may hide behind a Marxist ideology, Colombia's leftist guerrillas have ceased to be a political insurgency. They have traded their ideals for drug profits."[5] Similarly, President Álvaro Uribe declared in March 2004: "If Colombia [did] not have drugs, it would not have terrorists."[6]

Over the past three decades, eradication has been the centerpiece of Colombia's policy toward the drug economy, although the intensity of implementation has varied since the late 1970s. Generations of politicians have argued, like Fernando Londoño, Colombia's minister of justice and interior, that if the government eliminates the income that guerrilla groups derive from the cultivation of coca and opium poppy, "It [the insurgency] will be liquidated and nothing will be left."[7] The primacy of eradication over thirty years makes Colombia an ideal case for testing the central claim of the conventional view—that eradication bankrupts belligerents and paralyzes insurgencies. If eradication can succeed anywhere, it should have succeeded in Colombia, particularly since the 2000 launch of Plan Colombia, the most intensive aerial spraying campaign targeting illicit crops in history.

This chapter examines the conventional claims within the context of the broader interaction between military conflict and illicit economies in Colombia from the late 1970s to the present. The analysis encompasses the narcotics-related activities of leftist insurgent groups, notably the FARC (Fuerzas Armadas Revolucionarias de Colombia [Revolutionary Armed Forces of Colombia]), M-19 (Movimiento 19 de Abril [19th of April Movement]), and ELN (Ejército de Liberación Popular [Popular Liberation Army]); rightist paramilitiaries and their umbrella organization, AUC (Autodefensas Unidas de Colombia [United Self-Defense Forces of Colombia]); and the new paramilitary groups—or *bandas criminales* (criminal bands) or *grupos emergentes* (emerging groups), as the Colombian government prefers to call them—that have emerged since the official demobilization of the AUC in 2005. The analysis also extends to participation in non–narcotics-related illicit activities, such as kidnapping and extortion, making it possible to compare the payoffs associated with participation in different types of illicit economies.

On the basis of this analysis, I conclude that the conventional narcoguerrilla view fails to explain much of what has happened in Colombia. Consistent with the narcoguerrilla view, the FARC did gain considerable strength from its positive participation in the drug economy. However, its gains were not limited to enhanced military capability; they also included significant political capital. Moreover, despite the largest, most intense, and most sustained eradication program anywhere in the world, the Colombian government has failed to bankrupt or significantly weaken the belligerents through eradication. The important successes against the

FARC since 2005 have been largely and primarily due to direct military operations against the guerrillas, not to eradication. Eradication has instead hurt the government's counterinsurgency efforts by reducing the population's willingness to provide intelligence on the insurgents.

Colombia's experience with drugs and insurgency also reveals other weaknesses in the narcoguerrilla approach. While the conventional view treats drug traffickers and insurgents as virtually indistinguishable, often the groups are locked in conflict. Therefore, in order to defeat them, it is essential for the government to understand their distinct interests and strengths. At the same time, however, the distinction should not be over-drawn. Advocates of the narcoguerrilla view frequently contend that to the extent that traffickers and insurgents differ, ideology creates the dividing line. The implication is that insurgents can draw on greater popular support because they espouse certain political goals and an often nationalist ideology, whereas traffickers rely on coercion to maintain control. But in fact, Colombian drug cartels also succeeded in using drug-related activities to generate political capital, although not to the same extent as insurgent groups like the FARC.

THE RISE OF THE COLOMBIAN DRUG ECONOMY

Low-scale drug production and trafficking have existed in Colombia since the 1950s. Labs in Medellín processed heroin, cocaine, and morphine, which were transported to Cuba for distribution in Miami and to Mexico for distribution elsewhere in the United States.[8] In addition, by the early 1970s, marijuana cultivation was well established on the slopes of Sierra Nevada de Santa Marta and adjoining sections of the northeastern coastal region. However, the early and mid-1970s brought important changes in the international drug trade that contributed critically to a vast expansion of narcotics production. First, the United States undertook major drug suppression campaigns in Jamaica and Mexico, then the two main suppliers of marijuana to the United States. Those campaigns were temporarily successful, creating an opening for Colombia to increase its own production of marijuana. Second, Colombian smugglers decided to eliminate their Cuban counterparts in the United States and take over their business. By the end of 1978, Colombian crime organizations controlled wholesale distribution of cannabis in the United States.[9] Third, encouraged by its operations in Mexico and Jamaica, the United States pressured the Colombian government to undertake a similar marijuana eradication campaign.[10] In 1978, to divert suspicion that he himself was on the payroll of the traffickers, Colombia's president, Julio César Turbay Ayala, finally agreed to eradicate while the United States undertook interdiction at the U.S. border and on the sea. The effort to block the marijuana trade persuaded Colombian traffickers to switch their focus to cocaine, which was harder to detect and more profitable.

Initially Colombian traffickers obtained most of their coca leaf and paste from Peru and Bolivia. However, domestic cultivation grew at a steady pace, notably in the southeastern and southern plains and jungles of Colombia, in the departments of Putumayo, Caquetá, and Guaviare. As in Peru, coca had significant economic advantages over other crops. In addition to supporting higher prices, coca did not require transportation since traffickers picked it up right at the farm. It grew easily in acidic, poor-quality soil and did not require special irrigation systems and fertilizers. Finally, coca leaves were easy to process into nonperishable coca paste, while most licit crops required expensive canning or immediate consumption. As knowledge of coca's advantages became more widespread, the number of farmers participating in coca cultivation grew from perhaps 25,000 in the early 1980s to 300,000 by the late 1990s.[11] Many parts of the south were transformed into a pure coca economy. Between 1978 and 2001, when cultivation peaked, the area cultivated with coca in Colombia increased by almost 500 percent, reaching 169,800 hectares in 2001.[12]

The Growth of the Cartels

The emerging drug economy gave rise to the Medellín and Cali cartels, two of the largest and most notorious criminal organizations in history.[13] Headed by six Medellín-based drug lords, also called capos or, in Spanish, *narco-jefes* (Jorge Ochoa Vazquez and his brothers Fabio and Juan David, Pablo Escobar Gaviria, Carlos Lehder Rivas, and José Gonzalo Rodríguez Gacha) and two Cali-based *narco-jefes* (Gilberto Rodríguez Orejuela and José Santacruz Londoño), the traffickers established large processing laboratories,[14] smuggled the drugs overseas, organized distribution in the United States, and developed sophisticated money-laundering methods.[15] They built complex organizations, employing their own security forces and informers along with lawyers, economists, and financial experts who both handled the cartels' affairs and helped provide services, such as transport insurance, to smaller traffickers.[16] In addition, they diversified from the production and sale of coca into poppy cultivation and heroin processing.[17]

Together, the cartels earned an estimated $5 billion to $6 billion a year from cocaine sales.[18] By the late 1980s, Colombian traffickers had accumulated between $39 billion and $60 billion and controlled assets that were equivalent to those of Colombia's entire legal private sector at that time.[19]

Despite their brutality, they also had succeeded in using their role in the illicit economy as a platform for building popular support. That task was eased by the economic crisis that hit Colombia just as the drug economy took off. In the early 1980s, as Medellín's textile economy collapsed because of competition from Asia, the city's unemployment rate surpassed that of other cities, many businesses went bankrupt, and poverty became widespread. The cocaine economy brought hundreds of millions of dollars into Medellín, stimulating a miniboom in construction and in other sectors and considerably reducing Medellín's unemployment rate, generating 28,000 jobs in 1987 alone.[20] Thus, in the short term, the surging cocaine economy cushioned the impact of the economic crisis for many of Colombia's poor.

For the poor and disadvantaged, the drug economy also provided a path for advancing in a closed social system. Many of the capos came from poor backgrounds, and they became a symbol of how to make quick money.[21] As Mary Roldán put it, the drug trade became a vehicle for Medellín's least powerful to contest the distribution of power and economic privilege in an otherwise exclusionary system.[22] Many of the poor respected the traffickers for their wealth and success.

The major traffickers, especially those associated with the Medellín cartel, sought to build on the potential for popular support by investing in social projects and organizing social services. For example, Pablo Escobar built sports facilities, hospitals, and schools; planted trees; and organized sewer repairs in poor neighborhoods. Under the slogan "Medellín without Slums," he built 450 to 500 two-bedroom cement-block houses in a neighborhood that became known as Barrio Pablo Escobar. Escobar also reputedly donated a church to the town of Doradal in the Magdalena Medio (Middle Magdalena Valley). And while in prison in 1991–92, he donated large sums of money for public education, school transportation, and the most extensive water and sewer systems in the country at that time.[23] Escobar made sure that his services to the community were well advertised. The newspaper *Medellín Cívico,* which he owned, frequently ran articles contrasting Escobar's generosity with the selfishness of Colombia's traditional elite.

Other traffickers followed suit, albeit typically on a smaller scale. Gonzalo Rodríguez Gacha donated an outdoor basketball court to his hometown of Pacho and repaired the city hall's façade. Carlos Lehder organized and funded a major earthquake relief effort in the city of Popayán and built a housing project for the poor in his native city of Armenia.[24] Collectively, the Medellín cartel underwrote the provision of social services by rightist paramilitaries in Puerto Boyacá, including clinics and schools, visits of health brigades, road building and repair, and the construction of a communications center.[25] All of their handouts, of course, came at the price of extraordinary violence. In 1988, Medellín had the highest murder rate of any city in the world, with a homicide committed every three hours.[26]

Several traffickers attempted to build on their political capital and generate further power by participating in electoral politics. In 1982, Escobar ran on the Liberal Party ticket for Colombia's house of representatives and was elected as alternate representative for the Antioquia seat. (Minister of Justice Rodrigo Lara Bonilla, who blocked Escobar's further political ambitions within the Liberal Party, was assassinated on Escobar's orders in 1984.) After attempting unsuccessfully to win seats in the national senate and on Bogotá's municipal council, Lehder created a neofascist political party, the MCLN (Movimiento Cívico Latino Nacional [National Latino Civic Movement]). In addition to promoting a Nazi agenda and opposing communism, Zionism, neoimperialism, and neocolonialism, the party vehemently opposed extradition of traffickers to the United States (Lehder admitted that that was his main purpose in creating the party) and advocated the legalization of marijuana for personal use as well as the protection of Colombia's natural resources.[27] Lehder's campaign style consisted of trucking people from villages to his rallies, blasting disco music, and handing out money to attendees. In 1984, his party managed to win 12 percent of the regional electorate in Quindío, which translated into two of thirteen deputy seats in the departmental assembly, as well as eleven seats in various city councils.[28] The success of the party was enhanced by the collapse of the coffee economy in Quindío, which made Lehder's cash handouts even more attractive. (By the time the coffee harvest rebounded, Lehder was on the run and his party failed to win any seats in the departmental assembly in the March 1986 elections.)

Such efforts to build political capital met with some success. Escobar and others were widely praised for their generosity by the poor.[29] To Medellín's urban destitute, the traffickers were benefactors and employers whose criminal background could be overlooked. Especially during the economic downturn, Lehder's party did reasonably well. However, the traffickers' attempts to gain political power backfired by helping to trigger a crackdown by the traditional Colombian elite.

Throughout the 1980s, one of the major issues of contention between the cartels and the Colombian state was Colombia's policy of extraditing drug traffickers to the United States. Extradition, which many politicians perceived as a major encroachment on Colombia's sovereignty, was highly controversial, and the government's policy changed frequently. The bilateral extradition treaty was first signed in 1979, then deactivated between 1982 and 1984, then reactivated, then made unconstitutional by Colombia's supreme court in early 1987. In late 1987, it was reinstated by the Colombian government, which felt increasingly threatened by the traffickers' efforts to penetrate the electoral system.[30] The Medellín cartel responded with extraordinary violence, creating a group, Los Extraditables, that initiated what Escobar called an all-out war against the Colombian state. Scores of journalists and judges were assassinated or threatened, paralyzing the judicial system.[31] Politicians, especially those embracing extradition, also were targeted. The Medellín cartel assassinated five presidential candidates, including the Liberal Party candidate Luis Carlos Galán, a strong supporter of extradition who disqualified Escobar from participating in the 1990 presidential elections.[32] The traffickers also resorted to indiscriminate violence, exploding bombs in Bogotá and other cities and attacking hotels, banks, and political offices. One bomb destroyed the building of DAS (Departamento Administrativo de Seguridad [Administrative Department of Security]), the national domestic law enforcement and intelligence agency, killing 100 people. A bomb aboard an Avianca flight between Bogotá and Cali killed 119.[33]

Despite the violence, the Colombian government extradited more than twenty suspected drug traffickers to the United States between August 1989 and December 1990 and seized $125 million in drug-related assets.[34] Eventually, however, the government's hard line gave way. In 1991, President César Gaviria negotiated a deal that gave light sentences to most of the Medellín cartel's traffickers in exchange for their surrender. Escobar turned himself in, on condition that he be placed in a specially constructed prison, "La Catedral," near Medellín.[35] Escobar stayed in prison for thirteen months, while continuing to conduct his drug business and even leaving the prison on occasion. Ultimately, he escaped and was shot in 1993 on the rooftops of Medellín, thanks to a large-scale law enforcement operation facilitated by intelligence from the Cali cartel[36] and Los PEPES (Los Perseguidos por Pablo Escobar [People Persecuted by Pablo Escobar]), a paramilitary group that had been organized specifically to eliminate Escobar and his close associates.

Notably absent from that operation was intelligence provided by the local population. Escobar's popularity allowed him to move freely through various Medellín neighborhoods and the areas around his estates, despite the price on his head.[37] A private anti-Escobar group, Colombia Libre (Free Colombia), offered a $5 million reward for Escobar's capture, and the Colombian government offered $7 million. Nonetheless, Medellín's poor remained largely loyal to Escobar. Even after his death, instead of being remembered as a brutal terrorist who killed countless people, bombed city buildings, and organized an all-out war against the Colombian state, he was remembered as the man who distributed money and groceries to the poor and who built soccer stadiums.[38]

In the wake of Escobar's death and the demise of the Medellín cartel, the Cali cartel temporarily seized control of the drug trade in Colombia and the Western Hemisphere. In 1994, however, taped telephone conversations revealed that the presidential campaign of recently elected president Ernesto Samper had been heavily funded by the Cali cartel. Samper was widely criticized at home and became persona non grata in Washington. Relations between Bogotá and Washington reached a long-time low.[39] To clear his name and curry favor with the United States, Samper went after the Cali cartel, aborting peace negotiations that had been initiated by the capos in 1993, who, riding high on their cooperation with law enforcement efforts against Escobar, sensed an opportunity to come in from the cold, sanitize their criminal pasts, and become integrated into Colombia's official political system.[40] Gilberto Rodríguez and José Santacruz Londoño were arrested, with the help of U.S. intelligence, and other top members of the cartel turned themselves in.[41] The collapse of Colombia's second large cartel resulted in the emergence of hundreds of boutique cartels in Colombia and allowed Mexican trafficking organizations to gain dominance of the drug trade in the Western Hemisphere. The biggest of the Colombian boutique cartels has been the Norte del

Valle cartel, headed until 2007 by Wilber Varela ("Jabon") and Diego Montoya ("Don Diego").[42] Other major trafficking operations have coalesced around larger operators, such as Juan Carlos Abadía ("Chupeta"), Hermágoras Gonzales ("El Gordo"), Fabio Ochoa Vasco ("Carlos Mario"), Eduardo Restrepo Victoria ("El Socio"), and Daniel Barrera ("El Loco").[43]

INSURGENTS AND DRUGS: THE EARLY YEARS OF THE FARC

Compared with the two major cartels, the Fuerzas Armadas Revolucionarias de Colombia, like other insurgent groups, initially played a secondary role in the drug trade. But the drug economy was critical to the FARC's growth and success. Before it began to participate in the cultivation of coca and the production of cocaine, the group was small and largely powerless; following its embrace of drugs, it emerged as a dangerous challenger to the Colombian state.

The FARC, one of Colombia's oldest and most powerful guerrilla groups, originated in La Violencia, the civil war that swept over Colombia in the late 1940s and 1950s and resulted in the deaths of between 200,000 and 300,000 people. Triggered by the assassination of Liberal Party leader Jorge Eliecer Gaitán in 1948, La Violencia was rooted in a profound socioeconomic crisis and the weakness of Colombia's political institutions. The state was generally absent from rural areas, where lawlessness was widespread. Land distribution was profoundly inequitable.[44] The non-elites had little access to political representation and participation, and members of the elite were engaged in an intense power struggle.

The civil war, which pitted partisans of the Liberal Party against partisans of the Conservative Party, failed to remedy the country's institutional and socioeconomic problems. After a decade of conflict, the concentration of land in the hands of the wealthy had increased, the peasants remained politically powerless, the same dominant classes retained control, and the exclusionary two-party political system was resuscitated under a power-sharing arrangement known as the Frente Nacional (National Front).[45] But the struggle left a prominent legacy in the form of several guerrilla movements—including the FARC, the ELN, the EPL (Ejército de Liberación Popular [Popular Liberation Army]), and the M-19—that emerged from peasant self-defense organizations formed during the civil war.

The FARC was founded by Pedro Antonio Marín, who also went by the alias Manuel Marulanda Vélezor and the nickname Tirofijo (Sureshot). Marín began his guerrilla career in 1949 by joining a Liberal armed group that sought to protect the land interests of poor farmers from large landowners. The movement has been dominated by peasants since its earliest days. By the late 1990s, 70 percent of FARC members still were farmers, while the working class, students, and teachers represented another 20 percent and middle-class intellectuals the remaining 10 percent.[46] Hierarchically organized and highly cohesive,[47] the FARC originally sought to establish socialism, empower the lower classes (especially the peasantry), redistribute land, and bring economic development to the countryside. Since the fall of the Soviet Union, the FARC has modified its political agenda to downplay socialism, but it continues to advocate land redistribution and state ownership in many sectors.[48]

The FARC spent the first fifteen years of its existence significantly handicapped by its lack of physical resources, freedom of action, and political capital. During those years, the group's membership remained in the low hundreds.[49] The movement was incapable of fielding more than fifty combatants in a single operation, thereby ruling out major confrontations with government forces.[50] Any larger operation not only taxed its operational capacity but also threatened to wipe out a substantial portion of its membership. The FARC's military activities therefore were largely confined to long walks in the jungles, trying to avoid detection by military units. As Walter Broderick put it, the guerrillas were essentially engaged in an "imaginary war."[51]

In the mid-1960s, the FARC engaged mainly in isolated ambushes on small military units and raids on farms, while occasionally offering small farmers protection against unscrupulous landowners. While that strategy generated some legitimacy among the rural population, its effect was negated by the FARC's reliance on extortion to obtain vital supplies of food and other necessities—not just from large landowners but also from ordinary peasants—which caused even FARC-backed self-defense groups to turn against the movement.[52] The FARC initially hoped to use such groups to spread its message and consolidate its social base,[53] but in the late 1970s, it abandoned that effort and sought to dismantle the self-defense groups that were still operating.

In a nutshell, the 1960s and early 1970s were years of survival for the FARC, not expansion. Hardly more than a remote band of peasant fighters, the FARC could operate only in areas where the state presence was weak or nonexistent, such as in the intermontane regions and along the edge of the rainforest.[54] The group did not seriously threaten the government in Bogotá, nor could it take over parts of the country.

The FARC Embraces the Drug Economy

The FARC first encountered the drug economy around 1978 in the middle and lower regions along the Caguán River in the department of Caquetá. Seeing the use of drugs and the unrestrained capitalism, anarchy, enrichment of traffickers, and social violence that drugs brought to the region as counterrevolutionary, the Marxist group's original reaction was to oppose the cultivation of illicit crops. That policy, however, proved vastly unpopular with the local population.[55] Suddenly, even the traffickers and their security forces looked more appealing to the farmers than the guerrillas did.[56] Faced with the threatened loss of such support as it enjoyed, the FARC reversed course, and by 1982 it had embraced the illicit economy. The unpublished "Conclusions" of the FARC's Seventh Conference (the seventh planning meeting of the group leadership) laid out the movement's plans to protect coca production, tax traffickers, and recruit those involved in the lower levels of the drug business.[57]

At first, the FARC tapped only the most basic component of drug production, by imposing a "revolutionary tax" of 15 percent on coca farmers.[58] Progressively, however, the guerrillas sought to participate in other aspects of drug production, levying new tariffs on such related activities as importing precursor agents and refining cocaine. The FARC also collected a 20 percent fee from traffickers for use of the territory under its control and demanded payment for the protection of labs and the provision of airstrips.[59] In the 1990s, the FARC standardized its fees, charging $15.70 for every kilo of coca paste and $52.60 for every kilo of cocaine that traffickers produced in its territory. It charged $2,631 in protection fees for a domestic drug flight from one of its airstrips and $5,263 for an international flight.[60]

In the early 1990s, the FARC began to participate directly in drug production by acquiring coca plots and processing coca leaf into cocaine. It also diversified its portfolio by taxing the production of heroin and marijuana. By the late 1990s and early 2000s, the leftist guerrillas were believed to control approximately 70 percent of the opium poppy–producing municipalities.[61] By 2000, twenty-three (about one-third) of

FARC's *frentes* (fronts), organizational columns responsible for particular regions, were collecting payments in coca-growing regions and six were operating in opium-producing zones.[62]

Until the late 1990s, there was no evidence that the FARC had managed to participate in international smuggling operations or in distribution. In 1997, Drug Enforcement Administration officials testified before Congress that "to date, there is little to indicate the insurgent groups are trafficking in cocaine themselves, either by producing cocaine HCL and selling it to Mexican syndicates or by establishing their own distribution networks in the United States."[63] Evidence obtained in the early 2000s, however, revealed that the FARC had bypassed Colombian middlemen to some extent by developing contacts with international smuggling networks, including Mexican traffickers, that transport drugs into the United States, and with the Italian mafia, which handles traffic to Europe.[64] According to Colombian government officials, some of the Mexican cartels have acquired up to 55 percent of the cocaine shipped to the United States directly from the FARC.

The FARC and Drug Traffickers

Throughout that period, relations between the FARC and Colombia's drug traffickers remained tense and often violent, contrary to the predictions of the conventional narcoguerrilla view. The drug dealers initially benefited from the FARC's presence in drug-growing regions. The guerrillas established law and order in areas under their control and ensured that the farmers delivered on promised coca quotas;[65] they also protected the fields from Colombian and U.S. anti-narcotics squads.[66] The Medellín cartel contributed to FARC's efforts by giving the group arms "to protect airstrips and drug-processing plants in the southwestern plains from the army."[67] Yet progressively, the relationship between the guerrillas and the traffickers deteriorated as the FARC demanded more protection money and higher wages for the *cocaleros*.

Crucially, the FARC interfered with the traffickers' effort to launder money and buy themselves power and respectability by acquiring large landholdings. As traffickers began buying land in the Middle Magdalena Valley and northwestern plains, the guerrillas tried to limit their encroachment on farmers' holdings and force them to pay high protection fees. By 1984, the 100 top Colombian traffickers had issued a manifesto denouncing the guerrillas and declaring open war. The drug traffickers hired private security forces to eliminate the guerrilla presence in the regions where they owned land and processing labs or where the cultivation of illicit crops took place.

BENEFITS OF PARTICIPATION IN THE DRUG TRADE

Most credible estimates of the FARC's income from taxing the illicit economy in the 1990s fluctuate between $60 and $100 million a year.[68] In the early 1980s, the FARC already was believed to obtain about $3.8 million a month from the coca economy,[69] yet some estimates put its income far higher. According to them, the protection rents extracted by guerrillas from narcotraffickers amounted to $600 million in 1996 but dropped to less than $200 million annually in 1997 and 1998 as the paramilitaries expanded and were better able to protect the traffickers against the FARC.[70] Whatever the actual numbers, the consensus among analysts, based on interviews with captured FARC fighters, was that drug rents represented about 50 percent of the FARC's income. Extortion of oil companies and other large businesses generated an additional 34 percent, kidnapping brought in another 8 percent, and cattle rustling another 6 percent.[71] The rest came from bank robberies and other illegal activities.[72] For example, in the regions that they controlled, the guerrillas frequently "recommended" individuals for jobs in the local bureaucracy and collected a "facilitation fee" from their earnings, demanded payments for the award of public works contracts, and collected a cut of public expenditures.[73]

Military Capability: Physical Resources and Freedom of Action

The FARC converted its profits into a major increase in its fighting capacity. In 1979, three years before its decision to embrace the drug economy, the FARC consisted of nine *frentes*.[74] By 1986, it had approximately 3,600 fighters in thirty-two *frentes*, and by 1995, some 7,000 fighters in sixty *frentes*.[75] Five years later, the FARC's strength had nearly doubled, to 15,000 to 20,000 fighters in more than seventy *frentes*.[76] The FARC also expanded geographically. In 1979, the FARC had some presence in the departments of Huila, Cauca, Tolima, Putumayo, Caquetá, Antioquia, and Córdoba and in the Magdalena Medio region.[77] Four years later, the guerrillas controlled 173 municipalities, 13 percent of the country's total. By the mid-1980s, the guerrillas' influence had spread to the departments of Guaviare, Meta, and key regions of Sierra Nevada de Santa Marta, Serranía de San Lucas, and Bota Caucana.[78] By 1998, the guerrillas controlled 622 municipalities, 61 percent of the total. The group thus managed to operate in 40 to 60 percent of the country.

Drug profits allowed the FARC to arm its forces with up-to-date military equipment. In the late 1970s, it relied largely on old rifles, frequently dating back to La Violencia. Since then, the movement has acquired M60 machine guns, M16 rifles, AK-47 assault rifles, mortars, rocket-propelled grenades, M79 grenade launchers, land mines, explosives, and detonators. In May 2000, Colombian officials intercepted anti-aircraft and anti-tank rockets destined for the FARC. In addition, reports indicate that the FARC received man-portable missiles, such as SA-14s and SA-16s from Russia and antitank missiles from Venezuela,[79] as well as Redeye and Stinger missiles from Syria,[80] even though the group has not used such surface-to-air-missiles in the conflict. The FARC has also upgraded its communications equipment with Japanese and European voice scramblers and encryption technology.[81]

Its participation in the narcotics economy directly facilitated its acquisition of weapons by introducing the FARC to international arms smuggling organizations. In 2000, for example, Vladimiro Montesinos, then Peru's chief of intelligence, helped facilitate a cocaine-for-arms swap between the Russian mafia and the FARC, with the FARC purchasing 10,000 AK-47s and 3 million cartridges. According to U.S. intelligence officials, a single airdrop in October 1999 delivered 50 million dollars' worth of AK-47s deep in FARC's territory.[82] Positive involvement in the illicit economy therefore not only gave the FARC the financial means necessary to acquire sophisticated weapons but also greatly simplified procurement mechanisms and logistics.

In addition, positive involvement in the illicit narcotics economy resulted in greater freedom of action for the FARC. Drug profits gave the group the flexibility to develop highly specialized military units and to concentrate on strategic targets, as well as to develop bases in neighboring countries, including Ecuador, Venezuela, and Panama. Proponents of the conventional view have objected that participation in the illicit economy limits the mobility and freedom of action of the FARC.[83] According to such analysts, the FARC's ability to retreat from a drug-cultivation territory as a strategic maneuver has been compromised by its need to defend the coca plantations against government eradication squads. In fact, the

FARC did at times choose not to defend the coca fields and simply retreated, albeit at great cost to its political capital. More important, running away or defending a particular territory became options for the FARC only after it tapped into the drug economy—before it embraced the illicit economy, it had no option but to run.

Political Capital

Crucially, positive involvement in the illicit economy increased the FARC's political capital. For example, in response to local requests, the FARC stepped in to help improve conditions for *cocaleros* in the Caguán region in the late 1980s. It established local policing and increased security, making sure that farmers would not be robbed after receiving payment for their coca crops. The guerrillas also began to dispense justice and promulgate and enforce laws regarding the carrying of arms, fishing, hunting, working hours, liquor consumption, prostitution, drug abuse, and cutting of trees.[84] Equally important, the guerrillas came to provide protection, limiting the abuses of the traffickers and their intermediaries. They forced the traders to pay the farmers for coca in cash, not *basuco* (crack), and demanded that the traffickers pay better wages to the *cocaleros*.[85] The FARC also established quotas on the amount of land to be seeded with coca, and until the mid-1990s at least encouraged farmers to dedicate a part of their plots to food crops; the group also centralized purchases of coca leaf and controlled traffickers' access to the region.[86] Furthermore, the FARC limited the expansion of landholding by the drug traffickers, large landowners, and cattle ranchers at the expense of the coca farmers.[87] The guerrillas thus came to provide complex protection and regulation services for the illicit economy and the *cocaleros*.

The FARC also provided protection against the government's efforts to eradicate illicit crops. Colombia began spraying coca fields experimentally in late 1984, and by the end of 1985, 2,000 hectares of coca (10 percent to 15 percent of Colombia's crop at the time) had been eliminated through aerial spraying and manual eradication.[88] The FARC resisted eradication efforts by shooting at spray planes and attacking ground eradication teams, and it also protected traffickers' processing labs against government attack. In addition, the group frequently justified broader attacks on government military units, such as the destruction of the army base at Las Delicias in Putumayo, as counter–counternarcotics operations.[89] That strategy had both indirect and direct benefits: by driving counternarcotics forces from the area, often the FARC both freed farmers from the need to pay off corrupt government officials and protected the *cocaleros*' livelihood.[90]

However, the FARC's opposition to government counternarcotics efforts was not uniform. Somewhat surprisingly, up to the mid-1990s the group encouraged alternative development, even though it occasionally threatened alternative development workers and specific projects. In the Caguán region, for example, the FARC cooperated with local community groups and Colombian government organizations in the mid-1980s to implement an ambitious $25 million regional development plan, which included technical assistance for growing new crops, infrastructure development, a telecommunications system, new sewage and potable water systems, and the legalization of peasant landholdings.[91] Although the FARC's advocacy of alternative development is easily understood—it allowed the group to oppose eradication and stress the plight of the coca farmers while denying its participation in the drug trade—the logic behind its active cooperation with alternative development projects is less obvious. Although successful alternative development would undermine the illicit economy, limiting the FARC's income and its political capital, alternative development programs remained popular with the rural population in Colombia, to whom the FARC tried to appeal.[92] The FARC may have learned that it could embrace alternative development at no cost because alternative development projects during the 1980s and 1990s frequently failed to wean the *cocaleros* from their dependence on coca. So the FARC could take the politically correct position and still preserve its participation in the illegal coca economy.

The FARC also bid for public support by using drug money to provide otherwise absent social services. It established local clinics and vocational schools and organized public works, such as road paving. Indeed, in many municipalities, the FARC became the sole provider of essential public services.[93] According to a survey of 1,500 individuals in Colombia's war zones, in the late 1990s, 68 percent of the sample population used health services established by the FARC and many also used FARC dispute mediation services. At the same time, 91 percent of the population perceived local authorities as corrupt and 67 percent viewed them as incompetent in providing public services.[94]

Finally, the FARC's involvement in the drug economy helped the group build political capital by giving it an opportunity to exploit nationalist sentiment. The FARC frequently played the nationalism card by comparing the U.S.-sponsored drug eradication efforts, such as Plan Colombia (discussed below), with the U.S. intervention in Vietnam. In areas under its control, the movement put up billboards that read: *Plan Colombia: los gringos ponen las armas, Colombia pone los muertos* (Plan Colombia: The gringos supply the weapons, Colombia supplies the dead).[95] Similarly, the FARC exploited the controversy surrounding glyphosate, the substance used for coca spraying, as part of its nationalist appeal. Known under its trade name, Roundup, and produced in the United States, glyphosate has often been alleged to have a vast negative environmental impact and to be potentially harmful to humans.[96] The FARC endorsed such allegations, arguing that the gringos were conducting chemical warfare in Colombia.[97]

Collectively, the FARC's efforts generated significant political capital for the group. In areas where the group had previously had no foothold and had even been resisted by the population, it was welcomed after it embraced the illicit economy. Since the early 1980s, support for the FARC has consistently been strongest in the country's drug-producing regions. The major coca-growing departments of Guaviare, Caquetá, Putumayo, and Meta have been the FARC's principal strongholds, and the coca farmers of the south have been its most loyal supporters.[98] The bond between the FARC and the *cocaleros* persists today, even though the FARC's increasing brutality and mismanagement of the illicit economy in the late 1990s and 2000s significantly diminished its political capital.

GOVERNMENT COUNTERINSURGENCY AND DRUG ERADICATION THROUGH THE 1990s: THE EXPANSION OF THE CONFLICT

The increase in the FARC's military capability and political capital allowed the guerrillas to intensify the conflict with the government. Before 1980, they spent most of their time hiding in the jungles, trying to avoid encounters with the military. Between 1980 and 2002, when President Uribe launched a military offensive against the FARC, the guerrillas' willingness to confront the military substantially increased. Clashes between the guerrillas and the government forces grew in number from 94 in 1985 to 600 a year in the mid-1990s and to more than 2000 in 2002.[99] In 1995,

58 percent of Colombia's municipalities had a guerrilla presence and a quarter of municipalities had no police presence.[100]

The Colombian military was weak, poorly trained, underequipped, and badly structured. In 1997, the total number of soldiers in the navy, air force, and army amounted to 131,000; of those, only 22,000 were professional soldiers deployed for defensive purposes or rare offensive actions against the guerillas, while the rest were in administrative and logistical support, creating a tail-to-tooth ratio heavily skewed toward support staff.[101] With the FARC fielding approximately 7,000 fighters at the time, the Colombian military fell far short of the standard 10:1 ratio of government soldiers to insurgents. With only twenty helicopters, it also lacked mobility.

Overwhelmed by the struggle against the guerrillas, the Colombian military was initially reluctant to participate in counternarcotics operations. The military drew a clear distinction between its responsibility for battling leftist insurgents, notably the FARC, and counternarcotics operations, which it saw as the job of the police. While the military did not oppose interdiction and eradication policies, it did not want to have anything to do with them.[102] For example, in 1988, Defense Minister Rafael Samuel Molina argued, "The Army would have better results in the antiguerrilla struggle if it were not tied down in counternarcotics operations."[103] In the same spirit, in 1992 the military rejected a U.S. offer of $2.8 million to set up army counterdrug units.[104]

The army's reluctance to participate in antidrug activities was partially due to its tacit collusion with rightist paramilitary groups (described in detail below), which fought the guerrillas but also participated in the drug trade.[105] One Colombian colonel likened the uneasy and potentially embarrassing alliance to "the affair between a married man and his mistress. [He] has one, but doesn't bring her home to meet [his] family."[106] The paramilitaries and the army occasionally even fought alongside one another.[107] The paramilitaries increased the number of troops available to combat the guerrillas, and they could hold territory that the military was too thin to hold on its own. Moreover, army leaders believed that the paramilitaries could provide intelligence on the guerrillas and their supporters by shaking it out of the population.[108]

By the mid-1990s, however, the Colombian army had come to understand that by embracing counternarcotics operations, it would obtain U.S. aid, which was badly needed to beef up its anti-guerrilla fighting capacity. In 1998, Colombia and the United States signed an agreement to form an elite counternarcotics battalion within the Colombian army. The battalion, 950 men and thirty-three Huey helicopters strong, was to provide the security necessary for aerial eradication in the departments of Putumayo and Caquetá, two major drug-producing regions where providing security necessarily meant attacking the leftist guerrillas.[109]

Eradication was a top priority for the government of President Ernesto Samper. To shake off the drug scandal that plagued his presidency, Samper pledged in 1994 that all coca crops (close to 50,000 hectares) would be eradicated in Colombia within two years.[110] More coca (4,910 hectares) was eradicated in that year than in the preceding four years combined, and the area eradicated increased by close to 400 percent between 1994 and 1995.[111] The Samper administration billed eradication as the way to substantially weaken the guerrillas. A January 1995 editorial in one of Colombia's leading newspapers, *El Tiempo*, succinctly stated the government's case:

> If anything can persuade the guerrillas to negotiate a definitive and stable peace with the government, it is a substantial and prolonged reduction in the high revenues that they receive regularly from the [drug] traffic, which permits them to maintain and equip an expanding armed force. . . . In other words, no solution to the problem of armed insurgency in Colombia today is possible while the drug traffic continues to grow.[112]

However, eradication created widespread resentment, particularly in the absence of effective alternative livelihood programs to redress the *campesinos'* economic dependence on coca cultivation.[113] Eradication efforts frequently led to strikes and demonstrations in coca-growing regions and opportunities for the FARC to consolidate its support. In December 1994, 1,000 *cocaleros* occupied the airport in San José del Guaviare, the capital of the department of Guaviare. In Putumayo, where according to its governor about 135,000 of the department's 314,000 inhabitants depended directly on the coca crop for their livelihood, *cocaleros* occupied Ecopetrol pumping stations, disrupting the flow of oil and causing the loss of millions of dollars in revenue.[114] Florencia, the capital of Caquetá, was virtually under siege by the *cocaleros*.[115]

The FARC started offering a $200,000 bounty for every eradication helicopter or plane shot down, and the first was gunned down in February

1995.[116] Following large-scale fumigations in 1996, the FARC organized massive protest marches against the government, demanding suspension of forced eradication, adoption of voluntary eradication, and long-term development projects. Between 150,000 and 200,000 *campesinos* participated, powerfully demonstrating the FARC's political capital.[117] The army blew up the few roads leading to the areas where the *cocaleros'* protests were concentrated, thereby preventing the demonstrators from extending their marches but also sealing the FARC in with them and further constricting the state's presence in those areas.[118]

Most important, by espousing the *cocaleros'* cause, the FARC increased its access to intelligence on government forces. Between 1996 and 1998, intelligence provided by *cocaleros* helped the FARC inflict several major defeats on the Colombian army. In March 1998, for example, information provided by sympathizers in the Caguán region enabled the guerrillas to annihilate the 52nd counterguerrilla battalion of the Colombian army's 3rd mobile brigade.[119] The destruction of this elite unit greatly shocked the Colombian military. Progressively, the guerrillas succeeded in imposing increasing losses on the army, which suffered from a chronic lack of good intelligence on the guerrillas.[120] In 1984, the ratio of army casualties to guerrilla casualties was 1:1.52. By 1999, the ratio had risen to 1:1.21.[121] The first intensified wave of eradication thus failed either to weaken the FARC—instead, it strengthened the group—or to prevent the area under coca cultivation from doubling by the end of the 1990s (to 100,600 hectares in 1999) and spreading to twenty-seven of Colombia's thirty-two departments.[122]

Because military victory seemed nowhere in sight, Colombia's new president, Andrés Pastrana, began disarmament negotiations with the FARC shortly after his election in June 1998. As a gesture of goodwill, Pastrana gave the FARC a *zona de despeje* (demilitarized zone) covering 42,000 square kilometers, which the government fully vacated, though it had exercised no real control over the territory to start with. The territory became a de facto FARC state. During negotiations pursued intermittently over the next three and half years, neither the government nor the FARC presented any serious proposals; most of the discussions were about negotiation procedures. Encouraged by its military strength and the flourishing coca business in the *zona de despeje* and fearing that if its members demobilized they would be killed by the paramilitaries—who were not engaged in negotiations with the FARC or the government—the FARC was especially intransigent.[123] It used the demilitarized zone to train thousands of troops, build a command center, and hide kidnapping victims. The FARC's failure to participate seriously in negotiations clearly discredited it in the eyes of both the Colombian urban population and the international community. But the Pastrana government also committed mistakes and never developed a coherent negotiating plan. Pastrana never mobilized the support of the Colombian landowner and business class for the negotiations, nor, critically, did he obtain the support of the Colombian military.[124]

In February 2002, Pastrana ended the peace process and ordered the military to retake the *zona de despeje*. Violence erupted once again, and the FARC expanded its military attacks. The capital and the population felt under siege. Land travel throughout most of the country was paralyzed by the threat of FARC attacks, and while large swaths of the countryside were beyond the reach of the state, even the cities were not beyond the reach of the guerrillas and the paramilitaries. Some analysts estimated the strength of the FARC's urban branch at as high as 12,000 men and women, though others put it in the lower thousands, a more likely number.[125] Still, apart from several bomb attacks in 2002, including an attack on a disco in Bogotá, the FARC was generally reluctant to pursue terrorist operations in the cities, fearing that to do so would substantially reduce its legitimacy. Although Bogotá's electrical grid became a routine target, most of the FARC's actions remained concentrated on the outskirts of cities and in the countryside. Still, the sense in Colombia and abroad was that the FARC was on the march.

URBAN GUERRILLAS: M-19

In contrast to the rural FARC, the Movimiento 19 de Abril, another prominent guerrilla group, operated in the urban theater, with a strong presence mainly in Bogotá, where the state of the local economy was considerably better than elsewhere in the country. Like the FARC, M-19 also became involved with the drug economy. However, its focus was on extortion of drug traffickers, a choice that produced neither financial nor political gains.

M-19 emerged in the 1970s as a political-military organization presenting itself as an alternative to the traditional Conservative and Liberal parties. It took its name from the date of the 1970 presidential election, which it believed had been stolen by the Conservatives. M-19 espoused a nationalist agenda and opposed political fraud and corruption but never embraced any traditional left-wing or Marxist orthodoxy. It opened its military campaign by stealing the sword of Simon Bolívar from a Bogotá museum, proclaiming that it had taken up Bolívar's fight against the exploiters of the people.[126] Led by Jaime Bateman Cajón, its members were union leaders and students, often sons and daughters of the country's elite. However, the group also built up a following in the slums of Cali and other cities by providing services that the state had failed to provide and by engaging in Robin Hood tactics. In the early 1970s, for example, the group seized milk trucks and distributed the milk among the poor.[127]

M-19 did not seek to challenge state authority by holding territory; instead, in classic urban guerrilla style, it engaged in attention-getting operations in urban centers. Not only were such operations consistent with its ideology and its origins, but the group also was physically unable to carry out other operations. The weapons at its disposal came from occasional robberies of military arsenals. The military actions of the M-19 thus were limited to audacious but isolated acts such as the 1980 takeover of the Dominican Republic's embassy in Bogotá. By the late 1970s, M-19 was under tremendous pressure from the Colombian army, and many M-19 members were arrested. The group was stagnating at best and, as Robin Kirk put it, "waging war mainly through advertising campaigns."[128]

Used to acquiring funds from kidnapping, the M-19 decided in 1979 to begin extorting money from the major *narco-jefes*. As targets, they had two advantages: they were rich and they could not appeal to law enforcement for protection.[129] The first target was none other than Carlos Lehder, cofounder of the Medellín cartel, but although the group managed to seize him, he escaped. M-19 then shifted tactics to focus on the traffickers' relatives, abducting the three children of Carlos Jader Álvarez and the sister of Medellín trafficker Juan David Ochoa.

The traffickers convened a meeting, apparently under the leadership of Pablo Escobar, pledging support and money for the establishment of a security group, MAS (Muerte a Secuestradores [Death to Kidnappers]). MAS started a systematic campaign to hunt down, torture, and kill M-19 members and supporters. Without ever receiving any money, M-19 finally agreed to free Martha Ochoa in February 1982, but later executed Álvarez's children.[130] By that time, MAS's campaign against M-19 had halved the guerrilla group's membership, and those who remained had to go into hiding to avoid being eliminated.[131]

The extortion scheme failed to generate any political support for M-19 since it produced neither jobs nor resources for handouts for the population at large. Moreover, it produced no material benefits for M-19 and jeopardized the lives of its supporters and their families and acquaintances. Conceding defeat, M-19 changed strategy once again, eventually striking a cooperative deal with the traffickers.[132] At the time, the narcos were involved in a terrorist campaign designed to deter the government from extraditing detained traffickers to the United States. Among their principal targets were judges and policemen, who were offered the choice of *plata o plomo* ("silver or lead"—that is, a bribe or a bullet).

One suspected result of the deal between M-19 and MAS was the November 1985 assault on the Palace of Justice in Bogotá. On the day that Colombia's supreme court was supposed to rule on the extradition of a number of prominent drug traffickers to the United States, M-19 stormed the Palace of Justice, taking almost 400 people hostage, including the president of the supreme court, Alfonso Reyes Echandía, and twenty-four supreme court justices. The Colombian government responded with heavy force, defeating the guerrillas after a twenty-eight-hour siege. Approximately 100 people died, including nine supreme court justices as well as Reyes and most of the sixty M-19 guerrillas. During the siege, M-19 burned incriminating materials on the traffickers.[133] Nonetheless, the group denied that it had undertaken the action on behalf of the Medellín cartel, claiming instead that it sought to denounce the government of Belisario Betancur, which it blamed for the failure of the peace negotiations with various leftist guerrillas (including the FARC and M-19).[134]

Whatever M-19's motivation in taking over the Justice Palace, its actions once again failed to generate any political capital for the group. The public in Bogotá and elsewhere widely condemned the group and its actions.[135] One of Colombia's leading newspapers opined: "If there is in national public opinion a universally accepted opinion, it is the absolute lack of justification for that guerrilla operation."[136]

In 1989, the M-19 struck a deal with the government and demobilized. It returned the sword of Bolívar, disarmed, and ended whatever was left of its efforts to participate in criminal activities. It subsequently transformed itself into a political party, the Democratic Alliance M-19. At the same time, it negotiated another truce with MAS. M-19 promised to support a ban on extradition and amnesty for the paramilitaries, and MAS promised not to kill M-19 members, or at minimum, to give a twenty-four-hour warning before trying to assassinate any M-19 member.[137] Despite the fact that M-19's presidential candidate Carlos Pizarro Leongómez was assassinated by paramilitaries linked to MAS in 1991, the truce largely held, and between 1991 and 1994 the Democratic Alliance M-19 was the third-largest political party in Colombia.

RELYING ON EXTORTION: THE ELN

A third leftist group, the Ejército de Liberación Nacional, also sought to take advantage of illicit activities to expand its operations. But in contrast to the FARC, the ELN exhibited great reluctance to enter the drug business, due in part to its religious roots.[138] Its main focus was on extorting money from oil companies. Due to the non–labor-intensive character of that activity, it generated little political capital.

The ELN emerged in 1965. It was inspired by both the Cuban revolution and Christian liberation theology. The group's leaders sought to end the economic exploitation of the lower classes in Colombia and advocated economic redistribution. Its ranks included members of the urban working class and labor unions, farmers, middle-class workers, Catholic radicals, left-wing intellectuals, and students.

The ELN's original areas of operation were the northern departments of Bolívar, Antioquia, and Santander. Lacking both political support and physical resources, the ELN failed to mount military operations of any consequence and spent the most of its energy conducting internal purges. Amid the turmoil, several commanders turned themselves in and provided the army with intelligence that allowed it to capture a large number of ELN members by the end of the 1960s.[139]

In the mid-1980s, guerrilla priest Manuel Pérez revived the group by turning to extortion as its main source of income. The ELN's primary targets were the large oil companies that operated in northern Colombia. By kidnapping oil executives and holding them for ransom, it earned between $150 million and $200 million annually in the early and mid-1990s.[140] Those funds helped the group expand geographically into Cauca, Huila, and Boyacá and to grow from less than 500 guerrillas in 1979 to 3,000 to 5,000 in 1998.[141] Many of its troops, however, were part-time and lacked rigorous training. They were not especially adept at direct military combat and concentrated for the most part on undertaking isolated spectacular actions,[142] such as periodically attacking pipelines to protest "the theft of Colombia's national resources by foreign multinationals" and thereby causing hundreds of millions of dollars worth of damage.[143]

In addition to extorted cash ransoms in the neighborhood of $1 million per victim, the ELN forced multinational oil companies to invest in health, education, water, and sewage facilities and demanded that they hire local residents.[144] Since the 1994 passage of the National Law of Royalties, which requires a large portion of the royalties paid by oil companies to be returned to the regions where they operate, the ELN also attempted to use extortion to force regional governments to spend the rents in specified ways.[145] However, those benefits directly affected only a small number of people, and, in a critical failure, they did not offset the popular resentment generated by the ELN's decision to prohibit coca cultivation in areas under its control because extortion, not being a labor-intensive pursuit, generated few jobs. Therefore, by 1998 the ELN found itself at a significant disadvantage relative to rivals such as the FARC, the paramilitaries, and government forces.

By the late 1990s, much of the ELN leadership had reached the conclusion that the group's refusal to participate in the drug economy was no longer sustainable. Following Pérez's death in December 1997, the pragmatists prevailed.[146] In the late 1990s and early 2000s, drugs generated about 20 percent of the ELN's income.[147] While the group denied that it received payments from narcotraffickers, it provided paid protection to around 3,000 coca farmers in south Bolívar and north Santander and later in Arauca.[148] However, the ELN's embrace of the narcotics economy came too late. In 2000, when the ELN was engaged in negotiations with the Colombian government to obtain a demilitarized zone, at least 15,000 residents of the proposed zone protested vigorously against the plan (strongly encouraged, it must be said, by local paramilitaries).[149] In contrast, residents had generally welcomed the creation of a demilitarized zone for the FARC in 1998. Ultimately, the ELN's bid for a demilitarized zone failed, and many of its members defected to the FARC.

During the late 1990s and early 2000s, the group suffered critical hits from both the FARC and the paramilitaries. Those losses were augmented by the counterinsurgency effort mounted by President Uribe in 2002. From approximately 5,000 combatants in 2000, the ELN has been weakened to perhaps 2,500. Since 2002, the Colombian government has been engaged in on-and-off negotiations with the ELN about the group's demobilization and disarmament, yet so far the negotiations have produced no concrete results.

THE RISE OF THE PARAMILITARIES

While the relations between drug traffickers and leftist insurgent groups typically have been characterized by tension, the boundary between right-wing paramilitary groups and traffickers has been extraordinarily fluid. That is not to say that the relationship has always been easy, and on occasion open conflict has broken out between the two. Notably, as discussed before, a paramilitary group (PEPES) was instrumental in the destruction of the Medellín cartel. In many other cases, however, the two groups have merged or one has taken over the other's functions, notably when paramilitaries have eliminated independent traffickers from the areas under their control. By eliminating independent traffickers, the paramilitaries might have increased their take of the drug business, but they also limited their ability to generate political capital.

Private armies and militias have existed in Colombia for decades if not centuries, due to the state's inability to provide adequate security. Many paramilitary organizations originated as private protection units, usually referred to as *autodefensas* (self-defense groups), for cattle ranchers, coffee plantation owners, and owners of other large tracts of land; for emerald mafias; and for peasant communities tired of guerrilla attacks.[150] Since the early 1980s, drug traffickers have also relied on private security groups, such as the MAS, to protect them against the guerrillas. By the late 1980s, the narcos were using paramilitaries to protect their business interests in the departments of Santander, Antioquia, Norte de Santander, Cesar, Meta, Cauca, Casanare, Huila, Boyacá, Caquetá, Putumayo, and Córdoba.[151] Since then, the areas of most intense conflict between the FARC and the paramilitaries have remained the major coca-producing areas—Guaviare, Putumayo, Caquetá, and Nariño—which both movements seek to dominate.[152]

Frequently fighting in support of regular military forces, paramilitary groups initially focused on protecting their patrons against kidnapping by leftist guerrillas, extortion, cattle rustling, and land seizure. The strategy of the groups, which largely avoided encounters with the guerrillas, was to brutalize and intimidate the local population into abandoning the guerrillas and thereby forcing them out of the region. But as the 1980s progressed, the paramilitaries sought to become an independent political, military, and economic force. Crucial to their transformation was the prodding of Carlos Castaño,[153] a prominent commander associated with one of the most successful paramilitary groups, the ACCU (Autodefensas Campesinas de Córdoba y Urabá [Peasant Self-Defense Group of Córdoba and Urabá]). Under his leadership, many of the independent paramilitary groups became unified in 1997, created an umbrella organization, AUC (Autodefensas Unidas de Colombia [United Self-Defense Forces of Colombia]), and acquired a national mission. However, many other groups were only loosely affiliated with the AUC. They never fully bought into the national agenda and continued to function solely as protection armies.

The AUC's goals included acquiring land for itself through seizure (an activity that has contributed to the displacement of many Colombians, turning them into internal refugees), generating rents from drugs and other illicit economies, and eliminating the leftist guerrillas. In addition, its avowedly conservative agenda included support for the state, ostensibly promoted land reform (without fundamental redistribution), and opposed extradition of traffickers.[154] The paramilitaries stressed tradition, property, and order. In the late 1990s and early 2000s, their social discourse also included populist advocacy for the poor.[155]

Learning Curve

Beginning in the 1980s, the paramilitary groups realized that their participation in the illicit narcotics economy could encompass more than collecting protection money from drug dealers. They began to tax coca farmers, and some became directly involved in cocaine production and trafficking.[156] The demise of the Medellín and Cali cartels in the 1990s created further opportunities for the paramilitaries to become deeply involved in the drug trade. According to William Wood, a former U.S. ambassador to Colombia, the AUC came to control 40 percent of Colombia's drug trade, due in part to its control of Urabá and other areas close to the border with Panama.[157] The paramilitaries were also estimated to control about 26 percent of the country's heroin-producing municipalities.[158]

By the early 2000s, the AUC was selling drugs to Colombian, Mexican, and Brazilian trafficking organizations for distribution abroad.[159] Its expansion into trafficking was facilitated by the influx of prominent traffickers into the AUC. Diego Fernando Murillo ("Don Berna"), a long-time Medellín drug cartel capo; Víctor Manuel Mejía Múnera, a ranking figure in the Norte Del Valle drug cartel; Francisco Javier Zuluaga; and Guillermo Pérez Alzate ("Pablo Sevillano") all bought themselves leadership positions in the AUC to take advantage of the group's peace negotiations with the Colombian government and to avoid possible future extradition to the United States under drug trafficking charges.[160] Such ties also helped the AUC diversify into secondary illicit economies. The group came to control the illicit trade in gasoline, mainly siphoned from Colombia's pipelines, which is a key ingredient in processing coca leaves into cocaine paste.[161] In addition, the paramilitaries took over a large share of counterfeiting, prostitution, and urban gang activity.[162] Altogether, the AUC's annual income was estimated at roughly $110 million, some 70 percent of which stemmed from the group's involvement in the drug economy.[163]

Military Capability

The paramilitaries' positive involvement in the illicit economy resulted in a large expansion of their military capability. While ACCU (the predecessor of the AUC) could count only 93 members in 1986, it had between 4,000 and 5,000 in 1995;[164] the AUC, which had 12,000 members in 2000, could claim between 27,000 and 29,000 in 2006.[165] The paramilitaries have spread throughout the country, acquiring a presence in twenty-six of the country's thirty-two departments and 382 of its 1,098 municipalities.[166]

Although at first the AUC depended on the army for weapons, after tapping into the drug trade it independently acquired thirty-four small aircraft, including four cargo planes; fourteen helicopters with military equipment; and several speedboats.[167] Unlike the leftist guerrilla groups, which do not pay regular salaries to their fighters, offering only irregular special compensation instead,[168] the AUC paid its soldiers regular salaries that ranged between $250 and $1,000 a month, depending on rank, as well as a $10 bonus for each guerrilla killed.[169] In the 1980s, the paramilitaries depended on the army for logistical support and training; by 2000, they had built up an independent supply system and were able to hire private security companies to train their forces.[170]

The paramilitaries' military strategy was to extend their control by intimidating local officials and residents. Through the use of demonstrative massacres (during which they would kill local community leaders and those suspected of sympathizing with the guerrillas in front of other *campesinos*) and other intimidation techniques, the paramilitaries forced the local population to comply or to flee.[171] The paramilitaries thus adopted the coercion school of counterinsurgency operations. Instead of seeking to win the rural population's hearts and minds, they sought to physically destroy the guerrillas' base. In many areas, they succeeded. Typically, once they had "cleansed" an area of guerrilla sympathizers, the paramilitaries substantially decreased the level of violence against the local population.

Political Capital

In Colombia's drug-producing regions, the paramilitaries traditionally sided with the drug dealers, not the local population. They pandered to the narcos' interests by charging smaller protection fees, supporting the traffickers' efforts to acquire land, providing less physical protection to the *cocaleros,* and opposing farmers' efforts to get higher prices for their products. The decline in coca prices in Sur de Bolívar shows the typical pattern. Before the paramilitaries took control of the region in May 1999, coca paste was selling at about 2,200,000 pesos per kilo (about $1,100 at the time). Once the paramilitaries took over, the price of coca paste declined sharply, to 1,400,000 pesos ($700) per kilo, or more than 40 percent, despite the fact that traffic continued undiminished.[172] Moreover, the paramilitaries did little to enforce the contracts between the drug dealers and farmers, hence rendering the *cocaleros* vulnerable to price fluctuations and abuse.[173] The paramilitaries' failure to perform such regulatory roles for the illicit economy was especially prominent in areas where drug traffickers bought themselves leadership positions, thereby erasing the distinction between the paras and the narcos.[174]

The paramilitaries were more concerned with generating political capital when they expanded into areas where traditionally the guerrillas were strong. In such contested regions, they offered the *campesinos* higher prices for coca paste and reduced taxes. For example, when the paramilitaries took over in Mapiripán, they reduced the 10 percent tax charged by the FARC to 6 percent. (The paras, however, also conducted a notorious massacre in the same area in July 1997, when they used chainsaws and machetes to behead, dismember, and disembowel several *campesinos*.) Similarly, when they entered the FARC and ELN strongholds in southern Bolívar, they offered to eliminate the *campesinos*' debt to the FARC.[175] That was an especially effective technique for generating popular support and sympathy from the local population and mitigating the outrage at the paramilitaries' brutality, even though later, when the paramilitaries secured firm control of the region, they cut the price of coca paste.[176]

The paramilitaries also built political capital by providing social services, especially in northern Colombia, where they had a strong base.[177] In Puerto Boyacá, which became almost an independent paramilitary republic in the late 1980s, the ACDEGAM (Asociación Campesina de Ganaderos y Agricultores del Magdalena Medio [Rural Association of Ranchers and Farmers of the Middle Magdalena Valley]), a paramilitary group bankrolled by the Medellín cartel, ran its own clinics and schools, organized health brigades to visit surrounding villages, helped build and repair roads, and even constructed a communications center.[178] The *campesinos* increasingly turned to the paramilitaries for various proto-state services, such as the resolution of disputes related to property, debt, and political rivalry.[179] Such efforts partially reduced the resentment generated by the paramilitaries' brutality. However, overall the popular reaction to the AUC was one of passive tolerance rather than of active support.[180]

THE FARC'S ELIMINATION OF INTERMEDIARIES

Somewhat ironically, the growth of the paramilitaries since the early 1990s caused the FARC to emulate the paramilitaries' approach to the drug economy. As a result, the FARC saw its political capital decline. The destruction of the Medellín and Cali cartels and the weakness of the new boutique cartels that followed allowed the FARC to drive many independent traffickers out of business,[181] a course of action that was prompted also by the expansion of the paramilitaries and the increasingly common overlap between the traffickers and the paras. In many cases, for the FARC to allow traffickers to operate in a region would be equivalent to allowing the paramilitaries free rein to conduct their operations.

After displacing the small and medium-size drug traffickers in its territory, the FARC tightened its control of coca cultivation. Instead of forcing traffickers to pay the farmers higher prices for coca leaves and coca paste, the FARC imposed its own prices and forced the *cocaleros* to sell only to the FARC.[182] In some areas, such as in parts of Norte de Santander, it dictated the terms of coca cultivation, harvest, and processing, often against the wishes of the local population.[183] The FARC's monopoly on buying coca paste in many areas generated resentment on the part of the *cocaleros*. The FARC also came to oppose alternative development projects in various areas and created obstacles to projects to build roads and construct communications infrastructure that might heighten the government's presence.[184]

There have been increasing reports that the FARC has been forcing farmers in various areas to grow coca (and in the late 1990s and early 2000s, opium poppies also).[185] Since the launch of a major counterinsurgency campaign in 2004, *cocaleros* in Caquetá and Putumayo have reported that the FARC has required everyone to grow drug-producing crops (in addition to subsistence crops), even lending money to farmers against the proceeds of the next harvest.[186] Various indigenous groups have also reported that the FARC forces them to grow coca against their will.[187] Of course, claiming that they have been forced to grow drugs allows *cocaleros* to minimize their role as "criminals"; such reports may therefore not always be completely accurate.[188] Nonetheless, the frequency of the reports seems to be increasing. To the extent that the reports are accurate, the policy of forcing farmers to grow coca may have been reinforced by FARC founder Tirofijo's announcement in the late 1990s that the *frente* commanders were from that time on responsible for their own financing. Because each *frente* needs to contribute to its own financing, the FARC also switched its kidnapping methods; instead of concentrating mainly on prominent and wealthy people, it began to undertake "fishing trips"—erecting roadblocks and capturing travelers from all social strata and demanding ransom even from the poor, once again alienating the rural population.

Farmers in FARC-controlled regions also were exposed to more brutality in the late 1990s and early 2000s. In the late 1990s, the FARC often chose to avoid military encounters with the paramilitaries and did nothing to protect *campesinos* against AUC attacks. Preserving fighters was clearly a higher priority than preserving territory and protecting the population.[189] In addition, the FARC itself has come to commit more atrocities. In May 2002, the guerrillas launched a homemade bomb against a church in Bellavista, Antioquia, where refugees were hiding. The bomb killed 119 people, including 40 children, and injured another 98.[190] The AUC continued to kill many more civilians than the FARC until the AUC began negotiating demobilization terms with the Colombian government in 2004, but the level of civilian casualties caused by the FARC continued to rise.[191]

Finally, the FARC has been increasingly cooperating with the paramilitaries and their successors (discussed below) to manage the drug trade. Although vicious fighting between the two groups continued into the 2000s in many regions, there appeared to be at least tacit coexistence between them in some regions, such as Serranía de San Lucas. While the leftist guerrillas there controlled the cultivation areas, the AUC controlled the rivers and hence transportation of both coca paste and cocaine precursor agents. Nonetheless, smuggling out of the region continued,[192] something that could have happened only if the two groups were colluding. When the Colombian military captured "Sonia," the chief financial officer of the FARC's southern bloc, in February 2004, they found e-mails on her laptop asking the AUC to lend a helicopter to "transport arms and drugs through the jungle."[193] Since then Colombian authorities have interdicted shipments of drugs that belong jointly to the AUC, the FARC, and independent traffickers.[194]

As the FARC and the paramilitaries and their successors (the *grupos emergentes*) have moved closer together, the difference in their political capital has shrunk, and the rural population, including the *cocaleros*, has become willing to shift their support between the two groups.[195] The paramilitaries did not increase their political capital; instead, the FARC's capital declined. An important indicator is the reduction in the FARC's support among the *cocaleros*. In 1996, the FARC was able to draw 150,000 to 200,000 *cocaleros* to participate in massive protests against eradication. Five years later, the FARC sought to oppose eradication by ordering a stop to commercial and transport activity in Putumayo, but few *cocaleros* cooperated with the blockade, which was suspended without results after seventy days.[196] In 2006, after six years of aerial spraying, support for the FARC seemed to have rebounded somewhat, as demonstrated by its ability to mount protests at the local level, such as in the Policarpa municipality of Nariño. Overall, the FARC's political capital has clearly declined among the *cocaleros*, but it remains strongest in areas where the government is aggressively pursuing eradication.[197]

PLAN COLOMBIA

Eradication became the centerpiece of the government's counterinsurgency efforts with the launch of Plan Colombia in July 2000. By then, the FARC was sitting in the hills overlooking Bogotá. In many areas, the insurgents prevented normal economic and political activity, and attacks by armed groups along major roads prevented land travel in much of the country. Colombia also experienced very high levels of crime, with the murder rate averaging 62.2 per 100,000 during 1995–99 and one of the highest kidnapping rates in the world (3,200 a year at its peak in 1999).[198] Throughout that period, Colombia's security apparatus remained weak.

Plan Colombia is a joint effort of the Colombian and U.S. governments. Although designed to strengthen the state along multiple dimensions, it was launched fundamentally as a counterinsurgency plan that included at its core the most intensive aerial eradication effort ever undertaken. Washington and Bogotá had come to see the FARC as essentially a drug cartel that would be crippled if it lost its financial base. The key objectives of Plan Colombia therefore were defined as neutralizing the drug economy by "reducing the cultivation, processing, and distribution of narcotics by 50 percent in six years" and providing alternative development opportunities; strengthening the state presence and improving security throughout the country; strengthening the judiciary and fighting corruption; bolstering the economy; and improving governance. Its primary instruments were extensive aerial eradication and interdiction, at sea, on land, and in the air.[199]

Originally contained in a $1.2 billion aid package for counterdrug operations in Latin America that allocated $860 million to Colombia, U.S. support for Plan Colombia grew to more than $6 billion (through 2009), including more than $4.3 billion that was allocated through the Andean Counterdrug Initiative (ACI), the new name given to Plan Colombia in 2001.[200] As part of the effort, the Bush administration removed restrictions on the use of U.S. counternarcotics funds in order to permit the direct use of the funds for counterguerrilla operations and increased the cap on the number of U.S. military advisers and private contractors working in Colombia to 800 and 400 respectively. The military and drug eradication components of the plan soon dwarfed its socioeconomic and human rights components.[201]

The Failure of Aerial Eradication

At first, the eradication campaign seemed to be generating the desired results. According to the U.S. Department of State, in 2000, at the beginning of Plan Colombia, 136,200 hectares of coca were cultivated in Colombia, with an estimated cocaine potential of 580 metric tons.[202] In 2001, the numbers peaked at 169,800 hectares of coca and 839 metric tons of cocaine.[203] Then, after President Uribe allowed planes to spray crops with herbicides anywhere at any time, the cultivation of coca in Colombia fell 15 percent in 2002 and 21 percent in 2003.[204] From a total of 47,371 hectares sprayed in 2000, the number of hectares sprayed increased every year until 2006, when it peaked at 171,613 hectares; thereafter it declined, to 153,133 hectares in 2007 and 133,496 hectares in 2008. Over that period, manual eradication also increased substantially, with 66,396 hectares eradicated in 2007 and 95,732 hectares in 2008.[205]

Nonetheless, the counternarcotics component of Plan Colombia was, by the plan's own measures, mostly a failure. Six years after its launch, both coca cultivation and cocaine production were higher than in 2000. Coca cultivation has increased steadily since 2003, when it bottomed out at 113,850 hectares,[206] to 167,000 hectares in 2007.[207] Suppression efforts have nonetheless changed the regional distribution of coca cultivation, with areas of previously large-scale coca cultivation, such as Putumayo, seeing substantial declines and new areas of cultivation, such as Nariño, emerging.

Two principal factors have driven the recovery of coca in Colombia. First, coca farmers have adopted a variety of coping strategies to deal with eradication, including pruning coca plants after spraying; replanting with younger coca plants or coca plant grafts; cultivating areas where plants have a smaller chance of being detected (under dense foliage, for example) or that are off-limits to spraying (national parks and the ten-kilometer-wide belt near the border with Ecuador); interspersing coca plants with legal crops; decreasing the size of coca plots; and increasing the density of coca plants per hectare.

Second, the vast majority of coca farmers continue to lack viable legal alternatives. Many live in areas still controlled by the FARC, the ELN, and new armed groups, which frequently force farmers to cultivate coca or prevent the establishment of a state presence and the emergence of a legal economy. Lack of access to land, irrigation, roads, credit, technical assistance, and established markets make it impossible for farmers to switch to legal crops. The Colombian government's "zero-coca" policy further increases the hurdles facing farmers by conditioning all aid—including food security, technical assistance, roads, and so on—on the certified eradication of all coca in an entire area. If a single member of a community cultivates coca on a small plot, the entire community is disqualified from receiving assistance. Because of that, a paradoxical self-selection often takes place: the communities that are least dependent on coca and enjoy the greatest security eradicate coca to qualify for Colombian or U.S. government assistance whereas the communities that face the greatest insecurity and deprivation are left without aid. Most coca farmers are eager to abandon coca cultivation. They want to escape the insecurity that coca brings—by attracting brutal armed groups and crime organizations, for example—and they face significant negative economic repercussions due to aerial and manual eradication. Yet when sufficient opportunities to switch to legal livelihoods are lacking, coca farmers react to eradication by replanting, moving to areas that are not being eradicated, or even joining armed groups.

Moreover, even when communities qualify for aid, it often takes too long to pay off. Alternative livelihood programs take a long time to implement and even more time to start generating sufficient, sustainable livelihoods. Many marketable crops, such as cacao or coffee, take several years to produce harvests and generate income, and often the delay is increased by the need to address structural deficits, such as the lack of roads, land titles, credit, access to markets, and value-added chains. During the transition period, farmers frequently face a severe drop in income, some of which is offset by food security programs backed by the Colombian government and the U.S. Agency for International Development (USAID). However, the programs typically fall short of allowing families to provide for basic needs; consequently, farmers sometimes sour on the idea of alternative livelihoods and return to coca cultivation, permanently disqualifying themselves from any further assistance.[208]

Beefed-Up Counterinsurgency

Despite the failure of eradication, Colombian security forces have made important gains against the FARC. After coming to power in 2002, the government of President Álvaro Uribe launched Plan Patriota, a major military offensive against the guerrillas nestled within a broader concept, the so-called Democratic Security Policy. In addition to developing a network of informants in rural areas and establishing peasant militias,[209] the army sent 18,000 troops and special forces, backed by U.S.-supplied helicopters, to attack guerrilla strongholds in the southern jungles. Those efforts were supported by substantial increases in funding. Colombian government spending on defense rose to $6.9 billion in 2006.[210] By 2007, the number of professional soldiers had grown to 78,000 and important new military units were deployed, including two divisions, six brigades, twelve new mobile units, and six mountain battalions. The armed forces also acquired mobility assets, including more than two dozen helicopters.

The United States has been an important partner in the program. From 2000 through 2008, the U.S. government appropriated $4.9 billion for the Colombian military and police,[211] and U.S. forces also provided technical and signal intelligence to the Colombian military. As a result, the training, force structure, and mobility of the Colombian armed forces have greatly improved. In addition, the police maintain a presence in every municipality.

The vast improvements in the counterinsurgency capability of the Colombian forces have significantly enhanced their ability to strike at the FARC and force it to retreat. The FARC has lost much of its capacity to mount large-scale offensive actions, and it has been pushed further away from the roads and cities. Its areas of operation have shrunk to only 50 percent of the areas where coca is grown (down from 70 percent in the early 2000s), and the number of deserters has increased dramatically. The number of active FARC combatants has been reduced to perhaps 9,000, with only ten *frentes* remaining active.[212] Although revelations in late 2008 about so-called "false positives" (civilians killed by the armed forces, dressed in guerrilla uniforms, and later presented as important hits against the FARC) call into question the credibility of the military's reports of its activities, it is nonetheless clear that the FARC has been substantially weakened.

With the help of U.S. technical and signal intelligence as well as intelligence provided by FARC deserters, the military has scored crucial hits against both the top leadership of the FARC and its mid-level *frente* commanders.[213] By early 2005, some 800 FARC encampments had been destroyed, and twenty mid-level commanders removed from the battlefield.[214] The deaths in 2007 and 2008 of important commanders such as "J. J," "Negro Acacio," "Martin Caballero," and Raúl Reyes and of FARC founder Pedro Antonio Marín (who apparently died of natural causes) put the internal chain of command under tremendous pressure.[215] The dramatic special operations rescue in the summer of 2008 of fifteen of the FARC's highest-value political hostages, including former presidential candidate Ingrid Betancourt and three U.S. military contractors, struck a further demoralizing blow to the guerrillas.

Did Eradication Bankrupt the FARC?

To what degree did eradication contribute to the Colombian military's success? The evidence suggests that eradication reduced the FARC's income but not enough to cripple the insurgency. However, localized interdiction operations and the creation of military zones to encircle coca-growing areas, in which the FARC has been pinned down by the military, did disrupt its flow of income by preventing the group from selling coca base to local traffickers. Those measures also prevented the FARC from resupplying *frentes* operating outside the coca areas.

As coca cultivation declined between 2000 and 2004, FARC resources were hurt to some extent. But the guerrillas adapted by switching to other illicit economies, including extortion and kidnapping and even some efforts to trade in low-grade uranium.[216] In June 2007, the U.S. Office of National Drug Control Policy (ONDCP) estimated that Colombia's anti-drug efforts reduced the FARC's overall profits per kilogram of cocaine from the range of $320 to $460 in 2003 to $195 to $320 in 2005.[217] As a result, the group's drug income fell from $115 million a year to a still-sizable $65 million a year.[218] That estimate did not take into account other FARC activities, such as extortion, roadside kidnapping, and oil smuggling, which traditionally have constituted about 50 percent of the group's revenues. Therefore, at least before the coca cultivation rebound after 2005, eradication efforts had reduced the FARC's financial and physical resources but had not come close to bankrupting the group. Once coca cultivation rebounded, many FARC *frentes* relocated to areas of new or revived cultivation, where they continue to profit from the drug trade.

Some FARC *frentes* did suffer a significant resource crunch. Evidence from captured computers and guerrillas reveals that in some areas, FARC combatants lacked ammunition and other essential supplies, including clothing. But the primary cause of the *frentes'* weakness was not eradication but the Colombian military's success in encircling the *frentes* and thereby reducing their mobility and disrupting their communications and logistical channels. Those efforts had an especially significant impact on *frentes* operating outside the coca zones, which were cut off from sources of resupply.[219] But military encirclement and pin-down operations also interrupted the flow of resources to *frentes* operating in the coca areas. Deserters have revealed that in some areas, such as Guaviare, the FARC now gives the farmers IOUs (*bonos*) for their coca paste because it lacks cash. Despite the government's eradication campaign, coca is still cultivated in such areas in abundance, but military operations have made it difficult for the FARC to get the paste to traffickers.

The primary effect of eradication has been not to reduce the FARC's capabilities but to increase the alienation of *cocaleros* from the government. That has handicapped the counterinsurgency effort by depriving the government of human intelligence on the belligerents and by generating new recruits for the FARC. In the Magdalena Medio area, for example, after experiencing aerial spraying every year since 2000 (and twice in 2008), coca farmers refused to cooperate with local military forces, even suggesting that further eradication would drive them to join the FARC.[220] The farmers had no love for the guerrillas. They complained about the FARC's brutality, rejected the FARC's ideology, and were clearly aware that the FARC was under significant military pressure nationwide. But eradication drove the two groups together, particularly in the absence of alternative development programs or other assistance from the state. The Colombian military is keenly aware of that dynamic and frequently prefers to avoid or limit eradication operations in insecure areas.[221]

In contrast, in the Montes de Maria region, an area in which coca is not grown and that was only recently captured from the FARC, the population was willing to provide intelligence to the military, particularly after the local FARC *frente* began to turn increasingly to extortion of the population to make up for the disruption of supply routes originating within coca areas.[222] Similarly, in northern Nariño, a coca-growing area where the government has struggled to maintain a presence, farmers in one village began to cooperate with the military after their village was selected for an experimental alternative livelihood program run by Nariño's governor, Antonio Navarro Wolff. Villagers had been deeply hostile to the military before, but once the focus of government policy turned from eradication to alternative livelihoods, they began to provide government forces with intelligence on the FARC and paramilitary groups operating in the area.

In the absence of cooperation from the *campesinos,* the military's intelligence on the FARC in most coca-growing areas comes predominantly from signal sources and deserters.[223] That intelligence has proven to be of considerable value, given the FARC's reliance on cell phones and the U.S. ability to intercept such communications and provide real-time intelligence to the Colombian military. Armed with information, government forces have been able to strike hard at the FARC. But their success has come despite, not because of, eradication.

DEMOBILIZATION OF THE PARAMILITARIES AND THE RISE OF NEW "PARA" GROUPS

In addition to launching Plan Patriota against the FARC, President Uribe sought to deal with the paramilitaries by negotiating a demobilization deal that was signed into the so-called Justice and Peace Law in 2005. Prompted by the threat of extradition to the United States on drug trafficking charges, the paramilitary leadership agreed to disarm and demobilize, abandon drug trafficking, and disclose their crimes in exchange for lenient jail sentences and the government's commitment to forgo extradition. By the end of 2007, some 31,000 paramilitaries, including their most notorious commanders, had demobilized.[224] However, many of the top bosses continued to run the drug trade from prison; seventeen therefore were extradited to the United States in 2008 and 2009.

The demobilization of the paramilitaries, along with the substantial weakening of the leftist guerrillas, significantly improved security in both the countryside and urban areas. The number of massacres and attacks on the population, including community activists, fell dramatically. Highway traffic increased by 64 percent between 2003 and 2006, while the number of thefts and attacks on vehicles declined by 54 percent.[225] The number of attacks on electricity pylons fell from 483 in 2002 to 76 in 2007, and the number of oil pipeline bombings dropped from 184 in 2003 to 39 in the first eight months of 2007.[226] The number of homicides declined by 40 percent between 2002 and 2006, although it remained high by world standards.[227] Kidnapping declined even more impressively, by 80 percent, again from one of the highest levels in the world.[228] Overall, according to a Ministry of Defense analysis, the government was in full or partial control of 90 percent of the country by 2008, up from 70 percent in 2003.[229]

Parapolitics

Despite the government's successes, paramilitary groups continue to wield substantial economic and political power in Colombia. Some paramilitaries have transformed themselves into purely criminal organizations. Demobilized soldiers have joined city gangs, especially in Medellín. Ex-paramilitaries also continue to reap vast benefits from the drug trade and other illicit economies. Their drug networks remain unaffected, and they have not given up any substantial assets, including land, obtained through violence or illicit economic activities.

Similarly, the paramilitaries have retained and even expanded their political influence. Through intimidation and bribery, former paramilitaries have managed to acquire significant political power at the municipal and regional levels, getting their preferred candidates elected to some regional offices and buying off others.[230] The paramilitary influence is especially pervasive along the Atlantic coast, such as in César and Magdalena, along the Pacific coast, and in the major drug-exporting regions. There, extortion rackets linked to the ex-paramilitaries extend to many sectors of the formal, informal, and illegal economies, including transportation, gasoline smuggling, retail consumer goods markets, the health sector, gambling, real estate, and the hotel industry. At the national level, politicians supported by paramilitary leaders have been elected to the Colombian congress and exercise great political power. In 2005, paramilitary leaders claimed to control 35 percent of the congress. As of November 2008, twenty-two members of congress (which has a total of 102 senators and 166 representatives) had been jailed on charges of criminal links to the paramilitaries and another thirty were under investigation. Links to the paramilitaries are especially common in political parties linked to President Uribe.[231]

Paramilitaries also have infiltrated various ministries (forcing the resignation of Uribe's former foreign minister Maria Consuelo Araujo, among others) as well as Colombia's intelligence services and key law enforcement institutions, including DAS, whose former head, Jorge Noguera, was charged with collaborating with the paramilitaries.

New Paras and Their Complex Relationship with the FARC

New, equally pernicious, paramilitary groups are emerging. Demobilized paramilitary leaders continue to recruit among the urban poor and unemployed, offering $250 a month to new members.[232] Among the most notorious of the newly emerged armed groups (there are at least forty-three, operating in twenty-two departments) are the Aguilas Negras (Black Eagles), ONG (Organización Nueva Generación [New Generation Organization]), Los Rastrojos, Los Boyacos, and Los Pepes (a new group distinct from Los Perseguidos por Pablo Escobar).[233] The groups total between 5,000 and 10,000 members and operate throughout the key smuggling corridors and drug areas, including around Cúcuta and in Nariño, Bolivar, Magdalena Medio, and the Pacific and Atlantic coasts.[234] These *bandas criminales* or *grupos emergentes,* to use the government's terminology, have penetrated the drug trade and other illicit activities, such as the siphoning off and smuggling of gasoline. They have also been recruited to forcibly evict farmers from land wanted by agro-businesses or energy and mining companies.

Some of the groups appear to have directly inherited the leadership and organizational structure of the former AUC. Some are headed by top paramilitary leaders who did not demobilize, such as Vicente Castaño and Martín Llanos. Others are led by former AUC mid-rank commanders or have emerged from independent trafficking groups. Still others seem to be newcomers to the scene. In some areas, the groups compete with the FARC over territory and control of the drug trade. Elsewhere, they carve up territory and reach a modus vivendi or even collude with the FARC and local drug organizations.

COLOMBIA TODAY

Like the paramilitaries, the FARC lives on, albeit in a weakened state. Along with the ELN, it still operates in large swaths of the countryside.

In 2005 and 2006, after having been written off as near death, the FARC came back with a string of deadly attacks against the military. Since then it has suffered significant losses. Nonetheless, Colombia's military may be reaching the limits of its capacity as the fight against the FARC moves increasingly into punishing mountain and jungle terrain. In addition, it is unclear that the government will be able to maintain the current high levels of military spending.[235] Sporadically both sides make overtures for some form of negotiations. But those efforts have stumbled on the FARC's insistence on a demobilized zone, which the government is not willing to grant, and the government's belief that it can prevail militarily without strategic negotiations.

Several possible futures now lie ahead for the FARC: The group could collapse and splinter into small groups of drug traffickers and thugs; it could resort to asymmetric warfare and urban terrorism (some FARC members already are shedding their uniforms and focusing on selective killing of military and government officials and local community activists); or it could hunker down in the rural periphery as it did for the first two decades of its existence. Some combination of those alternatives also is possible.

In its current incarnation, the FARC is too weak to bring down the state or conquer large stretches of territory. Nonetheless, the threat that it and the new para groups pose continues to prevent economic and social development in many rural regions, particularly those where coca remains prevalent. In Nariño and the Magdalena Medio, even the major roads are not always secure. Armed groups frequently operate in areas as little as eight to ten kilometers away from the main roads, and government officials can venture into such areas only with the acquiescence of the groups. While the expansion of police to every municipality is an important achievement, coverage frequently remains thin, with one or two policemen in charge of a territory of several hundred square kilometers. That the Colombian state now believes that it has partial control of 90 percent of the territory does not mean that it has sufficient control.

Moreover, the underlying conditions that gave rise to the insurgency remain in place. Although Colombia's economy has made impressive gains since 2000, that progress has not translated into significant reductions in poverty or inequality. Colombia's $130 billion economy grew at 6.8 percent in 2006, the highest rate in twenty-eight years and two points above the Latin American average. Inflation fell from 16.7 percent in

1998 to 4.5 percent in 2006, and unemployment declined from a peak of 18 percent in 1999 to 12 percent in 2006.[236] However, 46 percent of the rural population remained in poverty in 2006, and Colombia continues to be an extremely unequal society despite a small drop in measures of income inequality.[237] For many *campesinos,* coca cultivation or other illegal activities continue to be the only opportunity for social advancement or sometimes even survival.[238] As new security challenges mount, it remains to be seen whether Colombia will manage to address the socioeconomic drivers of internal instability and rural underdevelopment and increase a multifaceted state presence throughout the country—or whether its failure to do so will allow potent new challengers to emerge and coca cultivation to persist.

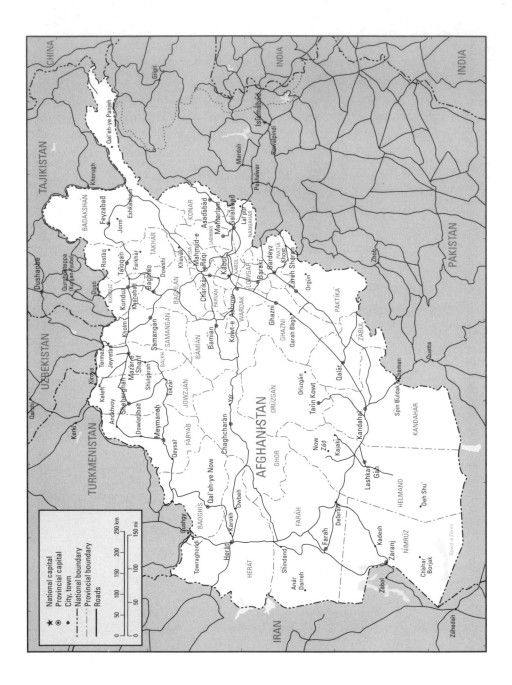

FIVE

AFGHANISTAN

Swimming in a Sea of Poppies

One of the poorest countries in the world, Afghanistan has been torn by war and insurgency since 1979. In the process, it has become the ultimate example of the "narco-state." In 2007 opium production climbed to a staggering 8,200 metric tons before declining slightly, to 7,700 metric tons, in 2008 and to 6,900 metric tons in 2009.[1] Afghanistan now supplies more than 90 percent of the global illicit market for opiates, up from no more than 50 percent in the mid-1990s, and more than 95 percent of the European market. Profits from drugs constitute more than one-third of the overall economy and equal more than half of the country's licit GDP.[2] Since 2001, opium poppy cultivation has spread to all thirty-four provinces of the country. Although eighteen northern provinces were declared opium-free in 2008 and twenty in 2009, that achievement remains tenuous, and marijuana cultivation already is replacing the former poppy fields in the north.[3]

Because the ruling elites in different regions have adopted different attitudes toward drugs, responses to the drug trade have covered the spectrum from de facto legalization and tacit acquiescence to interdiction and eradication. Policy within regions has also varied over time, often but not solely in response to changes in political control. In this chapter, I analyze the impact that different drug strategies have had on military conflict in Afghanistan since the Soviet invasion in 1979. The discussion encompasses four periods: the 1980s insurgency against Soviet occupation; the 1990s civil war; the U.S. invasion of 2001 that toppled the Taliban; and the postinvasion period, which has seen the rise of the Taliban insurgency and its allies against the U.S.-backed government of President Hamid Karzai. In addition, I examine the second major element of Afghanistan's underground economy—the smuggling of licit goods—and its interaction with the Taliban effort to take over Afghanistan in the 1990s.

I describe and analyze the condition of the illicit economy during each period, including its structure, operations, and evolution, as a result of both internal processes and exogenous shocks, such as changes in the intensity of military conflict. An accurate picture of the structure of the illicit economy is important in understanding how belligerents exploit illegal economies and what effects government policies have on the relationship between belligerents and the population.

THE SOVIET OCCUPATION AND MUJAHIDEEN INSURGENCY, 1979–89

Afghanistan first became a significant opium producer in the mid-1950s, after poppy cultivation was banned in neighboring Iran, which then became Afghanistan's principal market. But in the mid-1970s, when political instability and a prolonged drought disrupted the flow of drugs from Southeast Asia's Golden Triangle, Afghanistan and Pakistan began to supply large quantities of opiates to western Europe and North America.

Another turning point came when the Soviet Union, which had long been involved in Afghanistan as part of its competition with the United States for influence in Central and South Asia, invaded Afghanistan in December 1979. By the late 1970s, Moscow was Afghanistan's leading trading partner and source of economic aid. In a crucial move, the Soviets had modernized the Afghan army and co-opted many of its officers; they also had developed strong connections to Afghanistan's nascent communist movement. When the government of President Mohammad Daoud sought to redefine itself in the 1970s along more nationalist and traditionalist lines, the groundwork for a confrontation was laid. Daoud's government began to shed its leftist connections both at home and abroad, distanced itself from the Soviet Union, and threatened Afghan communists. That realignment precipitated a communist coup in 1978 known as the Saur Revolution, in which a leftist government intent on modernizing and secularizing Afghanistan was installed. Its reforms regarding land, credit, marriage, and mandatory education for both girls and boys threatened the socioeconomic foundations of Afghanistan's rural society: the family and the tribe and its khans (tribal leaders). A rebellion broke out, and by late 1979 the new government was about to collapse. Rather than see its investment vanish, the Soviet Union decided to invade.

The Soviet forces, which soon numbered more than 100,000, quickly became entrenched in the cities, while a resistance movement organized largely along tribal and religious lines emerged throughout the countryside. By the end of 1981, guerrilla warfare had broken out in all of the country's then twenty-nine provinces. Many of the mujahideen commanders who opposed the Soviet army were based in Peshawar, Pakistan, where they received aid from the United States and training and organizational support from Pakistan's Directorate for Inter-Services Intelligence (ISI).[4]

Despite their military superiority, the Soviet forces failed to win over the hearts and minds of the rural population. To defeat the mujahideen, they therefore turned to a scorched earth policy, systematically destroying agricultural resources and thereby forcing the rural population to leave for cities, which the Soviet forces controlled. The devastation was made complete by the warfare between different mujahideen factions, which mined each other's aqueducts and destroyed irrigation systems. By 1987, agricultural output was one-third of what it had been in 1978, and millions of Afghans had fled to neighboring countries. Among those who stayed, large segments of the population had no option but to turn to the cultivation of opium poppies, which could grow in the poorest agricultural conditions, and the production of opium.[5]

That development posed a dilemma for mujahideen commanders. On the one hand, poppy cultivation represented a substantial component of the economy, especially in Helmand, in the south, and in Nangarhar, in the east. On the other hand, opium consumption was *haram*—prohibited by the Koran—which meant that they could not endorse the drug economy without jeopardizing the Islamic credentials that legitimized their opposition to the communist regime.[6] Initially, most mujahideen commanders resolved the dilemma by tacitly acquiescing in the drug trade in the territories under their control and using any profits that came their way for personal enrichment. But three major resistance leaders—Gulbuddin Hekmatyar, Mullah Nasim Akhundzada, and Ismat Muslim—systematically exploited drug production for military purposes from early on. As they captured the prime agricultural areas of Afghanistan's south and east, they encouraged the local population to grow poppies, doubling the country's opium harvest to 575 metric tons between 1982 and 1983.[7]

Gulbuddin Hekmatyar, head of the largely Pashtun Hezb-i-Islami (Islamic Party), which was based in northeastern Afghanistan, used his drug profits to maintain one of the two largest resistance organizations in the country.[8] (He also was the leading recipient of covert aid from Pakistan and the CIA until the end of the 1980s.) Initially, Hekmatyar taxed only poppy cultivation. However, by the end of the 1980s, unlike other commanders who were satisfied to sell raw opium at bazaars in Afghanistan and Baluchistan, Hekmatyar, in partnership with Pakistani heroin syndicates, had invested in building processing plants.[9] By the late 1980s, he controlled at least six heroin refineries at Koh-I-Soltan, in southwestern Pakistan, that processed opium from Afghanistan's southern Helmand province.[10]

Within the Helmand Valley, Mullah Nasim Akhundzada emerged as another major sponsor of the opium economy. The Akhundzada family, which belonged to the principal tribe in Helmand, the Alizais, were based in Musa Qala in northern Helmand, a traditional poppy-growing area.[11] Following the Soviet invasion, Nasim quickly became a prominent commander in the Harakat-e-Inqilab-e-Islami, the leading jihadi party in Helmand, and his militias became a feared force. As a mullah (a local Islamic cleric) rather than a khan, Nasim had fairly modest social status. Nonetheless, his military successes and sponsorship of the opium trade helped him rise to a position of tribal leadership by the mid-1980s. Ultimately Nasim and his brothers came to control all of Helmand until the emergence of the Taliban in the mid-1990s. His power was so great that in 1988 communist-backed President Mohammad Najibullah singled Nasim out as a principal powerbroker in his appeal to seven major mujahideen commanders for a ceasefire.

As early as 1981, Nasim issued a fatwa (religious ruling) legitimizing poppy cultivation in Helmand.[12] "We must grow and sell opium to fight our holy war against the Russian nonbelievers," his elder brother, Mohammed Rasul, explained.[13] To ensure adequate production, Nasim issued quotas—decreeing in 1989, for example, that 50 percent of the land be sowed with opium poppies—and provided cash advances to farmers engaged in poppy cultivation and opium production. Any landlord who failed to fill his quota had to pay for the shortfall, a policy that drove many into debt. Farmers and landowners who did not comply were subject to harsh penalties, reportedly including torture and execution.

Nasim also sought to control as much of the trafficking component of the trade as possible, even maintaining an office in Zahidan, Iran, to handle the trade once it left Afghanistan.[14] He cut out traffickers in the areas under his control and directly and heavy-handedly regulated the opium economy in their place. But it would be a mistake to view Nasim as imposing cultivation primarily by force. Given the destruction of the agricultural infrastructure, opium poppy became by far the most lucrative and often the only viable crop even in the fertile Helmand Valley, and the population was driven to its cultivation by both economic and security pressures. The people wanted to grow poppies, but without Nasim's interference.

The third mujahideen leader to turn the drug economy to early advantage was Ismat Muslim, an Achekzai commander from the Kandahar district of Spin Boldak. Located on the border with Pakistan, Spin Boldak had a long history of involvement in smuggling. Ismat Muslim himself had engaged in smuggling, including heroin trafficking, between Kandahar and Quetta in Pakistan as early as 1979, and Achekzai smugglers, whom he favored over competitors from the Noorzai tribe, were a critical element of his political base.[15] Following a 1984 dispute with Pakistan's ISI over his smuggling activities, his resistance to ISI's control, and his refusal to join one of the Peshawar-based parties that the ISI insisted were to be the sole beneficiaries of Pakistani aid, Ismat Muslim defected to the Soviet-backed regime. His principal role in the regime was to control transit points and roads between Pakistan's Baluchistan and Kandahar.[16] Despite many attacks by mujahideen commanders and his notorious brutality and excesses, Ismat Muslim maintained complete authority over his territory. Together his military prowess and control of various illicit economies in his territory, including the drug trade, helped him to become the leader of the Achekzai tribe and, at the peak of his power, to claim the loyalty of 50,000 people.[17]

Benefits of the Drug Trade

In cases such as those sketched above, drug profits allowed belligerent groups to scale up their capabilities—for example, by replacing single-shot rifles with automatic weapons and light artillery.[18] Access to cash also liberated the mujahideen from their previous reliance on costly and time-consuming ambushes to secure weapons, ammunition, and other military

supplies and even food and clothing.[19] Such ambushes had to be conducted by large forces that had to maintain their positions for up to an
hour, exposing them to Soviet detection and possible destruction.[20] The
ability to buy arms from smugglers thus significantly increased the
mujahideen's freedom of action and helped them to become increasingly
independent of external sponsors.[21]

Equally important, control over the drug economy became a significant
source of legitimacy for the mujahideen. Traditionally, tribal elites in
Afghanistan derived legitimacy from their ability to provide security and
distribute goods among members of their communities. In order to achieve
and maintain his position of leadership, the khan was required to "provide food for others, arbitrate in their disputes and be unflinching in his
defense of the *qawm* [communal group]."[22] Positive involvement in the
illicit drug trade allowed the mujahideen commanders to deliver similar
goods and services to their communities. For example, in a 1987 interview, Mullah Nasim Akhundzada claimed to have established hospitals,
clinics, and forty madrasas in the Helmand Valley.[23] The ability to support
the community was all the more important given that many of the
mujahideen commanders lacked a prestigious tribal khan lineage. As
Olivier Roy argues, the "new notables" established their power as redis-
tributors: "The new notable creates a network of clients, strengthened by
matrimonial bonds, thanks to the goods he is able to distribute. These
goods do not come from extorting peasants, but from international
sources. . . . more recently, profits [come] from marketing weapons and
drugs (opium)."[24] Meanwhile, because traditional agricultural production and overall economic activity were destroyed, the traditional elites
had little to distribute, and therefore their power was undermined.

Growth of the Drug Trade

Several factors facilitated the growth of the narcotics economy in
Afghanistan through the 1980s. First, the success of those who first
became actively involved in drug production helped commanders shed
their religious inhibitions, obtain the knowledge necessary to exploit the
illicit economy, and become positively involved in the trade. A contagion
effect, in other words, was clearly at work.

Further sources of learning were the Afghan refugee community in
Pakistan and Pakistani government officials. Afghan refugees quickly
became proficient at smuggling a variety of commodities, including

weapons, consumer goods, and drugs. Mujahideen leaders with tight connections across the borders, such as Hekmatyar, were able to exploit those
channels to move opium and heroin into Pakistan, frequently with the
connivance of Pakistani officials. Trucks from the Pakistan army's
National Logistics Cell (NLC) often took CIA-supplied weapons from
Karachi to Afghanistan and returned loaded with heroin, which was protected from police search by ISI documents. [25]

The U.S. government also helped create more propitious conditions
for the drug economy by providing the mujahideen with Stinger surface-
to-air missiles, which ultimately ended the Soviets' air superiority. As the
mujahideen's air defenses improved, agricultural production picked up
but continued to center mainly on opium poppy cultivation. Together,
the United States and Saudi Arabia provided an estimated $6 billion in
arms and money to Islamist commanders fighting the Soviet occupation
throughout the 1980s. Additional aid came from Pakistan and Iran. Initially, foreign aid constituted a readily available alternative to the drug
economy for mujahideen commanders. But toward the end of the decade,
some leaders, such as Hekmatyar, greatly increased their participation in
the illicit economy, anticipating that eventually foreign aid would dry up.

WARLORDS AND THE ILLICIT
ECONOMY IN THE EARLY 1990s

The growing effectiveness of the mujahideen forces, backed by extensive
foreign aid, made it impossible for the Soviet occupying forces to consolidate their control over Afghanistan. The communist government in Kabul
had failed to win over the population or to bring about any significant
improvements in its well-being, and under Mikhail Gorbachev, the Soviet
Union's priorities shifted from the war in Afghanistan to internal reform
and the preservation of communist rule at home. In March 1988, the
Soviet government agreed to withdraw from the country over a period of
nine months, and withdrawal was completed on February 15, 1989.

But peace did not come to Afghanistan. The early 1990s were characterized by shifting and fluid alliances and constant infighting among warlords. Following the Soviets' exit, a three-year struggle pitted the
mujahideen against the regime of President Najibullah, who had been
elected in 1986. In 1992, Najibullah's government collapsed, and Kabul
was taken by the mujahideen, who immediately began fighting among

themselves. After being driven from the capital, Hekmatyar's Pashtun-dominated Hezb-i-Islami laid siege to the city, which was controlled by a coalition of Tajik forces under the military leadership of Ahmed Shah Massoud and the political leadership of Burhanuddin Rabbani, both of the Jamiat-i-Islami (Islamic Society), and Uzbek forces under the leadership of a formerly pro-communist general, Abdul Rashid Dostum.[26] Throughout the ensuing struggle, all sides relied on involvement in the illicit economy to augment their power.

For example, Massoud and Rabbani drew on resources from their regional base in Afghanistan's northeast, including the mining of precious and semi-precious gems, such as emeralds and lapis lazuli, and drug production and trafficking. Initially, Massoud refrained from active involvement in the drug trade, considering it anti-Islamic, but by the late 1980s he had overcome his inhibitions. His group levied a tax on opium cultivation that was paid directly to local commanders. Starting at around 2.5 percent, it climbed through the 1990s, eventually reaching 20 percent.[27] In addition, Massoud and Rabbani controlled trafficking routes through Tajikistan to Russia and Europe and cooperated with a major Iranian drug baron, Hadj Gulyam, to ensure that the trucks that they sent to Iran loaded with opium made the return trip carrying money and weapons.[28] Massoud and Rabbani used their revenues not only to finance their militias but also to build up regional government and military institutions that functioned independently of Kabul.

In contrast, Afghan commanders who sought to crack down on the drug economy faced serious challenges to their control. In the Helmand, Mullah Nasim struck a deal in 1990 with Robert Oakley, U.S. ambassador to Pakistan, to curtail drug production in exchange for $2 million in the form of U.S. Agency for International Development (USAID) development programs. Nasim kept his end of the bargain. Later that year, he invited U.S. embassy officials to inspect the valley. They found that Nasim's eradication efforts had been effective, noting that opium prices in nearby Baluchistan province, in Pakistan, had tripled.[29] However, the U.S. government, invoking U.S. laws against negotiating with drug traffickers, revoked the deal and did not deliver any aid to the Helmand region. Hard hit by Nasim's suppression of poppy cultivation and lacking economic alternatives, the population became restive. Moreover, the increase in opium prices angered rival leader Gulbuddin Hekmatyar, whose refineries relied on Helmand's opium. Hekmatyar ordered Mullah Nasim and five of his commanders gunned down. Nasim's brother, Mohammed Rasul, who inherited control of the Helmand Valley, annulled the prohibition on poppy cultivation.

Similarly, Haji Abdul Qadir, of the Arsala clan in Nangarhar, then the second-largest opium-producing region in Afghanistan, accepted an offer of international aid in exchange for cutting opium production by half. Haji Abdul Qadir and his brothers had sponsored Nangarhar province's skyrocketing expansion of opium production for several years, and they also were positively involved in another illicit economy: the tax-free smuggling of legal goods from Dubai to Pakistan. Their control of the Jalalabad airport ideally positioned them to participate in smuggling, in alliance with Afghan and Pakistani Pashtun truckers. Thus, although the ban on opium poppy cultivation curtailed their income to some extent, they were assured of another stream of revenue. But smuggling alone did not provide adequate employment for Nangarhar's large population, and after the crop-substitution funds ran out, the Arsalas were forced to rescind the ban.[30]

THE TALIBAN AND THE ILLICIT ECONOMY

In 1994, a new and powerful armed group arrived on the scene: the Taliban, composed of Islamic fundamentalists who became notorious for their unrestrained brutality, religious fanaticism, and ruthless oppression. Although led by Afghans, notably Mullah Omar, the Taliban was formed as a transnational network based in both Afghanistan and Pakistan. In Pakistan it drew primarily on a network of madrasas that educated Afghan refugees and on political parties belonging to the Deobandi movement, whose teachings are based on an austere interpretation of Islam. Adherents seek to purify Islam by embracing customs practiced during the time of the Prophet Mohammad, endorse a highly restrictive view of women's role in society, and oppose Western influences as corrupt. Although dominated by Ghilzai Pashtuns from Kandahar, the Taliban did not represent a particular ethnicity. Rather, as Barnett Rubin argues, it represented a social group—"the privately educated, rural ulama and their students affiliated to the Deobandi movement."[31] Highly centralized, secretive, and dictatorial, the group aimed to pacify and purify Afghanistan. Fundamentally anti-modernist, the Taliban sought to reconstruct the Afghan state and society by imposing a very strict, backward-looking interpretation of Islam.[32]

The Taliban made rapid military strides. In September 1995 it seized control of the province of Herat, and one year later it captured Kabul, ousting the power-sharing government led by Burhanuddin Rabbani (the president) and Gulbuddin Hekmatyar (the prime minister). In response, a group of predominantly non-Pashtun leaders, including Dostum, Massoud, and Rabbani, formed a loose anti-Taliban alliance known as the United Islamic Front for the Salvation of Afghanistan (UIF), or the Northern Alliance. The Northern Alliance's foreign backers included Russia, Iran, Turkey, India, and the United States.

Phase One: The Illicit Trade in Legal Goods

When the Taliban first appeared in 1994, its forces numbered in the hundreds and were poorly armed, frequently running out of ammunition. But within months, their numbers swelled to 15,000 as students from madrasas in Pakistan poured into Afghanistan. In addition to encouraging the influx of volunteers, Pakistan provided the Taliban with money, weapons, and military support. Early in the fall of 1994, a Pakistani artillery barrage helped the Taliban seize the important border town of Spin Boldak and the arms depot at Pasha, a major weapons cache that included rockets, artillery ammunition, tank ammunition, and small arms.[33] Further seizures of arsenals, including those at the Kandahar airport, where the Taliban acquired six MIG-21 fighters (only one of which was operational) and four MIG-17 transport helicopters, and at a Northern Alliance base at Sarkateb, where they gained twenty tanks and two additional MIG-17s, supplemented the logistical and infrastructure support that the Taliban was receiving from Pakistan and the money that it received from groups in Saudi Arabia.[34] By October 1996, the Taliban fielded at least 25,000 fighters in outfits complete with tanks, armored vehicles, helicopters, and fighter aircraft. The equipment was operated, in part, by veteran pilots, tank drivers, and technicians from Pakistan refugee camps who were paid in U.S. dollars and recruited with the help of Pakistan's intelligence service.[35]

Pakistan had two primary reasons for supporting the Taliban. First, the government preferred to have Afghanistan under the control of a pro-Pakistani force, rather than one that was close to Russia, India, or Iran. Its goal was to protect Pakistan's western flank from encirclement. At the time, Pakistan's military doctrine called for the use of Afghan territory to give Pakistan strategic depth in a military confrontation with India, so that its forces could recoup there if India should break through on Pakistan's eastern border. Second, Pakistan sought to secure trade access to and through Afghanistan and to end the constant harassment of its truckers by Afghan warlords, who charged exorbitant tolls on trade routes and sometimes took hostages.[36]

Without Pakistan's support, the Taliban would have encountered much greater difficulty in its efforts to take control of Afghanistan. But Pakistan was not the Taliban's sole source of financial and military resources; the group derived significant benefits from its involvement in the smuggling of legal goods between Pakistan and Afghanistan. That trade was an outgrowth of the Afghan Transit Trade Agreement, negotiated in the 1950s, which allowed goods to pass duty-free from the port of Karachi through Pakistan and over the border to Afghanistan. A buyer in Afghanistan would issue a letter of credit to import goods, such as refrigerators, through Karachi, and the appliances would then be driven through Pakistan into Afghanistan duty-free. The trucks would unload on the Afghan side and return to Pakistan empty. The tax-free goods would then be carried back into Pakistan illegally, sometimes on the backs of camels and donkeys. The reimported goods, which sold for far less than goods imported into Pakistan legally, were distributed through a trucking industry largely controlled by Afghan refugees in Pakistan. According to the World Bank, the value of such illicit traffic amounted to $2.5 billion in 1997.[37]

In order to transport the goods, the smugglers had to pay tolls to local warlords for the use of the roads and passes under their control, a practice that dated back to the previous century. The tolls climbed steadily in the early 1990s, threatening the interests of the transport mafia. For example, in Herat, the local warlord Ismail Khan doubled the charge for using his section of the highway from 5,000 rupees ($125) to 10,000 rupees ($250) per truck. On any route, a truck could be stopped and forced to pay tolls as many as twenty times, and sometimes local warlords stole the goods. Although the warlords were not consciously trying to destroy the smuggling economy, their capriciousness and greed made it increasingly difficult for the smugglers to conduct business.

The emergence of the Taliban significantly lowered the smugglers' transaction costs and allowed them to conduct business in a much more predictable fashion. As early as fall 1994, when the Taliban first emerged around Kandahar, it cleared chains from the roads, set up a one-toll system for trucks entering Afghanistan at Spin Boldak, and patrolled and protected the highways against the warlords. In a crucial decision, the Taliban also declared that it would not allow goods bound for Afghanistan to be carried by Pakistani truckers, thus satisfying a key demand of the Afghan transport mafia.[38] The traffickers paid the Taliban handsomely for its support. The Taliban was reported to have collected 6 million rupees ($150,000) from transporters in Chaman in a single day in March 1995 and twice that amount the next day in Quetta.[39]

Apart from improving procurement, logistics, and salaries, such funds helped the Taliban buy off some of its opponents, and bribery became a key feature of the Taliban's strategy.[40] In addition, the Taliban's support for smuggling generated a certain amount of political capital. Many traffickers were important regional powerbrokers who helped sway the territory where they operated away from local warlords and toward the Taliban. Moreover, the vibrant smuggling economy helped revitalize some aspects of the licit economy. For example, there was increased business for teahouses and rest stops serving truckers, which benefited those living close to the smuggling routes. But because the trade was not labor intensive, the number of people who benefited directly was limited; consequently, the associated increase in popular support for the Taliban also was limited. Writing prior to the Taliban's sponsorship of the labor-intensive opium economy, Olivier Roy remarked that the Taliban's legitimacy came essentially from the weapons that it controlled.[41]

Phase Two: Efforts to Eradicate the Illicit Opium Poppy Economy

In late 1994 and early 1995, the Taliban spread from Kandahar through the south in a blitz campaign. The fighting was bitter, with casualties for the Taliban running into the hundreds for the first time. As Anthony Davis argued, "neither [the Taliban's] moral authority nor cash accounted for much" in Helmand.[42] Ultimately, however, the Taliban succeeded in taking over the region after a two-month military campaign.

The Taliban's opponent in Helmand was Ghaffar Akhundzada, the brother of the late Mullah Nasim and Mohammad Rasul Akhundzada. Ghaffar was an experienced fighter who had fought against the Soviets during the 1980s and emerged in the early 1990s as one of the country's leading warlords. The Taliban forces facing him were still relatively weak: their numbers were small, their military equipment very limited, and their military tactics poor. But Ghaffar's military efforts were hampered by lack of popular support. Wanting to dominate the illicit economy to the fullest extent possible, he and his brothers had taken it upon themselves to directly regulate cultivation, set prices, and punish (frequently brutally) villagers who failed to deliver their quotas. Rather than protect the farmers against drug traffickers, the Akhundzadas took on the traffickers' role. The population also became economically squeezed after Mullah Nasim's short-lived effort to eradicate poppy cultivation. By the time the Taliban emerged as a competitor for power, many farmers saw it as an acceptable alternative to the Akhundzadas.

After the Taliban secured control of Helmand, the group's first impulse was to prohibit poppy cultivation. In a series of communiqués about Taliban goals, its leaders banned cultivation of both opium poppy and marijuana. They also cracked down on hashish addicts, who were subject to harsh penalties.[43] The ban, combined with large opium stockpiles, high wheat prices, and bad weather, led to a nearly one-third drop in opium production between 1994 and 1995. The United Nations and the United States both were hopeful that if the Taliban succeeded in taking over the country, it would stem Afghanistan's opium and heroin production. In 1996, Giovanni Quaglia, then director of the UN Drug Control Policy (UNDCP) office in Pakistan, declared, rather cavalierly as it turned out, that "in these circumstances, the [drug] problem [in Afghanistan] can be dealt with in ten years."[44]

However, despite the ethnic ties between the Taliban's Pashtun fighters and the local population, the Taliban's efforts to end poppy cultivation quickly threatened its position in Helmand province and control of the region shifted back and forth between the Taliban and local warlords throughout 1995. The Taliban encountered a similar situation in 1997 when it attempted to proscribe the informal traffic in timber in the provinces of Paktya and Kunar. There smugglers were chopping down hundreds of acres of high-quality hardwood, pine, and cedar and hauling the wood off through Nangarhar to Pakistan to be processed into cheap furniture and window frames. After taking over the two provinces and expelling Nangarhar's commander, Haji Qadir, the Taliban first attempted to levy a tax of $750 per truck before altogether banning the trade;[45] however, the ban generated widespread resistance.[46] In fact, Haji Qadir, who was exiled in Peshawar, capitalized on the popular resentment by launching a military attack into Kunar with the help of two local warlords. Although the Taliban ultimately prevailed, the scale of the unrest in the province seriously rattled its leadership.

Phase Three: From Laissez Faire to De Facto Legalization

The Taliban's prohibition of the narcotics trade did not last. Driven by the need to secure its vital base in Helmand province, the Taliban rapidly altered course, and by 1996 the ban on cultivation was lifted. At first the group adopted a laissez-faire approach to drug cultivation, but progressively it became positively involved in various aspects of the opium economy, taxing farmers as well as protecting and taxing traffickers.

The Taliban's new edict stated that "the cultivation of, and trading in *charas* (cannabis, used for hashish) is forbidden absolutely. The consumption of opiates is forbidden, as is the manufacture of heroin, but the production of and trading in opium is not forbidden."[47] In practice, despite the announced ban, heroin labs were not destroyed and heroin traffic was not interdicted. The 10 percent tax on opium, formerly paid to the village mullahs, was now directed to the Taliban's treasury, generating an estimated $9 million in 1996–97.[48] A 10 percent tax was also levied on the traffickers. Those taxes were eventually increased to 20 percent, bringing in between $45 million and $200 million a year.[49] In addition, by 1999 the Taliban was taxing heroin labs.[50]

Despite paying higher taxes, drug traffickers benefited, on balance, from Taliban control. Compared with the greedy and unpredictable local warlords who had previously controlled and taxed the trafficking routes, the Taliban significantly lowered transaction costs for the traffickers, brought stability to the industry, and helped to streamline it. Moreover, the traffickers benefited from the increase in poppy cultivation under Taliban rule. In 1994, Afghanistan produced 3,400 metric tons of opium. As a result of the Taliban's initial ban and other market and weather factors, production fell to 2,300 metric tons in 1995, but by 1999 it had climbed to 4,600 metric tons.[51]

Drug profits paid for the Taliban's weapons, ammunition, fuel, food, and clothes; they also paid for salaries, transport, and other perks that the Taliban leadership allowed its fighters.[52] However, the change in the Taliban's approach to the drug economy was not driven by financial need. There were no indications that the Taliban was hurting financially before it retreated from its poppy ban. According to World Bank estimates, its profits from smuggling legal goods were $75 million in 1995, enough to comfortably sustain the Taliban's military effort.[53] However, the group lacked widespread popular legitimacy and support, and participating in the drug economy offered a solution to that problem. Once the Taliban reversed its policy toward poppy cultivation, it was able to consolidate its control over southern Afghanistan, and Helmand, along with Kandahar, became its key stronghold.

The opium economy proved to be a rich source of political capital because it provided reliable and relatively lucrative employment to a vast segment of the population. Approximately 350 person days are required to cultivate one hectare of poppy plants in Afghanistan, compared with approximately 41 person days per hectare for wheat and 135 person days per hectare for black cumin. Harvesting alone requires as much as 200 person days per hectare for poppy.[54] Therefore, even those who did not have access to land could be hired as itinerant laborers during various parts of the growing season.

For many people, opium poppy cultivation was the only livelihood in an otherwise devastated economy.[55] Ruined by the war against the Soviet Union in the 1980s, Afghanistan's economy remained in critical condition throughout the 1990s. All legal economic activity, other than subsistence production and the microeconomic spillover from illicit activities, came to a halt. Against that backdrop, opium revenues in Afghanistan totaled $102 million in 1994, $54 million in 1995, $183 million in 1999, and $1,200 million in 2002.[56] Typically, the yearly net earnings for small sharecroppers amounted to several hundred dollars and rose to more than $1,000 for landowners.

Prices for opium were often, though not always, considerably higher than prices for legal products, such as wheat and fruit.[57] Moreover, opium was relatively easy to produce and did not require a functioning agricultural infrastructure. Because irrigation systems were ruined in most of the country, it became very difficult to cultivate more wheat and fruit than the amount necessary to meet immediate needs, and food had to be imported from Pakistan and Iran. Transportation networks around the country had collapsed, making it problematic for farmers to be able to deliver perishable crops to market at a profit. Light, easy to transport, and nonperishable, opium was either picked up by traders at the farm gate or was transported over much shorter distances. In addition, opium poppy growers had access to advance credit under a system known as *salaam*. Over time, creditors in Afghanistan came to lend money against a guaranteed amount of opium to be delivered by the farmer at harvest time. Such microcredit provided farmers with money to purchase food, clothes, and medicine for their families during the winter months. No other micro-finance opportunities existed for the majority of the rural population.

Moreover, the flourishing illicit narcotics economy supported other forms of microeconomic activity. Service businesses, such as rest stops and fuel stations, sprang up to serve drug smugglers,[58] and much more reconstruction took place in areas where opium poppies were grown than elsewhere in the country.[59] Many people therefore developed a stake in the illicit narcotics economy and appreciated the Taliban's positive involvement—traders, smugglers, shopkeepers, moneylenders, local warlords, and religious elites whom the Taliban tolerated and allowed a cut of the business, and most important, the large rural population.

In the limited interviews conducted in Afghanistan during the 1990s, farmers emphasized the Taliban's sponsorship of the illicit economy as a crucial source of the group's legitimacy. Ahmed Rashid's 1997 interview with Wali Jan, an elderly farmer near Kandahar, provides one example. Wali Jan earned around $1,300 a year, a small fortune by the standards of Afghan farmers, and he knew whom to thank for his prosperity: "We cannot be more grateful to the Taliban. The Taliban have brought us security so we can grow our poppy in peace. I need to grow poppy crop to support my 14 family members."[60]

The statements of the Taliban itself, even if only partially genuine, further attest to the political salience of the illicit narcotics economy. In 1997, Abdul Rashid, the head of the Taliban's counternarcotics force in Kandahar—which existed to regulate the opium economy and enforce edicts, such as that against consumption of opium—explained: "We let people cultivate poppies because farmers get good prices. We cannot push the people to grow wheat as there would be an uprising against the Taliban if we forced them to stop poppy cultivation. So we grow opium and get our wheat from Pakistan."[61] Elsewhere Rashid maintained: "Everyone is growing poppy. If we try to stop this immediately, the people will be against us."[62]

The importance of the drug economy to the Taliban's political control is further underscored by the fact that the Taliban did not yield on any other doctrinal issue nor did it reverse any other of its extremely unpopular repressive policies. As the Taliban expanded its control throughout the country, it instituted a highly restrictive form of sharia law. The Taliban forbade women to attend school, work outside the home, or receive medical care; it also imposed purdah, the mandatory veiling of women from head to toe. Participating in sports, playing music, flying kites, dancing, or reading anything published outside of Afghanistan became illegal. Religious police from the Ministry for Promoting Virtue and Preventing Vice patrolled the streets, looking for offenders, such as men who failed to grow sufficiently long beards. Women found walking on the streets without a male relative or whose ankles were showing were lashed on the spot, frequently by boys or men wielding car antennas or electrical cords. Punishments for offenses were brutal. The Taliban frequently packed the stadiums with crowds of tens of thousands to witness amputations, floggings, and executions. Thieves had their right hand and left foot amputated; murderers were killed, sometimes by members of the victim's family; and adulterers were stoned to death with their children watching from the front of the crowd.

The Taliban also destroyed almost all vineyards, insisting that grapes were used to make alcohol, a substance prohibited by the Koran.[63] But although it never relented on any of its other prohibitions and draconian measures, the Taliban did reverse its poppy prohibition. And while all other economic employment opportunities and many social activities for women were banned, women were permitted to engage in various stages of poppy cultivation and opium production, including planting, weeding, thinning, lancing the capsules and collecting the resin, cleaning the seeds, and processing byproducts such as oil and soap.[64]

Not only did the Taliban refuse to yield on any other social, political, or economic issue except for opium cultivation, once in power it proved fundamentally uninterested in state-building or economic development. Its goal was to purge any sign of modernity from the country and enforce its fundamentalist cultural norms. The Taliban essentially abdicated all but the bare minimum of its governing responsibilities, except for providing security. It never set up social services or a functioning bureaucracy; furthermore, it allowed the existing social services and state administration to completely disintegrate. But once again, it made an exception for the opium economy. In that domain, it provided a variety of extension services to farmers, such as issuing licenses for cultivation and providing fertilizers.[65] It put its money into its military forces and bribes for troublesome tribes and hoarded the rest for future jihad, though not for personal enrichment.

In short, the benefits that the Taliban reaped from positive involvement in the drug economy were so vast that they trumped both religion and ideology, but that was a lesson that the group learned the hard way. The Taliban's initial ban on cultivation severely reduced its political capital and undermined its strength. But once the Taliban began to support the illicit economy, its political capital greatly increased. In fact, the Taliban's support of the drug trade was a key source of its legitimacy in poppy-growing areas.

In contrast, in areas where the Taliban was unable to buy political legitimacy by supporting the narcotics economy, it had to resort to much greater brutality. The Taliban was much harsher in its treatment of cities, perhaps with the exception of Kandahar, than in its treatment of villages. Although drug and other illicit traffic no doubt went through the major cities, far fewer people benefited from the trade in urban areas.

Phase Four: The 2000 Eradication Campaign and the Subsequent Return to Laissez-Faire

It was therefore all the more surprising that the Taliban banned poppy cultivation in 2000. The ban, which was enforced by village elders (maliks) and supervised by mullahs, resulted in the largest reduction of opium poppy cultivation in a country in any single year. Cultivation fell from an estimated 82,172 hectares in 2000 to less than 8,000 in 2001, thereby contributing to a 75 percent drop in the global supply of heroin.[66]

The ban severely depressed the economic prospects of vast segments of Afghanistan's rural population. In the words of one U.S. Drug Enforcement Administration (DEA) official, the ban was "bringing their country—or certain regions of their country—to economic ruin."[67] The ban drove the majority of landowners, farmers, and sharecroppers heavily into debt; unable to repay their debts, they were driven to borrow further or flee to Pakistan. The experience of a seventy-year-old sharecropper, recounted by David Mansfield, a prominent drug expert who has conducted extensive fieldwork on poppy cultivation in Afghanistan, illustrates the destructive effects of the Taliban's new policy. The sharecropper, from Nad-e-Ali, Helmand, had planted two to four jeribs (each equal to about one-fifth of a hectare) of poppy to support his ten-member family. Because of the Taliban's ban, he was unable to repay the $1,800 that his landlord had lent him against his promise to deliver a certain amount of raw opium after the growing season. The landlord, whose land he tilled, agreed to extend another loan on the condition that the farmer accept a reduced share of the profit—one-sixth of the next opium crop instead of the traditional one-third—and agree not to leave the area, even if only to visit his extended family. The farmer was thus de facto consigned to bonded labor but felt that he had no option but to accept the terms if he wanted to feed his family. He believed that if the Taliban did not destroy his crop of opium in the upcoming growing season, he could repay his outstanding debt; if it did, he would have to flee to Pakistan, leaving his family to ruin.[68]

Why did the Taliban undertake such a politically counterproductive policy? Part of the answer seems to lie outside the country. Combined with its record of gross violations of human rights, the Taliban's toleration of the drug trade had made the regime an international pariah. By 2000, only three countries—Pakistan, United Arab Emirates, and Saudi Arabia—recognized it as the legitimate government of Afghanistan. By responding to the UNDCP's repeated appeals to curb opium production, the Taliban apparently hoped to gain international recognition. However, despite the vast fall in opium poppy cultivation, the effort failed.

In addition, the Taliban may have been motivated by the desire to boost the price of opium. As poppy cultivation exploded during the 1990s, farm gate prices for opium plummeted, but the 2000 ban on cultivation and the resulting 75 percent contraction in supply substantially increased those prices. The total farm gate value of opium production in Afghanistan went from $56 million in 2001 to $1,200 million in 2002.[69] Moreover, when the poppy cultivation ban went into effect, hundreds to thousands of metric tons of opium and hundreds of metric tons of heroin were stockpiled in Afghanistan—enough to supply the western European market for at least two years.[70] According to DEA spokesman Will Glaspy, the Taliban regime was believed to be stockpiling as much as 65 percent of each year's harvest.[71] Captain Saif Riaz, a veteran of Pakistan's drug enforcement efforts, claimed that "they have sufficient stockpiles to last at least 10 years."[72] The Taliban therefore could expect to profit financially from its ban on cultivation.[73]

But the political costs of the ban for the Taliban were substantial. Although the group enforced the ban in regions where it had firm control, it encountered widespread popular resistance. That resistance was neither assuaged by the hefty subsidies that the Taliban offered to affected tribes that it did not fully control[74] nor deterred by its brutal punishment of individuals caught violating the ban, and it led to the weakening of Taliban control in such areas as the Shinwari and Khogiani districts of Nangarhar province.[75] Mullah Mohammad Hassan Akhund, the governor of Kandahar and an influential member of the Taliban regime, argued that implementation of the ban for a second year would require "many people to be killed and others to face starvation."[76] By the spring of 2001, with the ban still in place, farmers started violating the ban and planting poppies once again.[77]

In September 2001, the Taliban rescinded the ban. Some analysts have argued that the reversal was driven by the Taliban's need for additional financial resources to fight the United States after 9-11.[78] However, the ban's success in raising the price of heroin and the Taliban's access to large stockpiles of drugs cast doubt on that explanation. Instead, it seems likely that the decision was driven by the political costs of the anti-drug policy. The Taliban already faced widespread resentment; meanwhile, the Northern Alliance, which remained active in northern Afghanistan, continued to support opium production. Taliban leaders likely feared that if they extended their ban, the Northern Alliance, with U.S. support, might capitalize on popular disenchantment to mount a serious threat to their regime.

THE U.S. INVASION AND ITS AFTERMATH

The Taliban's fears were soon realized. The 9-11 al Qaeda terrorist attacks in the United States and the subsequent refusal of the Taliban leadership to hand over Osama bin Laden and other al Qaeda operatives based in Afghanistan precipitated the U.S. invasion of Afghanistan. Operation Enduring Freedom, which began in October 2001, rapidly toppled the Taliban regime and took over most of the country within a few months. However, the top al Qaeda leadership, as well as the Taliban's Mullah Omar and other top officials, managed to escape, despite major offensives aimed at their capture, such as Operation Anaconda in the Tora Bora region.

Many observers were surprised by the speed of the Taliban's fall in its main stronghold, Afghanistan's south. Contrary to expectations, many southern Pashtuns rose up and fought against the Taliban.[79] Their lack of support for the Taliban can be attributed in large part to the poppy ban of the previous year, which hurt Pashtun tribal chiefs and ordinary villagers alike. In fact, some farmers in Helmand province later alleged that Afghan anti-Taliban forces had promised to let them grow poppy in exchange for their help in toppling the Taliban regime.

By the end of 2001, with the Taliban on the run in Pakistan, attention turned to the task of building a new Afghan government. Meeting in Bonn under United Nations auspices in December 2001, the leading anti-Taliban factions created the thirty-member Afghan Interim Authority, which would be succeeded after six months by a Transitional Authority—to be established by an emergency *loya jirga* (grand council)—and ultimately by a new elected government. Pashtun leader Hamid Karzai became the first chair of the Interim Authority and then Afghanistan's interim president in 2002. The 2004 presidential election confirmed him in office; it was followed in 2005 by parliamentary elections.

The Bonn conference also created the International Security Assistance Force (ISAF) to help provide security around Kabul and support reconstruction efforts in Afghanistan. ISAF was not a UN force but a coalition of the willing deployed under the authority of the UN Security Council. ISAF, which has been led by NATO since 2003, gradually expanded its peacekeeping mission from the area surrounding Kabul to the entire country. In 2005, NATO-ISAF absorbed most of the U.S. forces originally deployed under Operation Enduring Freedom. Only U.S. troops tasked specifically with special counterterrorism missions continue to operate independently, outside the NATO command structure.

The Opium Economy Rebounds

Under international pressure, the Afghan Interim Authority banned opium poppy cultivation in one of its first acts. The new decree, which was issued in January 2002, also banned processing, trafficking, and consumption of opium and related products. But in taking on the drug trade, the government was facing an uphill battle. The structural conditions that nourished the opium economy had long been in place, beginning with Afghanistan's endemic poverty. Afghanistan's per capita GDP was one of the lowest in the world. In 2004, it was estimated that around 6.4 million people, or more than 20 percent of the population, did not have enough to eat on a yearly basis and that 37 percent of Afghan citizens were unable to satisfy their basic needs.[80] Not surprisingly, at least one-third of the farmers surveyed by the UNDCP office reported alleviation of poverty as a principal reason for their decision to grow poppies.[81]

Moreover, a devastating drought that lasted from 1998 to 2005 caused most crops to fail, dramatically worsening the situation in the countryside. But even after the drought came to an end, farmers had few incentives to cultivate legal crops, given their lack of access to essential infrastructure, irrigation, markets, and microcredit. Increasingly, opium production became a prerequisite for participation in the rural economy. Rent, share-cropping contracts, and land tenure terms came to be calculated in opium, and it became increasingly difficult to obtain access to land without promising payment in opium.[82]

Moreover, opium offered farmers a relatively good income. In the 2004 growing season, an Afghan farmer could expect a gross income of $12,700 per hectare under poppy cultivation. With roughly one-third of a hectare under cultivation, the average poppy farmer could generate a gross income of around $3,900 for his family ($594 per capita) if he sold all of his opium production immediately after harvest and even more if he sold some later.[83] That sum represented twenty times as much as he would earn by growing wheat, and it was a fortune in a country where many people lived on less than one dollar a day.

Equally important, opium delivered a steady income. Although daily opium prices fluctuate by up to 30 percent, over the long term they tend to be relatively stable.[84] Prices for legal products, especially those that have intense external competition, tend to be more volatile over the long term, making such products considerably more risky. In surveys conducted in poppy-growing villages, farmers highlighted risk management as a crucial consideration when deciding which crops to plant each year.

Earnings from poppy cultivation also outstripped earnings from non-agricultural activities. During 2003, for example, when farmers could earn as much as $12 a day cultivating poppy, the USAID offered only between $3 and $6 a day to its Afghan employees[85] while a tailor earned a daily wage of 30 cents.[86] Earnings from growing poppies allowed farmers to acquire goods that satisfied more than their basic needs—including televisions, electric generators, motorcycles, and even cars—and to finance medical care in Pakistan and large dowries for their daughters. Planting poppies thus offered not simply survival in the face of grinding poverty, but also upward mobility.

It was therefore hardly surprising that despite the Interim Authority's ban on poppy cultivation, opium production quickly returned to pre-2000 levels. After hitting a low of 190 metric tons in 2001, opium production rebounded to 3,400 metric tons in 2002 and peaked at 8,200 metric tons in 2007. In 2008, opium poppies were cultivated on 157,000 hectares in Afghanistan.[87] The number of poppy-growing villages has increased dramatically since the fall of the Taliban, and new areas, such as Badakshan in the north, have emerged as major producing regions.

The United Nations estimates that 2.9 million Afghans—12.6 percent of the population—are involved in poppy cultivation.[88] Yet that number fails to capture the true size, scope, and economic importance of the drug economy. It does not include the itinerant laborers hired during harvest time and their families; individuals involved in selling imported or local goods, whose business depends on drug profits; or workers and entrepreneurs who benefit from the development of local services, such as rest houses, for traffickers. The real estate boom and business activity visible in many Afghan cities are financed in large part by profits from the drug industry.[89]

Approach I: Laissez Faire

Despite the prevalence of poppy cultivation—or, perhaps more accurately, owing in part to its prevalence—the U.S. military initially took a hands-off approach to the drug trade. That approach was rooted in the U.S. reliance on Afghan warlords for assistance and desire to cultivate local support. At their peak in 2001–02, U.S. forces contributing to the war in Afghanistan numbered no more than 8,000, double the size of the 2001 deployment; consequently, they relied heavily on local proxies. Afghan warlords, who often had sizable militias numbering in the thousands, were used not only for intelligence gathering but also for direct participation in military operations against al Qaeda and the Taliban. In what President George W. Bush called one of the biggest bargains of all time, CIA and special forces officers handed out $70 million in $100 bills to local warlords, including Ismail Khan in the west; Abdul Rashid Dostum, Mohammed Fahim, and Ustad Atta Mohammed in the north; and Hazrat Ali in the east.[90] Many of the warlords were deeply connected to a variety of illicit economies, including the drug trade.

U.S. policy was to turn a blind eye to these activities, and the late 2001 arrest and subsequent release by U.S. forces of Bashir Noorzai, one of Afghanistan's major drug traffickers, epitomized that approach. Although Bashir was known to be a major player in the illicit trade and closely linked to Taliban leaders, he was released in exchange for providing intelligence to the United States.[91]

In October 2002, General Tommy R. Franks affirmed publicly that the U.S. military would stay clear of drug interdiction.[92] Similarly, when asked about counternarcotics operations, the U.S. military spokesman at the Bagram military base, Sergeant Major Harrison Sarles, commented:

"We're not a drug task force. That's not part of our mission."[93] Privately, U.S. officials acknowledged that drug-suppression efforts would compromise the anti-Taliban effort. Western diplomats admitted that "without money from drugs, our friendly warlords can't pay their militias. It's as simple as that."[94] Thus, the U.S. military did not interfere with drug convoys or bust the drug labs and storage depots that it encountered.

That approach allowed many powerful warlords to consolidate their power.[95] A notorious example was that of Hazrat Ali, a powerful commander from eastern Afghanistan backed by 18,000 militiamen. Ali rose to prominence when he was hired by the U.S. military to hunt down Osama bin Laden in Tora Bora. Despite the failure of that mission, Ali's cooperation greatly facilitated information gathering and U.S. troop operations in the area under his control. As Major James Hawver, a reservist in Jalalabad in 2002, commented, "He [Ali] was sort of our benefactor. He let it be known that if anybody messed with us, he'd deal with them."[96]

Ali threatened his rivals with U.S. air strikes while appointing himself the security chief of Nangarhar province, and from that position he consolidated his control over the drug trade. Poppy farmers from Nangarhar reported that Ali's men came to their villages in pickup trucks to buy raw opium. Although at first they transported it across the border to Pakistan for processing, they later processed it into heroin in labs that sprang up in Nangarhar itself.[97]

Sponsorship of the illicit economy generated substantial political capital for Ali. A 2003 interview by Ron Moreau and Sami Yousafzai with a thirty-five-year-old farmer named Ghulam Shah illustrates the attitudes of the local population. During the Taliban ban on opium cultivation, Shah was barely able to feed his family and became heavily indebted. However, after the removal of the Taliban, Shah went back to poppy cultivation, succeeded in breaking out of debt, and expected to make about $9,000 from twenty-five kilograms of opium—an immense fortune for him. With that money, he could afford to take his teenage daughter to Pakistan for a kidney transplant. He praised God and Ali for his good fortune: "We are all Hazrat Ali's soldiers. We all work for him."[98]

Another prominent warlord believed to be deeply involved in the drug trade was Mohammad Atta. While giving interviews about his extensive eradication efforts and disarmament measures from the governor's mansion in Mazar-I-Sharif, Mohammad stashed away large quantities of weapons and protected drug smuggling into Uzbekistan. When the Karzai-appointed chief of police seized a large shipment of opium, Mohammad arrested him and kept him locked up in his house for several days.[99] Mohammad Atta also engaged in large-scale fighting with the Uzbek warlord Abdul Rashid Dostum, who also was deeply involved in the drug trade, over the control of opium poppy fields and smuggling into Uzbekistan. Similarly, Gul Agha Sherzai, a prominent warlord who captured the city of Kandahar from the Taliban in 2001 and who governed Kandahar province until 2004, was also alleged to be involved in drug trafficking. He was reputed to provide military and police escorts to protect the fifty-to-seventy-vehicle drug convoys heading from Kandahar to Iran. In addition, militia commanders under his control bought opium poppy from farmers.[100]

Backed by substantial firepower and manpower, many warlords became provincial governors and police chiefs. Once in power, they gained the loyalty of police and military officials by allowing them to participate in such activities as taxing various aspects of the drug trade. Most warlords charged traffickers fees in the neighborhood of 15 percent to 18 percent for securing transportation routes and taxed heroin labs at rates ranging from 12 percent to 15 percent.[101] On average, farmers reported that they paid one-tenth of their opium harvest to local warlords, either in kind or in cash.[102] But the closer the relationship between the warlord and the farmer, the smaller the tax. Typically farmers from the same ethnic group as the warlord paid the lowest taxes.

By giving their own ethnic group preferential access to the drug market—through lower taxes, better protection, and greater marketing opportunities—the warlords strengthened their independent power bases and contributed to the centrifugal forces that continue to threaten Afghanistan's stability. The Karzai government attempted to counter that tendency by removing prominent warlords from their regional government positions and giving them positions in the national government or in provinces where they did not have a tribal affiliation or patronage networks.[103] While the co-opted warlords have become integrated into the Afghan political system, few have fully severed their connections to the drug trade. Many have learned to manipulate counternarcotics policies to appease Kabul and the international community while continuing to reap multiple benefits from the illicit economy.

Approach II: Compensated Eradication and Interdiction

While the U.S. military maintained a laissez-faire approach to drugs and remained reluctant to share intelligence on drug depots and processing plants,[104] official counternarcotics policy in Afghanistan followed a different track. After being assigned lead responsibility for counternarcotics by the UN Assistance Mission in Afghanistan (UNAMA), the United Kingdom adopted a two-pronged strategy combining compensated eradication and interdiction to combat the Afghan drug trade.[105] Its goal, as announced in 2002, was to reduce cultivation by 70 percent in five years.

Under the compensated eradication program in place during the 2002–03 growing season, U.K. officials promised to pay $350 in compensation for each jerib of poppy that was eradicated. Altogether the government committed approximately $37 million in U.K. funds and another $35 million in international funds to the program.[106] However, several major problems soon emerged. First, money was not distributed to farmers directly but given to local authorities, who, more often than not, simply pocketed the money. Many farmers who eradicated their fields received no compensation and quickly soured on the scheme, accusing Karzai and the international community of betraying them. The following comments from a Nangarhar farmer, quoted by John Burns, reflect the alienation of the rural population:

> When the Taliban fell, we were happy, because they took away our freedom, they forced us to go to mosques, they made us grow long beards. But now we are not happy, because the governments that control Karzai, the American and the British, are cruel. They freed us from one evil, and now they have delivered us into another one.[107]

Local commanders also demanded bribes from farmers who wanted to evade eradication. As a result, the 2002–03 eradication campaign, like subsequent eradication drives, generally targeted only the poorest and most vulnerable farmers, while the poppy plantations of wealthy and influential growers were left alone.[108] The farms that were spared often included fields owned by the local officials in charge of compensated eradication. More broadly, fraud became a major problem. Due to the poor security situation, there was no independent verification procedure in place to ensure that the fields had in fact been eradicated or even planted with poppies in the first place or whether farmers received compensation;

the British authorities simply relied on the input of local authorities to determine the amount of money to be disbursed. Accordingly, local commanders declared that much larger areas of land had been cultivated with poppy than actually had been. Local commanders thus benefited in three ways from compensated eradication: by pocketing vast sums intended for compensation, by collecting bribes to forego eradication, and by strengthening their political capital with the landlords and farmers whose fields they spared.

Not surprisingly, the money quickly ran out. As a result, the compensation per jerib shrank steadily, from the original $350 to $40 per jerib.[109] At that level, the promised compensation was insufficient for farmers to make ends meet. Moreover, the compensated eradication scheme did not address the structural drivers of poppy cultivation. The case of a thirty-three-year-old farmer in Nangarhar illustrates the dilemma that many others faced. He expected to obtain $5,000 from his poppy harvest. If he participated in the compensated eradication scheme, he would receive less than $1,000, a considerable loss. Moreover, he owed $1,160 to a local trader and faced ruin and punishment if he failed to repay. Under the circumstances, compensated eradication was not a real option for him.[110]

Moral hazard also emerged as a major weakness of the compensated eradication approach. Not only did local authorities overdeclare the amount of land cultivated with poppy in order to claim compensation for eradicating it, but farmers started growing more than they would have otherwise. Because collecting opium milk from poppy capsules is very labor intensive, the number of acres that an individual farmer can seed with poppy is limited by the number of family members who can be employed during harvest time and by the financial resources available to hire itinerant laborers. As a result, many farmers plant only a portion of their land with poppy. However, once they were being paid by the government to destroy their poppy plants, they had an incentive to expand the area under cultivation.

Moral hazard also became a regional issue. Because of different climatic conditions, cultivation in Nangarhar, in the east, takes place several months earlier than in Badakhshan, in the north, where poppy is a spring crop. Farmers in Badakhshan witnessed the compensation scheme in the east and substantially increased their own production, expecting to be compensated at the same rate. Paying compensation for eradication thus increased cultivation.

Finally, the eradication strategy generated violent protest and civil unrest. Farmers in Helmand province, disgruntled with the government's eradication efforts, alleged that during the U.S. military invasion, Hamid Karzai had promised to let them grow poppy in exchange for their help in toppling the Taliban regime. The Karzai government denied their allegations.[111] In the subsequent anti-eradication protests, the police killed eight farmers and wounded dozens of others, generating widespread anger. Similarly, in Nangarhar, up to 10,000 farmers blocked roads and attacked police and eradication teams with stones. The spontaneous protests in Nangarhar coalesced into more systematic organized violence against the fragile state as several tribes joined forces to stop eradication.[112] The assassination of Vice President Abdul Qadir Arsala and attempted murder of Mohammed Fahim, then the minister of defense, also were blamed on the opponents of eradication.[113]

In short, compensated eradication vastly increased the financial resources of local commanders and alienated the farmers from the Karzai government and the international community. It thus accomplished exactly the opposite of what it had promised, which was to limit the resources of the warlords and reduce opium poppy production. In fact, opium cultivation expanded dramatically while the compensated eradication scheme was in place. Furthermore, the eradication scheme contributed to the destabilization of key regions in Afghanistan.

Meanwhile, interdiction against traffickers and the destruction of their labs, nominally under way, failed to make any serious progress. British interdiction efforts were clearly at odds with U.S. laissez-faire policy, and the United States maintained the upper hand. As domestic and international criticism of British ineffectiveness in stamping out drug production mounted, British officials became increasingly frustrated with the unwillingness of the U.S. military to cooperate in any way with counternarcotics operations. U.S. forces even refused to share intelligence on prominent traffickers, which prompted Prime Minister Tony Blair to raise the issue with President Bush. To improve effectiveness, in early 2004 Britain established an elite interdiction unit, the Afghan Narcotics Special Force (ANSF), nominally responding directly to Karzai's cabinet but operating under the control of British special forces. In its first year, the unit seized seventy-five tons of opiates, destroyed eighty labs, and dismantled two opium bazaars.[114] But even those successes had no significant impact on Afghanistan's drug trade.

Approach III: Forced Eradication and Beefed-Up Interdiction

In 2004, the pendulum began to swing back toward more intense drug suppression policies. Forced eradication and beefed up interdiction replaced compensated eradication. Ironically, the policy shift was driven largely by criticism of failed anti-drug efforts emanating from the United States. Amid a host of U.S. newspaper articles reporting on the "explosion" of opium poppy cultivation in Afghanistan and editorials urging strong action, pressure mounted from Republicans in Congress to make greater progress toward eliminating poppy cultivation in Afghanistan.[115] Democrats also weighed in, with presidential candidate John Kerry castigating the Bush administration for failing to stamp out drugs in Afghanistan, as did international officials. Antonio Maria Costa, the executive director of the UN Office on Drugs and Crime (UNODC), declared that "opium cultivation, which has spread like wildfire throughout the country, could ultimately incinerate everything—democracy, reconstruction, and stability. . . . The fear that Afghanistan might degenerate into a narco-state is slowly becoming a reality."[116]

In the summer of 2004, the Pentagon undertook the first major revision of its Afghanistan policy, expanding the mission of the U.S. military to include help for President Karzai in uprooting the drug trade. Written by Robert Andrews, a retired CIA and Defense Department official, the Pentagon report concluded that "the narcotics problem has become a major impediment for ridding Afghanistan of warlords, the Taliban, and al Qaeda."[117] Under new guidelines that were officially announced in March 2005, U.S. forces in Afghanistan were to provide support for counternarcotics operations, including "transportation, planning assistance, intelligence, [and] targeting packages," as well as in extremis support for Drug Enforcement Administration and Afghan officers who came under attack.[118] Lieutenant General David W. Barno, then the top U.S. commander in Afghanistan, had foreshadowed the new policy direction by announcing in December 2004 that the U.S military was conducting three wars in Afghanistan: the hunt for al Qaeda and the Taliban leaders; the campaign against the Taliban and al Qaeda networks; and the campaign against provincial warlords, drug traffickers, and other centrifugal forces.[119]

Although the U.S. military mission was expanded to include some support for interdiction, there was nonetheless a strong sense in the Pentagon that participating in eradication efforts (until then conducted by the Afghan government under the supervision of the British UNAMA assistance team) would severely jeopardize U.S. military operations by alienating the population. Many of the British troops operating in Afghanistan under NATO command shared that sentiment. As a British soldier returning from Afghanistan commented after the U.K. government announced that British soldiers would now also be employed in interdiction: "The guys have been out there, building relationships with local people that bring in crucial intelligence and keep us safe. If the same guys start kicking down doors and reporting on ordinary people who are just trying to earn a living in difficult circumstances, then they are not going to see us as friends anymore."[120] Winning the hearts and minds of the population was clearly seen by the counterinsurgency forces as incompatible with participating in eradication.

In contrast, the U.S. State Department's Bureau for International Narcotics and Law Enforcement Affairs believed that uncompensated and "resolute" eradication was an essential tool in the effort to eliminate narcotics from Afghanistan. In April 2004, Robert B. Charles, then the assistant secretary of state for international narcotics and law enforcement affairs, testified before Congress that the opium economy was "a cancer that spreads and undermines all we are otherwise achieving in the areas of democracy, stability, antiterrorism, and rule of law."[121] In a later statement, he charged that British eradication efforts were overly soft-hearted:

Criteria such as requiring alternative development to be in place and a preoccupation with avoiding any possibility of resistance may restrict our ability to collectively reach key eradication goals. . . . if there is heroin poppy there which needs to be eradicated, we shouldn't be delaying, we shouldn't be making it conditional upon providing an instant and available additional income stream. [For some farmers] it is just survival, but what we have to do is to make it crystal clear there is such a thing as a rule of law. . . . the point being that our priority should not be, it seems to me, some kind of misplaced sympathy.[122]

In November 2004, Charles announced that previous efforts would give way to an aggressive eradication program named Plan Afghanistan, similar to efforts under way in Colombia.[123] He pushed the administration's case with the UN Office on Drugs and Crime, suggesting that funding from the United States—UNODC's largest contributor—would be jeopardized unless it expressed clear support for eradication. Responding in a letter dated November 11, 2004, Costa stated: "I am happy that large-scale eradication is under consideration."[124]

Similarly, the United States put strong pressure on President Hamid Karzai, who had just won the country's first free presidential elections, to tackle narcotics. At a major counternarcotics policy conference in Kabul in December 2004, attended by U.S. vice president Richard Cheney, Karzai declared a jihad against poppies, describing the Afghan opium trade as a worse "cancer" than terrorism or the Soviet invasion of 1979 and promising to eradicate all poppy in Afghanistan in two years.[125] Not everyone in Karzai's government was comfortable with the anti-drug jihad. Afghanistan's finance minister, Ashraf Ghani, announced a multi-pronged approach to counternarcotics including interdiction, economic growth, an agricultural strategy, and judicial reform, but he warned against premature eradication, arguing that "destroying that trade without offering our farmers a genuine alternative livelihood has the potential to undo the embryonic gains of the past three years. The likely results would be widespread impoverishment, inflation, currency fluctuations, and capital flight."[126] Karzai nonetheless reaffirmed the prohibition against growing poppy, while Afghanistan's National Council of Ulemas issued a fatwa against opium cultivation and trade.[127] The Karzai government also undertook a bureaucratic restructuring, upgrading the Counternarcotics Directorate to the Counternarcotics Ministry and designating the Counternarcotics Police as Afghanistan's main narcotics law enforcement agency.

Despite that flurry of activity, the United States considered the Afghan counternarcotics agencies too unreliable and the British too squeamish about the political fallout to entrust them with executing Plan Afghanistan. Instead, the United States turned to private contractors. Several months earlier, the U.S. government had provided Dyncorp with a $50 million contract to train an Afghan eradication team consisting of four units of 150 men each. The team, the Central Poppy Eradication Force (CPEF), would take guidance directly from the United States through the Ministry of the Interior, sidelining the Counternarcotics Ministry and the British. Ironically, the main U.S. contact at the Ministry of the Interior was Lieutenant General Mohammad Daoud, the deputy minister of the interior for counternarcotics, an ex-warlord from the north who was reputed to have major connections to the drug trade.[128] The United States also set up a similar interdiction unit, a covert squad of special agents known as Task Force 333. At the same time, in an effort to maintain some influence over counternarcotics strategy, London and Kabul established the Central Eradication Planning Cell (CEPC) under the Ministry of Interior with the goal of shaping the deployment of the Central Poppy Eradication Force to "ensure that eradication by CPEF is targeted in a way which takes account of alternative livelihoods."[129]

In 2004–05, the CPEF forcibly eradicated 217 hectares in Kandahar before retreating in the face of armed opposition.[130] In the Maiwand and Panjwayi districts of Kandahar province, protesters blocked roads and opened fire on the eradication teams. The protests nearly sparked a provincial revolt, and the eradication teams did not dare come back. The U.S. embassy in Kabul blamed the Karzai government for the failure. In a memo sent in advance of Karzai's visit to Washington and leaked to the *New York Times,* embassy officials criticized Karzai for being "unwilling to assert strong leadership" in eradication and doing little to overcome the resistance of "provincial officials and village elders [who] had impeded destruction of significant poppy acreage." The memo went on to criticize Karzai for being unwilling to insist on eradication "even in his own province of Kandahar."[131] Western diplomats admitted that Karzai did not want to generate further instability before the September 2005 parliamentary elections. Meanwhile, the local Kandahari leaders who opposed eradication acquired a large amount of political capital with the local population. After Karzai placed a new governor in Kandahar province, eradication appeared to increase in 2005–06 and the total area of cultivation decreased by 3 percent.[132]

Deployed in safer areas, the Afghan National Police eradicated 888 hectares of poppy in 2004–05, while provincial government eradication efforts, especially in Nangarhar, resulted in the destruction of 4,007 hectares.[133] During the same period, eradication in Helmand province reduced the area of cultivation by 30 to 40 percent but had little impact on the overall health of the drug trade. Local officials used eradication to eliminate competition while boosting their own opium profits by pushing up prices. Provincial authorities also benefited by imposing a double "tax" on cultivators: the first tax was paid so that officials would not eradicate early in the season and a second tax was paid at harvest time.[134] Selective enforcement resulted in the consolidation of opium production in the hands of a few large traders with good connections to, if not formal positions in, the national or provincial governments. It also gave local officials ample opportunity to accumulate political capital by sparing the poppy fields of other influential individuals and of their fellow tribesmen while targeting competitors from other tribes.

Similarly, local authorities have manipulated interdiction policies to acquire control of the drug trade, displace intermediaries, and buy political allegiance. Local officials charge traffickers for protection against both government seizure of their cargos and rival traffickers.[135] They also are widely reputed to capture trading convoys, take half of the opium, sell it to other traders, and release the remaining opium and the captured traders for a fee. In one reported case, a ton of opium was seized and ostensibly burned in public when in fact a substitute of some sort was burned and the genuine opium was sold to traders.[136] Typically the victims of such tactics are small traders, while large, influential operators partner with government officials to increase their domination of the drug industry. In fact, many have resorted to buying themselves positions that involve counternarcotics operations just to get in on the take. The job of district police chief, for example, regularly sells for $100,000. Therefore, like eradication, interdiction policies create opportunities for well-placed elites to reap greater profits while building stronger political ties.

Interdiction conducted by national government forces—whether Task Force 333 or the Counternarcotics Police—suffers from a similar bias. It frequently targets smaller traffickers and local bazaars while ignoring powerful ex-warlords and local government figures, who often are one and the same.[137] Thus, once again, the effect of national interdiction operations is to displace small-scale local traffickers and concentrate control of the trade in the hands of powerful political elites.

Alternative livelihood programs to provide legal economic alternatives have been slow to reach the vast majority of Afghanistan's population and often have failed to address the structural drivers of opium poppy cultivation. A legal microcredit system, for example, is still lacking in most of Afghanistan. USAID refused to give it priority, and although the national Microfinance Investment Support Facility for Afghanistan (MISFA) has been highly successful, it has covered only 8 percent of projected credit needs.[138] Instead, preference has been given to high-visibility, quick-impact, but often unsustainable projects to buy popular support, such as projects to build clinics and schools (for which doctors or teachers often are lacking) and to temporarily employ potential recruits for poppy cultivation or the Taliban, such as cash-for-work programs to clean irrigation canals. Within U.S. reconstruction efforts in Afghanistan, which from 2001 to mid-2009 amounted to $7.8 billion, systematic rural development has long been underemphasized. It was not until mid-2003 that USAID started its first national agriculture program, and even then it was given only 5 percent of the annual reconstruction budget.[139] Moreover, the lack of security and increasing insurgency in the south have halted many of the alternative livelihood projects and delayed the operation of a hydropower plant at Kajaki Dam in Helmand. The plant was USAID's flagship program for the south and took much of its money for the entire region. Some agro-projects, such as the restoration of pistachio orchards in several areas and the export of Afghan pomegranates to Dubai, have been successful, but the successes have been too small and isolated. Moreover, many projects have been poorly designed as well as undermined by the corruption and incompetence of Afghan officials and local and international contractors.[140] While some road projects, such as the rebuilding of the Ring Road, which connects major Afghan cities, have been completed, the lack of security has jeopardized travel on them. Several National Priority Programs, such as the National Solidarity Program (NSP), MISFA, and National Rural Access Program (NRAP), have been considerably more successful. Many of those programs have focused on getting money directly to the people by working at the village level through community development councils, but scaling them up to the provincial and national level remains a challenge.

The meager successes of the alternative livelihood efforts in Afghanistan should not be interpreted as implying that no legal alternatives at all are available. Farmers who live in secure areas, have an irrigation system, own land, and are close to markets, such as Jalalabad in Nangarhar in the east and major cities in the north, may have the opportunity to grow legal crops, such as vegetables, at a substantial profit. Many such "resource-rich" farmers have abandoned opium poppy cultivation, even in areas where opium had been thought to be entrenched. In some of those areas, vegetable traders have been reducing transaction costs for farmers of legal crops by absorbing the cost of transport and collecting crops at the farm gate, providing advances on the cultivation of crops, and distributing seeds, thus mimicking what the opium traders have been doing for years for poppy farmers. Greater security and improvements in physical infrastructure have facilitated such undertakings and allow them to be sustainable. However, the vast majority of Afghan farmers are resource-poor and depend on opium poppy for their basic subsistence.[141] For them, eradication in the absence of robust and well-performing rural development spells economic disaster.

During the 2008–09 growing season, alternative livelihood efforts in the south of Afghanistan were essentially reduced to crop substitution. Motivated by the unusual price ratio of wheat to opium, with opium prices being very low due to several years of overproduction and wheat prices being unusually high, Afghan officials and international advisers began handing out free wheat seed to poppy farmers in parts of Helmand. It is too early to assess the effectiveness of the policy since aerial survey data of cultivation patterns have not yet been released and almost no monitoring of the program was carried out in the field, but there already are indications of short-term problems. While some farmers did in fact plant wheat, many farmers also cultivated poppy along with the wheat, and at least some farmers sold the wheat seed in the local market for cash, undermining local agricultural seed markets.[142] More important, there are good reasons to doubt the long-term effectiveness of the program. First, the price ratio of wheat to opium cannot be sustained. Second, many farmers do not have enough land to generate sufficient income from wheat, even at currently high prices. Third, because wheat cultivation is far less labor intensive than poppy cultivation and opium harvesting, requiring only 12 percent of the labor that poppy cultivation requires, a wholesale switch of the rural agricultural economy to wheat cultivation would mean a significant loss of jobs. Fourth and most fundamental, the program fails to address the many factors other than price that favor poppy cultivation in the region. But because handing out free goods became an important political tool in the run-up to the August 2009 presidential elections, Kabul embraced the program and extended it throughout the south. And because of its apparent simplicity, many international development advisers also liked the scheme and planned to promote it in the future.

THE RESURGENCE OF THE TALIBAN

The decision to intensify eradication and interdiction took place against the backdrop of an upsurge in armed opposition to the NATO- and U.S.-backed Afghan national government. The insurgency, located mainly in the south and east of the country along the border with Pakistan, is a complex amalgam of shifting alliances among several actors, with the Taliban at the core. Gulbuddin Hekmatyar's militias; Jalaluddin and Sirajuddin Haqqani's fighters; various al Qaeda affiliates and other foreign jihadists; and Pakistani Pashtun insurgent groups such as Baitullah Mehsud's[143] and Maulana Fazlullah's organization, the Tehrik-i-Taliban-Pakistan, have in varying degrees joined or supported the "Afghan" Taliban. The groups are motivated by their common goals of driving the United States and NATO forces out of Afghanistan, undermining the Afghan and Pakistani governments, and achieving political control over the Pashtun areas that span the Afghan-Pakistan border.[144] Most of them also seek to restore the supremacy of the Pashtuns over the northern Tajiks, whom they consider to be too prominent in the post-Taliban regime, and to reconstitute a strict interpretation of Islam as the law of the land on both sides of the border between Afghanistan and Pakistan. Increasingly, the Taliban appears to be coordinating its efforts with al Qaeda, which has become entrenched in the mountainous region of Pakistan.

The Taliban insurgency greatly benefits from having safe havens in Pakistan, such as Quetta, where a part of the Taliban leadership, including Mullah Omar, is believed to be hiding; the Federally Administered Tribal Areas; and the North West Frontier Province. Despite repeated U.S. Predator strikes, the Taliban continues to maintain training camps, recruiting centers, and staging areas in Pakistan.[145] But it also has become internally self-sustaining in Afghanistan, where its strength is estimated to number between 5,000 and 10,000 combatants.

Since 2005, its forces have contributed to growing instability in the rural Pashtun belt in the south and east of Afghanistan. The non-Pashtun north of the country also has become destabilized, however, with insecurity increasing and former warlords rearming, allegedly in response to the Taliban's growth.[146] Throughout the country, daily attacks on Afghan government officials, NGO workers, and coalition forces have been increasing both in scope and intensity, and the announcement of an amnesty for rank-and-file Taliban in January 2005 has had no impact on the frequency and intensity of the attacks.[147] Instead, the insurgency has become more effective as it has adapted to coalition countermeasures. Instead of massing in large bands of up to several hundred fighters, the insurgents have shifted to using smaller units to attack vulnerable targets, such as NGOs and local government officials. They also have adopted Iraqi jihadist methods, including the use of remotely detonated roadside bombs and suicide bombings, which allow them to blend in among the population and avoid detection. In addition, they continue to threaten and intimidate the local population through such tactics as burning down coeducational schools and issuing so-called "night letters," in which they warn the population against cooperating with the Afghan government and international forces.[148] The insurgents have managed to seize and temporarily hold several towns, and many districts of the south have become a no-go zone for government officials, international advisers, NGOs, and increasingly even for local Afghan district chiefs.

Government and coalition forces have been unable to provide adequate security across vast areas of Afghanistan. At least until mid-2009, when the Obama administration conducted a major policy review and issued new guidelines for conducting counterinsurgency operations in Afghanistan (the effectiveness of which has yet to be seen), NATO forces typically reacted quickly with overwhelming airpower when they encountered a Taliban group. However, they have not been able to field sufficient troops to mount regular ground patrols and provide sustained security in rural villages and increasingly even in cities in the Pashtun belt. The Afghan National Army (ANA) is widely praised by the population and the international community, but it is still too weak to take on the Taliban insurgency on its own and faces significant retention problems. The lack of NATO and ANA ground forces has resulted in overreliance on air power and a large number of civilian casualties. To reduce reliance on air power, another 21,000 U.S. soldiers deployed to Afghanistan in 2009 to join the 43,000 U.S. and 32,000 international troops already there, while the ANA was expected to grow to 140,000 troops. At the end of summer 2009, Washington was again reviewing the number of troops necessary to secure the country, with the U.S. military calling for further increasing U.S. forces by perhaps many thousands of troops and for increasing the combined Afghan military and police forces to 250,000.

ASSESSING THE IMPACT OF ERADICATION

Many frustrated U.S. officials have attributed the resurgence of the Taliban to the rebound in poppy cultivation. Noting that the Taliban operates in the south and east, which historically have been the largest areas of poppy cultivation, and arguing that the Taliban earns some 20 to 50 percent of its income from drugs, they have called for massive eradication to end the insurgency. Among the leading advocates of that approach was William Wood, U.S. ambassador to Afghanistan from 2007 to 2009. In an unclassified message, Wood called for a massive spraying campaign that would wipe out 80,000 hectares of poppy in Helmand, a hotspot of the insurgency, and deliver a fatal blow to both the drug trade and the Taliban.[149] But such analyses misidentify both the sources of the Taliban's resurgence and the proper policy response.

It is certainly true that since 2005 the Taliban has been able to tap into the drug trade, in no small part due to mismanaged interdiction and eradication policies, and the group is deriving substantial profits from the drug trade. Although the actual amount is elusive, it could easily be in the tens of millions of dollars a year, but not likely the hundreds of millions that some estimates toss about. But the Taliban has many other sources of income. In rebuilding their base from 2002 to 2004, Taliban leaders relied on donations from Pakistan and the Middle East as well as profits generated by smuggling licit goods between Pakistan and Afghanistan. Today, other funding comes from gem smuggling, illegal logging, illegal trade in wildlife, ransoms collected from the families of kidnapping victims, and general taxation of economic activities in areas under its control. Crime groups unrelated to the Taliban, tribal elites, and Afghan government officials also profit from the many illicit economies.[150] In addition, much to the frustration of U.S. and NATO officials, the Taliban continues to receive aid from Pakistan's ISI, including financial assistance, medical assistance to wounded fighters, and intelligence.[151]

Equally important, the insurgents have tapped into popular resentment of the Karzai government over growing insecurity, the rise of crime, the slow pace of economic reconstruction, the vast corruption among government officials, and the breakdown of the rule of law. Common complaints focus on the judicial system's ineffectiveness at settling local disputes, rampant extortion by members of the Afghan National Police, and the general practice among government officials of skimming profits from both legal and illegal economic activities.

Drug eradication efforts are another important source of support for the Taliban. Ironically, forced eradication has created opportunities for the Taliban to reenter the drug trade. Afghan officials in charge of eradication and interdiction routinely target competing local elites when carrying out those policies. In response, those targeted have often joined forces with the Taliban. Some tribal elders have declared themselves sympathetic to the Taliban, accusing the provincial government of being corrupt and exploitative. Some, as in the Sangin region, a hotbed of poppy cultivation, have joined the Taliban outright. Such alliances are especially prominent in Helmand province, but they also are emerging across the greater Pashtun belt.

In some regions, drug traffickers have hired Taliban forces to protect their drug convoys and poppy farms. In addition, the Taliban has offered its protection to poor opium farmers. In southern Afghanistan, the Taliban has hammered posters on walls offering to protect the poppy fields and warning eradication forces against destroying the crops;[152] it also has killed members of eradication teams. More broadly, the insurgents have sought to rechannel spontaneous protests against eradication into organized opposition under their leadership. In the process, they have shown surprising sensitivity to local sentiment. In one telling episode, the Taliban came to a village near Kandahar in the spring of 2006 and told the villagers to pack up and leave because there was going to be fighting.[153] The villagers asked the Taliban fighters to postpone the operation for a few weeks so that they could harvest their opium crop. The Taliban agreed, retreated, and came back to the village only after the crop had been harvested.

Even in areas where eradication has been temporarily successful, it has helped the Taliban by discrediting pro-Kabul elites and antagonizing the population. In Nangarhar, for example, cultivation of opium poppy fell an impressive 95 percent during 2004–05 under the supervision of Governor Haji Din Mohammad, a younger brother of former governor Haji Qadir, and police chief Hazrat Ali.[154] With promises of international aid, threats of eradication, and the imprisonment of miscreants, local authorities managed to persuade many farmers not to cultivate opium poppy. Yet the promised aid did not materialize. The cash-for-work program backed by the Afghan government and USAID failed to reach the poorest and most vulnerable farmers, and many farmers who participated in it were unable to offset their losses.[155] Many participating households lost as much as $3,400 in income that year, representing 90 percent of their total cash income.[156]

The suppression of opium also caused downturns in trade in various nonagricultural sectors, including transport, construction, and retail.[157] Pauperization was widespread, alienating the farmers from both local authorities and the Kabul government. Shah Mahnoud, an influential tribal leader in Nangarhar, explained: "I made the decision this season that it would be forbidden to plant poppy. So none of us did. Now I'm not so happy about that . . . farmers will grab my collar and say, 'You said that we could get aid for not growing poppy and we got nothing!'"[158]

Many farmers became further indebted as a result of the ban on opium poppy cultivation, and their anger at the government grew. As one farmer explained:

> With my tailoring work, I cultivated some poppy fields; but this year as the government forbade poppy cultivation, I didn't cultivate the land because wheat cannot meet the costs [of renting land]. I don't own land. I am indebted, too. Thus, I wonder how to pay off the debt. The state hasn't helped us at all. We were very optimistic for the [2004 presidential] election, assuming that a good government would be set up, and it would heal our wounds; but they kill us because they grab our livelihood and kill us through hunger. They satisfy their foreign lords and forced us to stop poppy cultivation.[159]

Farmers who were unable to repay their debts faced three options: death at the hands of their creditors; liquidation of their productive assets and the sale of their livestock and even their daughters (as young as three) to cover the debt; or flight into Pakistan.[160] Many of those who fled found shelter in the same Deobandi madrasas that swelled the ranks of the Taliban in the early 1990s.[161] Today, the refugee networks in Pakistan are once again replenishing the Taliban ranks.

Following the 2004–05 anti-opium campaign, poppy cultivation in Nangarhar increased by 346 percent in 2006 and returned almost to its pre-ban level in 2007.[162] The following year, governor Gul Agha Sherzai imposed a new ban on opium poppy and eradicated the fields of those who did not comply.[163] To gain cooperation, he paid off some tribal elites and imprisoned others. He also threatened that NATO would bomb the houses of those who failed to comply, and NATO forces did in fact confiscate some opium as they conducted house searches for insurgents.[164]

As a result of these efforts, poppy cultivation in Nangarhar again dropped dramatically, from 18,739 hectares in 2007 to none in 2008, and Nangarhar's anti-poppy campaign was hailed as a major success to be emulated elsewhere in Afghanistan. But because the benefits promised to result from alternative livelihood programs failed to materialize, the economic consequences for many in the province were devastating. Development projects are complex undertakings that require many years of effort, and in this case the timeline was unrealistic; the scope and geographical range of the projects were too limited; and the projects were undermined by lack of security and dedicated resources. The governing authorities suffered a severe depletion of their political capital, while the Taliban's stock rose. Many tribes, such as the Achin, Shinwari, and Khogiani, which received virtually no development aid, broke with the government and began to rearm despite their deep dislike of the Taliban. Previous agreements to limit the Taliban's movements through the region were rescinded. There were even reports that some individuals had invited the Taliban to establish a local presence in return for the promise to their protect poppy fields.[165] In listing the government's alternatives, one tribal leader commented, "Next year there will either be poppy here or the Taliban."[166]

The same dynamics have been replicated in the south. In Helmand and Kandahar, support for the Taliban has been strongest in areas where the Taliban has protected the poppy fields against eradication. In 2008, the Taliban managed to limit eradication in Helmand to only 1,000 of the more than 100,000 hectares cultivated with poppy, strengthening the sense among farmers that the Taliban offers a viable alternative to the government. When questioned about the prospect of aerial spraying, farmers in Helmand, Kandahar, and Nangarhar frequently threatened to take direct action against the government or to join the Taliban. As one respondent put it: "If the government sprays, there is only one way and that is to join the Taliban."[167]

Even villagers who hesitate to join the Taliban are increasingly reluctant to cooperate with government and allied forces. Despite intensified counterinsurgency efforts, including foot patrols in local villages, the provision of local intelligence on Taliban forces has not increased. NATO troops typically return from local information-gathering missions with only vague promises of cooperation and staunch denials of any knowledge of Taliban activities. The U.S. military at times has resorted to threatening to cut off aid to local areas if information is not provided, to little avail.[168] The lack of intelligence has been especially marked in areas that have recently been subject to eradication, such as Nangarhar in 2006 and again in 2008.[169]

U.S. and NATO military officials, while under tremendous pressure from both counternarcotics agencies and politicians back at home to reduce the cultivation of poppy, clearly understand the large costs of any such action for the counterinsurgency effort. In 2006, U.S. General Benjamin Freakley, who was responsible for the eastern front, halted DEA and Afghan counternarcotics operations in Nangarhar in an effort to head off further destabilization. In a similar attempt to diminish the Taliban's appeal, the commanders of the 101st Airborne Division informed the U.S. ambassador in 2008 that they would permit crop eradication in Nangarhar only if the State Department compensated farmers for the loss of their opium crops.[170] And in Helmand, British forces have issued leaflets and radio broadcasts to inform the deeply antagonized population that they were not conducting eradication.

Approach IV: Scaled-Up Interdiction and Robust Alternative Development

Under mounting pressure do something about drug production in Afghanistan, in October 2008 NATO agreed to target Taliban-linked drug traffickers. Although the details of the policy are still being worked out, this new interdiction effort will seek to deprive the belligerents of drug income by targeting fifty designated Taliban-linked traffickers and possibly bringing down entire trafficking networks linked to the Taliban.[171] The latter will require extraordinary amounts of intelligence and manpower, and its success is far from certain. Although the goal is to provoke a split between the traffickers and the Taliban, the effort may backfire in a number of ways: the bond between the traffickers and the Taliban may be strengthened; the Taliban may replace the deposed traffickers and become more directly involved in the drug trade; and new turf wars may erupt among the various actors involved in the trade, thus greatly compounding the lack of security in the country.

In addition to stepping up interdiction efforts, NATO is planning major military operations to engage the Taliban in the main poppy cultivation areas in Helmand and Kandahar. In addition to the 21,000 U.S. troops deployed to Afghanistan in 2009 to support the effort, more may be under way. If the Taliban can be eliminated from the poppy-growing areas without interfering with poppy cultivation, one of the insurgents' main sources of political capital—the ability to prevent eradication—will disappear. But if NATO operations interfere with poppy cultivation, local opposition to the Afghan government and its allies will increase, and active support for the Taliban may grow.

Compared with such possible outcomes, the financial impact of the Taliban's ouster from the poppy-growing areas is likely to be small. The extent of the Taliban's losses will depend on its ability to continue providing protection to traffickers, if not farmers, as well as on the extent to which poppy cultivation moves to new areas accessible to the Taliban, such as Farah province. Moreover, its losses will be cushioned by continued access to funds raised in Pakistan and the Middle East and funds from other illicit economies.

The Obama administration has elevated rural development to the forefront of its counternarcotics policy while disavowing large-scale eradication. Richard Holbrooke, the U.S. special envoy for Afghanistan and Pakistan, has embraced the view that eradication is deeply counterproductive to the counterinsurgency effort: "It wasn't just a waste of money. . . . This was actually a benefit to the enemy. We were recruiting Taliban with our tax dollars."[172] Underwritten with $380 million in U.S. aid, the intensified alternative livelihood program in southern Afghanistan's core poppy-growing areas is to focus on improving the yields of legal crops and on ensuring that enough food is grown to feed the population instead of on generating off-farm income (as did the previous cash-for-work programs); the program also hopes to create value-added chains for high-value export fruit.[173] While the details of the policy remain to be determined, past experience suggests that the critical challenges will include addressing the underlying drivers of opium poppy cultivation (of which the new administration appears much more aware than the Bush administration was) rather than simply offering replacement crops and integrating counternarcotics efforts within a broader plan for rural and socioeconomic development. While the farm-level assistance emphasized in the new program, which was neglected in previous efforts, is very important, care needs to be taken not to throw the baby out with the bath water. Experience in Latin America and Asia suggests that alternative livelihood efforts that focus simply on subsistence and local markets are not highly effective; attention also must be given to generating value-added chains and ensuring that national and international markets exist for products. The alternative livelihood effort will depend critically on the reestablishment of security and a substantial weakening of the Taliban; if successful, it will reinforce efforts to stabilize the country and promote its economic development, lending support to the long process of state-building in Afghanistan.

SIX

CONCLUSIONS AND POLICY IMPLICATIONS

To varying degrees, Peru, Colombia, and Afghanistan have all served as testing grounds for the narcoguerrilla perspective, and in all three cases, the conventional government wisdom has proven to be sadly deficient. Eradication of illicit crops has not fatally weakened any of the insurgencies active in these countries. Instead, as the political capital model of illicit economies and military conflict predicts, aggressive drug suppression measures have served primarily to increase the guerrillas' legitimacy and political support among the populations involved. When governments have succeeded in bringing belligerents to heel, as in the case of Colombia's FARC, success has been a result of direct military engagement, not a counternarcotics campaign.

Efforts to combat illicit economies have yielded the greatest gains for insurgents in poor regions dominated by labor-intensive illicit activities, such as opium poppy cultivation. By protecting and regulating such activities, belligerents can transform themselves in the eyes of the local people involved from thugs or wild-eyed revolutionaries into defenders of the people and their right to a basic livelihood. In contrast, groups—including governments—that seek to combat labor-intensive illicit activities typically fail to increase either their political capital or their military strength. However, governments need not abandon all counternarcotics efforts to prevail over an insurgency. While eradication typically backfires by antagonizing the rural population and driving farmers into the insurgents' arms, interdiction, laissez-faire, alternative livelihood programs, and licensing have proven to be effective under some circumstances. When well designed, all four policies can reduce the insurgents' political capital and make the local population more likely to cooperate with governing authorities, notably by providing intelligence on guerrilla forces.

The lessons learned apply with equal force to Peru, Colombia, and Afghanistan, even though the structure of the drug economy, the roles played by key actors, and the nature of the threat to the state vary across those cases:

—In Peru, the traffickers initially were small- and medium-scale intermediaries who operated in the jungles without ever really threatening the Peruvian elite. What threatened the Peruvian elite was the Shining Path insurgency, especially once it undertook its urban campaign. The major traffickers that emerged in Peru, such as Vladimiro Montesinos, already were members of the elite.

—In Colombia, the heads of the Medellín and Cali cartels directly threatened the traditional landowning elite by buying or expropriating land as a way to launder their profits. The top traffickers also sought to force their way into the established political system through corruption and violence. It was that threat, as much as the drug-related activities of left-wing insurgents, that led Colombia's government to internalize the international anti-narcotics norms promoted by the United States and to endorse eradication to a much greater degree than was done in either Peru or Afghanistan.

—In Afghanistan, almost all of the principal players have had ties to the drug trade since the mid-1980s. The drug trade and other illicit activities, such as smuggling, have become the primary source of patronage in the country, making eradication especially problematic and significantly complicating the government's efforts to consolidate its position.

This chapter synthesizes the key findings from each of the three principal cases. I also briefly extend the analysis to two cases, Northern Ireland and Burma, that further illuminate the relationship among political capital, illicit economies, and military conflict. I close with a discussion of the policy implications of the analysis.

PERU

Sendero Luminoso (Shining Path), Peru's largest leftist insurgent group, earned tens to hundreds of millions of dollars a year from the illicit drug economy after overcoming its initial ideological aversion to the trade. As the narcoguerrilla view would predict, those profits were crucial to the Shining Path's ability to expand its operations beyond isolated attacks and gain control of large areas of Peru. However, that perspective ignores an equally important dynamic: the Shining Path exploited the farmers' dependence on the drug economy to win political support. By protecting coca growers against abusive traffickers and government eradication efforts, the movement gained legitimacy in local eyes. The Shining Path was consistently more popular in the drug regions than elsewhere in the country; as a result, Sendero had less need to resort to brutality in those regions, further cementing its position.

Sendero's relationship with Peruvian drug traffickers was more complex. Although the guerrillas protected traffickers from government interdiction efforts, the two groups never developed identical goals. In fact, because Sendero also protected the *cocaleros* against traffickers and attempted to displace the traffickers from various areas of the drug trade, their interests often were in conflict. Consequently, once the government scaled back its eradication and interdiction campaigns, it found that many traffickers were willing to provide intelligence on the insurgents. The possibility of thus turning traffickers and insurgents against each other is typically ignored by the narcoguerrilla view, which maintains that insurgents and traffickers represent two sides of the same coin.

More broadly, the case of Peru highlights the weakness of the central argument of the narcoguerrilla view: that by stamping out the drug trade, governing authorities can bankrupt and defeat an insurgent movement. When the Peruvian government adopted that approach in the early and mid-1980s, the military lost ground to Sendero. The government's eradication efforts threatened the livelihood of coca farmers, who turned to Sendero for support; as a result, Sendero consolidated and extended its control over the countryside. In contrast, when the government halted eradication and the military prevented the police from interfering with coca cultivation, the *cocaleros* no longer needed Sendero's protection. Like the traffickers, they became willing to provide vital intelligence to government forces, allowing the military to score key successes against the Shining Path. Meanwhile, an urban intelligence operation led to the capture of the Shining Path's founding leader and the subsequent collapse of the movement. Only after Sendero was defeated did the illicit economy shrink significantly in size.

Since the mid-1990s, the remnants of Sendero have been financing their activities through illicit logging. Government laxity in enforcing the prohibition against illicit logging, as well as the small number of the remaining Senderistas, has made it difficult for the Shining Path to rebuild its political capital. However, the group has a new opening for growth in the government's decision to return to a policy of aggressive coca eradication, which began in 2002. Today, eradication is again antagonizing and radicalizing the *cocaleros,* and Sendero has once again offered itself as their defender.

COLOMBIA

A similar relationship between illicit economies and insurgency characterizes the case of Colombia, on an even greater scale. Like the Shining Path, the leftist FARC initially tried to suppress drug cultivation. But after reversing course, it grew rapidly from a band of a few hundred guerrillas on the run in the southern jungles into a 20,000-strong group that largely controlled the southern and south-central parts of the country. Drug profits contributed directly to the FARC's rise, but the political capital that the group developed through its participation in the drug economy played at least as large a role. The FARC gained legitimacy and political support by protecting coca farmers against traffickers and eradication teams, providing a regulatory framework for the illicit economy, and offering social services to the population.

The FARC was not alone in providing such services. In the 1980s, Colombia's major drug cartels also built substantial political capital by taking over a variety of state roles. The circumstances surrounding the death of Pablo Escobar, the head of the Medellín cartel, illustrate the significance of that support. Despite Escobar's amply demonstrated brutality, many Medellín neighborhoods closed ranks around him when he was on the run. Despite the temptation of large government bounties, neighborhood residents refused to share information about Escobar with law enforcement officials. (Ultimately, intelligence provided by the rival Cali cartel brought him down.) The depth of popular support for Escobar debunks another key claim of the narcoguerrilla view: that once belligerents become involved in the drug trade, they cease to be motivated by ideology and hence lose political support. According to that logic, since the

Medellín cartel was never motivated by ideology, it should not have been able to accumulate any political support. And yet it did—in fact, enough to motivate the Medellín population not to provide intelligence on it to the government despite the cartel's brutality. This is yet another demonstration that even nonideological crime organizations can gain considerable political capital by using illicit economies to take on various security and protection functions of the state.

However, involvement in illegal activities does not necessarily lead to a substantial increase in political capital, as examples from both ends of the political spectrum show. Colombia's right-wing paramilitary groups used drug profits to fuel their growth from a few hundred men in the mid-1980s to almost 30,000 in 2006. Nonetheless, rather than protect coca farmers against traffickers, they typically took on the traffickers' role and abused the population. They also provided relatively few social services. Their political capital therefore remained limited.

Meanwhile, two leftist groups, M-19 and the ELN, failed to generate much political capital due to the nature of their illicit activities and, in the case of M-19, the relative wealth of its region of operation. M-19's involvement in the drug economy first took the form of kidnapping drug traffickers' relatives for ransom; later it shifted to protecting the traffickers by opposing extradition and destroying evidence that could be used against them. Those activities failed to generate much in the way of financial resources; they also failed to generate political capital because they were not labor intensive and hence benefited relatively few people. Moreover, they were so violent that they antagonized M-19's original urban base.

Similarly, the ELN's strategy produced too few benefits for the broader population to create significant legitimacy or support. By extorting payoffs from landowners and major businesses, especially oil companies, the ELN earned as much as $150 million a year. Some of those profits were invested in the provision of social services, but since the group's main activities— kidnapping and extortion—generated little rural employment, the ELN built little political capital. Worse, it sacrificed political capital by trying to suppress the drug economy, which it opposed on religious grounds.

The Colombian government has fared little better than the ELN in its efforts to end coca cultivation, despite pursuing eradication for almost three decades and carrying out the most intensive aerial fumigation campaign in history over the past nine years. After decreasing temporarily, the area under coca cultivation has rebounded since 2005 to pre-eradication levels, and there has been no substantial decline in the supply of Colombian cocaine. Nor has eradication managed to bankrupt or destroy the FARC. The FARC has been greatly weakened, but not as a result of eradication. The credit for that achievement belongs to a military campaign— underwritten by U.S. financial assistance, training, and signal intelligence provision to the Colombian military through Plan Colombia—aimed at encircling individual FARC *frentes*. In combination with localized interdiction efforts, that strategy has significantly disrupted the FARC's access to resources. Eradication, on the other hand, has increased the FARC's political capital, which in the absence of eradication would be at an all-time low. Critically, eradication has hampered local intelligence flows to the military, forcing the government to rely on signal intelligence and information from captured and deserted guerrillas. In short, the government has struck great blows against the FARC—but despite, not because of, eradication.

AFGHANISTAN

It remains to be seen whether the government of Afghanistan, with the assistance of the international community, will be able to report success similar to Colombia's in beating down the Taliban. Given the unprecedented dependence of the country's economy on illicit poppy cultivation and the size of the population dependent on the illicit economy for its basic livelihood, since the early 1980s few actors in Afghanistan have found it possible to resist participating in or at least tolerating the poppy economy. During the 1990s, even the Taliban chose to become deeply involved, despite its initial efforts to stamp out what it regarded as an un-Islamic activity. Only after the Taliban abandoned eradication was it able to consolidate its control over the Pashtun south as well as non-Pashtun regions. Since the fall of the Taliban in 2001, the ubiquity of the drug economy has greatly complicated government and allied efforts to consolidate Kabul's control of the country and defeat the Taliban insurgency. During the first two years of Operation Enduring Freedom, the U.S. military took a laissez-faire approach to poppy cultivation and drug trafficking, arguing that that strategy would facilitate information gathering, military operations, and the effort to win local hearts and minds. However, under international pressure, the Afghan government has intensified its efforts at eradication and interdiction since 2004, sparking protests, riots, and social instability.

Bans on poppy cultivation and eradication campaigns have failed to bankrupt potentially restive warlords, instead increasing both their financial profits and their political capital. Local elites in charge of eradication have strengthened their positions by destroying the poppy fields of their opponents and protecting those of their supporters. And ironically, eradication has allowed the Taliban to inject itself back into the illicit economy. The government's anti-drug campaigns have strengthened the previously loose connection between the Taliban and traffickers, generating vital political capital for the Taliban by allowing the group to capitalize on the resentment aroused by eradication and to offer its services as a defender of the people.

Similarly, interdiction efforts have been counterproductive. Instead of limiting the coercive and corruptive power of criminal actors, they have led to the vertical integration of the drug economy in Afghanistan and facilitated the rise of powerful capos with good connections to the government or the Taliban or both. Nonetheless, even greater resources will be poured into interdiction in the near future. In October 2008, NATO amended the mandate of its forces in Afghanistan to permit interested countries to conduct interdiction operations against traffickers linked to the Taliban. The goal of the policy is to bankrupt the belligerents, possibly by eliminating entire trafficking networks; to succeed, however, it will require extraordinary amounts of intelligence and manpower. So far, worldwide interdiction efforts have by and large failed to accomplish their goals. As the Colombia experience shows, even with the dedication of an extraordinary amount of resources, such efforts manage to capture about one-third of drug flows at most, usually with little impact on the income of traffickers and belligerents.

In conjunction with the stepped-up interdiction effort, NATO plans to focus its military activity in the key poppy cultivation areas in Helmand and Kandahar. The objectives are to force the Taliban to fight, not melt away as it has done elsewhere when encountering significant NATO forces, and to push the belligerents out of the poppy-growing areas in order to reduce their income. If NATO succeeds in expelling the Taliban from those areas without interfering with poppy cultivation, the insurgents will lose a critical source of political capital—the ability to protect villagers' poppy fields against eradication. But if the allies' decision to escalate the struggle impedes poppy cultivation, the local population may turn against the government and embrace the Taliban. Moreover, even if the Taliban is pushed out, it is not likely to go bankrupt because it will continue to get funds from Pakistan and the Middle East, from illicit logging, and from smuggling legal goods—all important current sources of income.

The core pillar of the Obama administration's new counternarcotics strategy for Afghanistan—development of alternative livelihoods that focuses on rebuilding Afghanistan's agriculture while eradication is greatly scaled back—is a courageous break with ineffective efforts in Afghanistan and more broadly with the conventional government policy applied for decades in Latin America as well as in Asia. The new counternarcotics policy will be able to sever the links between the Taliban and the population, thus facilitating intelligence flows and enhancing the counterinsurgency effort. How quickly the new policy will result in reducing the size of the illicit economy in Afghanistan will depend on progress in security, without which rural development cannot take off, as well as on how well-designed and well-funded the development effort is. But without doubt, the undertaking will require many years to reach its goals.

NORTHERN IRELAND

The difficulty of bankrupting belligerents by targeting illicit economies is underscored by the experience of a very different country: the United Kingdom, which battled insurgents in Northern Ireland for decades. This case also highlights the important role that the state of the overall economy plays in shaping the relationship between participation in illicit economies and political capital.

In relatively wealthy regions, several factors limit the legitimacy and support that belligerents can gain by supporting an illicit economy. First, because most people have the opportunity to pursue legal livelihoods, the importance of the illicit economy is diminished. Second, the forms of illegal activity that predominate in such regions typically are not very labor intensive and thus benefit relatively few people: drug distribution, for example, is far more common than the cultivation of illicit crops. Third, residents of wealthier regions can afford to give greater weight to moral sanctions against participating in an illicit economy than can residents of poorer areas. For a farmer in Peru's Upper Huallaga Valley, for example, opting out of coca cultivation could condemn his family to starvation.

Fourth, law enforcement is typically more effective in wealthier regions, limiting the extent to which belligerents can exploit illicit economies.

As a result, belligerents in developed countries derive fewer benefits from their participation in activities such as the drug trade. Sometimes they choose to forgo participation altogether in order to avoid the loss of legitimacy that such activities can entail. However, even in developed countries, where the state has myriad well-developed law enforcement tools at its disposal, cutting off the flow of resources to belligerents remains a significant challenge.

The case of Northern Ireland illustrates those observations. For many decades, the region was torn by violent conflict between armed groups claiming to represent the predominantly Roman Catholic Nationalists—such as the Provisional Irish Republican Army and its post-1997 splinter group, the Real Irish Republican Army—and those claiming to represent the predominantly Protestant Unionists or Loyalists, such as the Ulster Defense Association and Ulster Volunteer Force. In general, Nationalists sought to reunite Northern Ireland with the Republic of Ireland, while Unionists, who formed a small majority of the population in Northern Ireland, wanted it to remain part of the United Kingdom.

Armed groups on both sides have participated in the drug trade as a way to finance their activities. On the Nationalist side, the Provisional IRA was involved in drug trafficking in the late 1970s and 1980s—an activity that, while lucrative, was condemned by Catholic clergy and community leaders. To stem the resulting loss of political capital, the Provisional IRA abandoned its efforts at drug distribution (and turned to armed robbery instead).[1] As former Provisional IRA member Eamon Collins explained:

> The IRA—regardless of their public utterances dismissing condemnations of their behavior from church and community leaders—tried to act in a way that would avoid severe censure from within the . . . community; they knew they were operating within a sophisticated set of informal restrictions on their behaviour, no less powerful for being largely unspoken.[2]

The Provisional IRA also sought to rein in splinter groups, such as the Irish People's Liberation Organization, that continued to participate in the drug trade. And to build further political capital, the Provisional IRA even began an intimidation campaign aimed at ordinary drug dealers in Northern Ireland.[3]

In contrast, the Real IRA, a republican splinter group, remained involved in drug trafficking and distribution. Largely moribund today, the Real IRA, even at its height, had much weaker ties to the Irish Catholic communities than did the Provisional IRA; it therefore had relatively little political capital to lose as a result of its drug activities. Nonetheless, even the Real IRA went to considerable lengths to hide and deny its participation.

Loyalist groups also became involved in the drug trade, particularly in the 1990s. Until that point, they relied on a variety of illicit activities, such as robbery, tax fraud, smuggling, counterfeiting, and the collection of protection money, to finance their operations. The most profitable activity involved siphoning money off from legal pubs and drinking clubs. By the time the authorities began to crack down on the clubs, Loyalist paramilitaries had raked off tens of millions of dollars.[4] Once they lost that source of funding, they turned increasingly to drugs.

As the 1990s progressed, Loyalist groups came to control as much as 60 percent of Northern Ireland's drug trade.[5] In addition to taxing drug dealers operating in their territories, they ultimately took over the traffic from Britain, forcing local drug dealers to buy from them.[6] But the Loyalists too feared community reprobation. Many members opposed involvement in the drug trade, which remained largely the domain of individual groups, such as Billy Wright's Mid-Ulster United Volunteer Force, a local group that operated under the national Ulster Volunteer Force umbrella. Initially the umbrella Loyalist organizations tried to skirt the issue. As Andrew Silke points out, they were "painfully aware that the practice carries the heaviest political cost of all of the various fund-raising activities."[7] But ultimately, the magnitude of the political costs led Loyalist leaders to curtail participation in the drug trade in the late 1990s and to step up their involvement in loan sharking, counterfeiting, fuel rackets, and other frauds. Thus, as soon as one source of funds was cut off or abandoned, new illicit alternatives arose to take its place.

BURMA

The case of Northern Ireland underlines the difficulty of combating insurgents by targeting illicit economies. In contrast, the case of Burma suggests an alternative approach that may ultimately bring about a reduction in both conflict and illicit activities, although possibly at significant cost to the government's standing in the international community as well as to the

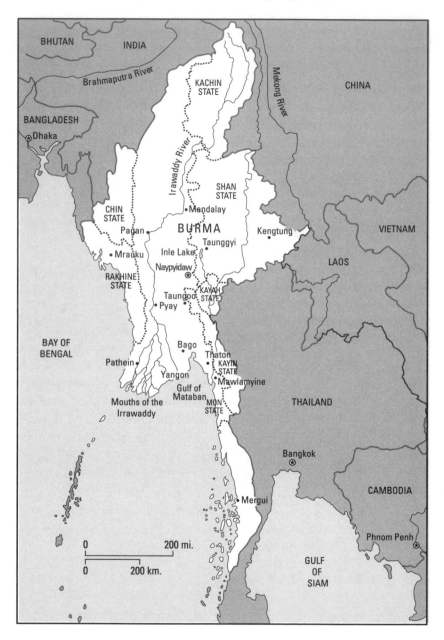

human security of marginalized populations. After unsuccessfully battling multiple insurgencies over four decades, in the late 1980s the Burmese government abandoned eradication of opium poppy fields in favor of a laissez-faire policy toward illicit economies coupled with cease-fires. Once it had prevailed upon many belligerent groups to disband and disarm, it succeeded in imposing eradication.

Opium poppy has been grown in Burma, a part of the Golden Triangle, for centuries. However, cultivation greatly increased after the country became independent in 1948. Over the following five decades, Burma was the predominant supplier of opiates for the international market. It was also the scene of constant military conflict as several insurgencies broke out almost simultaneously with independence. The belligerents included ethnonationalist insurgencies, such as the Shan, Karen, and Kachin, which sought autonomy, independence, and the reconfiguration of administrative boundaries; a communist insurgency, led by the Communist Party of Burma (CPB) with support from the People's Republic of China; and the Chinese nationalist Kuomintang, which was driven into Burma after Mao's victory in China.[8] Overall, more than forty belligerent groups emerged in the second half of the twentieth century. Some, such as the CPB and the Mong Tai Army, led by the notorious opium warlord Khun Sa, numbered around 15,000 men. Others, such as the ethnonationalist Kayan Newland Party, had as few as one hundred members. All the belligerents, as well as Ka Kwe Ye, a government-sponsored paramilitary group, became positively involved in a range of illicit economies, including illicit logging, illicit mining, and smuggling. Drug activity was especially pervasive, as insurgent groups entered the trade for financial and political profit and drug lords bought themselves armies to control land and narcotics production.

The military government's counterinsurgency policy focused on cutting the belligerents off from resources. Introduced in the late 1960s, the so-called "Four Cuts" policy was meant to limit the rebels' access to food, funding, recruits, and intelligence. It included both forced relocation of the population and eradication of poppy fields, carried out via aerial spraying with U.S. support.[9] (Eradication was selective: the fields of belligerents aligned with the government were spared.) But the policy had little impact, and the main insurgent groups continued to grow opium poppies and to derive funds and political support from doing so.

In the late 1980s, two crucial changes took place. In 1988, anti-government protests, fueled by a collapsing economy and the desire for democracy, broke out in many parts of the country, including Rangoon, which was then the capital. As a result, the military government of Ne Win was replaced by a new junta, the State Law and Order Restoration Council, which brutally put down the demonstrations.[10] The following year, the Communist Party of Burma, which had ceased to receive support from China in 1981, splintered along ethnic lines into five major factions: the 12,000-strong United Wa State Army, the 2,000-strong Myanmar National Democratic Alliance, and three smaller groups in the states of Kachin and Shan.

Fearing that the new insurgencies would join forces with pro-democracy activists, the junta proceeded to negotiate a series of ceasefires.[11] To sweeten the deal, it acquiesced in the belligerents' participation in illicit economies, and over U.S. protests, the junta also suspended eradication of opium poppy.[12] In Kachin state, various rebel groups—the Kachin Defense Army; New Democratic Army, Kachin; and Kachin Independence Organization—were allowed to harvest timber and opium poppy and to mine gems and gold. In Karen state, the Democratic Karen Buddhist Army was granted the right to tax opium poppy cultivation and to traffic in opium and timber. The government took a similar laissez-faire attitude to drug-related activities in Shan state and legalized cross-border trade with China, Thailand, and India in the ceasefire zones, as long as government checkpoints were established and taxes were collected.[13] (Drugs were officially not taxed, but they were not interdicted.) In a few cases, the junta even granted significant autonomy to insurgent leaders such as Sai Lin, who was given control of Special Region Number 3, bordering Yunnan province, China. The junta also struck similar bargains with prominent drug lords, allowing them to invest their profits in legitimate businesses such as construction, paper mills, beer factories, banking, and supermarkets.[14] In addition, the traffickers-turned-businessmen received contracts to repair ports and construct major roads.[15]

The ceasefires have held for over a decade, aided by the junta's success in pressuring many belligerent groups to disarm in the wake of the ceasefires.[16] Today only a few rebel groups, each numbering in the hundreds, remain engaged in armed struggle; such groups operate in Mon and Karen states and in the remote regions along the border. However, various rebel groups continue to exercise autonomy within their territory and either maintain large standing armies or have the capacity to raise them again.[17]

The United Wa State Army, for example, boasts 20,000 soldiers while the Kachin Independence Army claims to have 4,000 men under arms.

Surprisingly, the laissez-faire policy did not result in a massive increase in poppy cultivation. Between 1991 and 1996, cultivation and production levels stayed at about the same level (160,000 hectares, equivalent to 2,350 metric tons of opium, in 1991 and 163,100 hectares, or 2,560 metric tons, in 1996).[18] Nonetheless, under pressure from the United States and China—where addiction rates were growing and increasingly powerful drug traffickers were beginning to pose a threat to the authority of the Chinese Communist Party in the border regions—the Burmese junta finally undertook large-scale eradication of poppy in the late 1990s and early 2000s.[19] It also forced former rebels in autonomous territories, such as Sai Lin in Special Region Number 3, to carry out eradication. Groups that had disarmed had little choice but to comply. Under the supervision of the U.S. Drug Enforcement Administration (DEA), for example, Special Region Number 3, once a hotbed of opium cultivation, was essentially cleared of poppy.[20] Nationwide, production fell in 2005 to 30,800 hectares of poppy (equivalent to 312 metric tons of opium) and in 2008 to 28,500 hectares (410 metric tons, due to higher opium resin yields that year).[21] Overproduction of opium in Afghanistan, which saturated the international market, helped sustain those gains.

Eradication has radically impoverished the rural population. Many people have left the hill regions where poppy cultivation was the dominant activity; others have turned to unrestrained logging, forest foraging, and illicit trade in wildlife. Many former opium farmers now have food security for only eight months a year and require foreign food aid to survive for the remaining four months.[22] Previously, their dire plight might have led farmers to join forces with local insurgents, but after the conflict between the government and belligerent groups ended, they had nowhere to turn.[23]

In contrast, the former belligerents have not suffered. They have managed to maintain their income by switching to production of synthetic drugs, mainly methamphetamines, known locally as *yaa baa*. In Shan state alone, more than fifty meth factories have been discovered.[24] Unlike opium poppy fields, such factories are easy to hide and consequently difficult to destroy. But since production of synthetic drugs is not labor intensive, this illicit economy provides no relief to the population at large. Nor did it generate significant political capital for the belligerents, an outcome that the groups could tolerate because the conflict between them and the government was over and they fully controlled the local populations. In summer 2009, the junta began to pressure the belligerent groups to speed up their disarmament and to adopt a new constitution in 2010 that would diminish their autonomy; the result was renewed military conflict between the groups and the government. Any spread of the conflict may once again alter the drug trade pattern in the country and in Southeast Asia.

The case of Burma thus represents a twist on laissez-faire. The junta used this approach to end the military conflicts not by winning the hearts and minds of the population but by buying off the insurgents. Subsequently, it implemented an eradication campaign that dramatically suppressed poppy cultivation. However, the cost of that policy was substantial, because the government gave up control of significant parts of Burma's economy as well as its territory in order to bring the many insurgencies to an end. The policy also has been extraordinarily costly in human terms since it greatly immiserated already poor and marginalized populations.

THE CASE AGAINST PREMATURE ERADICATION

Taken together, these case studies show that aggressive efforts to suppress illicit economies, such as crop eradication, have not succeeded in fatally weakening belligerents. The discussion in this book focuses on how such policies affect the political capital of insurgent groups. But even setting that issue aside, it is extraordinarily difficult to use eradication and related strategies to cut off funding for belligerents. Suppression efforts typically raise the price of illicit commodities; thus, even when those efforts are partially successful, insurgents may see no change in their income, especially if they have stockpiled drugs. Belligerents may also have reserve funds to tide them over in difficult times.[25] And most important, suppression efforts rarely succeed for long. The participants in the drug trade are extraordinarily adaptable. Farmers often replant after eradication teams have moved on. They can offset losses from eradication by increasing the number of plants per hectare and evade detection by planting under tree cover deep in the jungles or under cloud cover at higher elevations. Similarly, traffickers can easily adopt new smuggling routes or modes of transportation in response to interdiction attempts.

Source-country suppression policies, such as eradication coupled with interdiction, have succeeded in disrupting supply for about two years at most.[26] Without reductions in global demand, supply inevitably recovers—whether in the same locale or elsewhere (the so-called balloon effect). The destruction of the "French connection" in the 1970s, which interrupted heroin smuggling from Asia through Turkey, resulted in a sharp increase in heroin production in Mexico. A subsequent eradication campaign dried up the flow of heroin from Mexico, facilitating the rise of the Golden Crescent and increases in production in the Golden Triangle. Meanwhile, Mexican farmers shifted to cultivating marijuana. Eradication with the herbicide paraquat, which was believed to have carcinogenic effects, then drove down U.S. demand for Mexican marijuana, allowing cannabis cultivation to take off elsewhere in Latin America. The expansion in marijuana cultivation, accompanied by a vast increase in demand for drugs in the United States, paved the way for a major increase in Latin American coca cultivation and cocaine production in the late 1970s and early 1980s.[27] Since then, eradication and interdiction efforts in the Andean region have been largely a shell game, with cultivation rising and falling in different areas while remaining remarkably stable—at around 200,000 hectares over the past twenty years—in the aggregate.

The failure of such policies can be highlighted by examining patterns in consumption and prices. Successful suppression policies should cause prices to rise and consumption to fall. In fact, since the 1990s consumption of cocaine and heroin has been more or less stable in the United States, while consumption of marijuana and methamphetamines has increased. Cocaine consumption has increased in Europe over the same period. Many non-Western countries, such as Iran and Pakistan, remain very important markets for narcotics, and countries that previously had little internal consumption (despite significant trafficking), such as Russia and Brazil, have developed a taste for illicit drugs that rivals the West's.[28] Even in regions where suppression of traditional drug production has been relatively successful, as in Burma or Laos, demand has not disappeared. Instead, many users have switched to home-cooked synthetic drugs.[29] Meanwhile, drug prices have been dropping. In the United States, the retail price of heroin fell steadily, from $1,887 per gram in 1981 to $364 per gram in 2007 (the latest year for which data are available), and cocaine prices fell from $613 for two grams in 1981 to $121 for two grams in 2007.[30] In other words, over a quarter-century, prices for both drugs have fallen by roughly 80 percent.

More of the Same?

Supporters of eradication argue that the solution is even more comprehensive and consistent eradication campaigns. They also suggest that despite eradication's disappointing results to date, prices would be even lower and consumption even greater in the absence of aggressive supply-side measures. Those arguments reveal the difficulty of drawing inferences about policy effectiveness when comparisons to control cases cannot be made. Imagine the following scenario: a sick patient has been taking a pill as treatment, but is not getting better. Does that imply that the active ingredient in the pill is not effective? That is one plausible answer, and indeed it may be correct. But there are also other possibilities. The active ingredient may in fact be effective, but the dosage needs to be higher. That is the argument for more and more intense eradication. Or the active ingredient may be at least partly effective, meaning that without it, the patient would be much sicker. On the negative side, the treatment may be not only ineffective but also counterproductive and detrimental to the patient's health. Or the treatment may be wiping out the targeted disease (like eradication aimed at particular crops) but, like chemotherapy, compromising other aspects of the patient's health along with it.

Aggressive suppression policies can indeed have negative side effects, beyond the creation of political capital for government opponents, as examples from Colombia and Mexico suggest. In Colombia, the government's success in destroying the Medellín and Cali cartels led to the emergence of numerous "boutique" cartels, smaller-scale organizations that are much harder to detect and combat. Moreover, the elimination of the cartels enabled the expansion of right-wing paramilitary groups with the potential to pose an even greater threat to state security and to the human security of the population. The demise of the cartels was, of course, a critically important achievement that greatly reduced the power of organized crime vis-à-vis the Colombian state. Nonetheless, it also had grave unintended consequences.

Similarly in Mexico, the government's recent decision to crack down on major drug traffickers, after decades of tolerating and even collaborating in their activities, has provoked a wave of violence.[31] In going after the top capos of the major drug trafficking organizations—the Tijuana organization, also known as Arellano Félix organization; the Federation, at the core of which is the Sinaloa organization; the Juárez organization; the Gulf organization; and La Familia—the government not only encountered large-scale armed resistance but also triggered a major turf war among the traffickers. The fighting claimed the lives of 6,290 people in Mexico in 2008, and the tally of victims is expected to be even higher in 2009.[32] The violence and accompanying increases in kidnappings and other crimes, especially in the states of Chihuahua, Baja California, Michoácan, and Guerrero, have created enormous insecurity. The government clearly was unprepared for the challenge, and President Felipe Calderón had to deploy more than 45,000 military personnel, including upward of 10,000 to the city of Juárez, to suppress the violence.[33] How successful the state will be in this effort and in reducing the power of the cartels remains to be seen.

An Incomplete Solution

Even if eradication could be implemented without such negative effects— and further, even if it could be implemented in a way that would result in the permanent elimination of illegal crops—there is no guarantee that belligerents relying on the drug trade would be forced into bankruptcy. Belligerents always have the option of switching to other forms of drug production, such as cooking methamphetamines, or other illicit economies, such as extortion, illegal logging, and smuggling. Moreover, groups rarely rely on drugs to provide their entire income. Even Colombia's FARC has derived only 50 percent of its finances from drugs.

Equally important, a temporary drop in income would not necessarily cripple a belligerent group's military operations. Insurgents could, for example, choose cheaper military tactics, such as the use of primitive explosive devises. They may be able to defer the replacement of equipment until a new income stream is found. Even in the absence of new income, belligerents may well be able to carry on a deadly military campaign for a number of years; that is especially true of terrorist groups numbering in the hundreds or less that engage sporadically in spectacular attacks. Al Qaeda, which often is cited to justify the need for eradication in Afghanistan, is a pertinent example.[34] The September 11 attacks in the United States were estimated to cost between $300,000 and $500,000.[35] It would take a moderately competent terrorist group only a year to earn enough from taxing drug production or trafficking to finance many such attacks, and perhaps as little as participation in only one international smuggling run to earn the money for one such attack.[36]

MAKING ERADICATION MORE EFFECTIVE

Although eradication has not been effective in suppressing overall production of any major drug or in substantially weakening any major belligerent group, it has succeeded at suppressing production in particular regions for certain periods, as in Afghanistan in 2000 and in Burma over the past several years. Those examples suggest the conditions that must hold if governments are to realize even such less ambitious goals. First and foremost, the government must have control over the entire area where eradication is to take place. It must be able to detect and eliminate new areas of production, and it must maintain a presence on the ground to prevent replanting. Any armed opposition must be overcome before eradication takes place. Second, the government must choose one of two approaches. Either it must be willing to couple eradication with repression and crack down harshly on any opposition, or it must have in place a comprehensive alternative livelihood program that does not just promise a future legal livelihood but guarantees an existing legal livelihood to former or potential cultivators of illegal crops before extensive eradication is undertaken.

Eradication and Repression

The repression model so far has been only temporarily successful. Poppy cultivation in Afghanistan picked up within one year of the Taliban's 2000 ban. In Bolivia, which carried out an eradication campaign between 1995 and 2000, production has been increasing since despite a combination of repression and localized alternative development programs.[37] Forced eradication also contributed to instability in Bolivia and to the 2005 election of *cocalero* leader Evo Morales, who suspended forced eradication. In Burma, forced eradication appears to be holding to date despite the tremendous hardship that it has imposed on former poppy farmers, but the policy's success is due in large part not to eradication but to two unrelated facts: Afghanistan's poppy plants yield more opium than Burma's, and Afghan opium has a higher alkaloid content than Burmese opium. Afghan opium therefore has displaced Burmese opium in the international market.

Eradication and Alternative Livelihoods

The second model, based on alternative livelihood programs, has been successful at a local level but less successful countrywide, in part because most alternative livelihood programs have not lasted long enough or have not been well funded and managed.[38] Thailand provides the most significant success story. There, three decades of multifaceted, comprehensive, well-funded, and well-managed rural development—accompanied, crucially, by impressive economic growth—have led to the elimination of poppy cultivation.[39] Cultivation fell from 17,920 hectares at the peak in 1965–66 to 288 hectares in 2008.[40] However, Thailand's poppy problem was relatively small; at its peak, cultivation was about one-tenth the current level in Afghanistan. Moreover, Thailand remains host to a flourishing traffic in synthetic drugs as well as in opiates from other countries.[41]

For alternative livelihood programs to be effective over the longer term, first of all security must be established; military conflict must be brought to an end in order to give the programs a chance to work. Equally important, alternative livelihood programs cannot be construed solely as crop substitution. Their goal should not be to find replacement crops that generate as much revenue as illicit commodities but to create economic conditions that allow farmers to earn a decent livelihood in the legal sector.

The relative prices of legal and illegal products are only one factor driving the cultivation of illicit crops. Often other factors, such as insecurity and lack of access to such critical aspects of a functioning economy as credit and markets, are even more important. For that reason, farmers in the Shinwar and Achin regions of Afghanistan or the Shan hill areas of Burma continue to plant illicit crops even when legal crops, such as vegetables, fetch greater prices.

For alternative livelihood programs to have any chance to take off, they must address all the causes of participation in illicit economies. They must encompass the promotion of high-value, highly labor-intensive crops; infrastructure building; distribution of new technologies, such as those involving better fertilizers and seeds; marketing help and the development of value-added chains; facilitation of local microcredit; access to land and land titles; and development of off-farm employment opportunities, to name a few of the most prominent components. They also must encompass provision of education, health, and other services to marginalized populations and undertake the political integration of those populations into the broader society. Alternative livelihood programs really mean comprehensive rural and overall economic and social development. Accordingly, they require enormous inputs of time and resources as well as basic security, a critical component.

LICENSING AS A POLICY ALTERNATIVE

As an alternative or supplement to eradication, some governments have experimented with licensing the illicit economy for legal purposes. In

Turkey, the licensing of opium poppy cultivation for medical opiates (mor-phine, codeine, and thebaine), which began in the mid-1970s, eliminated the illegal cultivation of poppies. Licensing was adopted after several years of eradication had failed to limit poppy cultivation but succeeded in gen-erating political instability. None of the belligerent groups active in the country, such as the Kurdistan Workers' Party, or terrorist groups, such as Dev Sol, ever managed to penetrate the licit opium poppy market, although they continued to traffic in illicit opiates from Asia. Licensing has also been adopted to control illicit logging, as well as the mining of and trade in dia-monds in Africa—in the latter case, with the goal of cutting off financing for belligerent groups such as those in Sierra Leone, Liberia, and Congo.[42]

Nonetheless, licensing and related policies such as legalization and laissez-faire are not always the appropriate response to illicit economies. Nor are suppression policies always the wrong choice. There are, after all, good reasons why some economies and activities remain illegal, even if bans can have undesirable consequences. The fact that murder is illegal creates demand for killers and establishes a highly lucrative market for professional hit men. Belligerent groups who provide such services can reap large financial profits; however, the solution is not to legalize murder. Similarly, smuggling of the materials needed to build weapons of mass destruction must remain prohibited, since the consequences could be cat-astrophic if such materials fell into the hands of terrorists. Legalization of the consumption of illicit drugs is likely to lead to increased consump-tion—a serious and important reason to eschew such a policy.[43]

Licensing or blanket legalization may also result in the depletion of irre-placeable resources. Illicit trade in wildlife is a highly lucrative illicit econ-omy, and belligerent groups, such as the National Union for the Total Independence of Angola (UNITA), have profited from killing and selling wildlife, especially endangered species. A laissez-faire approach to poach-ing might well reduce the belligerents' financial profits, but it would also result in the irretrievable loss of many species.

Moreover, the fact that licensing is feasible and effective in one context does not mean that it would be equally effective elsewhere. Several factors made a critical contribution to the success of opium licensing in Turkey. The government had firm control over the territory where licensing was undertaken, enabling it to comply with the Single Convention on Nar-cotics Drugs, the cornerstone of the international narcotics regime that governs licensing. Turkey also adopted a particular technology, the so-called poppy straw method, that makes it very difficult to divert morphine into illicit channels. India adopted a different method that proved far less effective at preventing diversion.[44] In addition, Turkey had a guaranteed market for its opiates in the United States, which had agreed to purchase 80 percent of morphine-based medical opiates from Turkey and India. Nonetheless, both India and Turkey are being displaced from the licit market by countries such as Australia, a new industrial supplier of medical opiates that do not contain morphine and hence are not subject to U.S. law. The growing competition, along with the relative weakness of the state, would greatly complicate efforts to adopt similar licensing schemes in Afghanistan or other countries today.[45]

Finally, even when licensing is possible, the existence of a licit economy does not necessarily translate into the elimination of the related illicit economy. The legal market for cars in the United States has not prevented the existence of an illicit market for cheaper stolen cars (which Mexican drug traffickers exploit to launder funds).

Given the limitations of licensing and legalization, more aggressive strategies, such as carefully implemented eradication and interdiction policies, remain important government options. But it is essential that those policies be well-crafted, judiciously applied, and properly sequenced in combination with other measures. For example, once alternative livelihood efforts have created the resources that farmers need to switch to sustainable licit livelihoods, eradication may be an important tool for completing the transition. Such smart eradication will be socially viable and can strengthen the rule of law. But premature eradication—in the context of insurgency and without alternative livelihoods in place—will be counterproductive and ineffective, as the cases discussed here have shown.

Similarly, well-crafted interdiction efforts remain crucial not because they will necessarily significantly reduce the income of belligerents or limit drug supply, but because they allow the state to prevent crime organizations from accumulating excessive power and threatening a country's security, political integrity, and the rule of law. However, poorly designed interdiction measures can have the opposite effect. They can facilitate the vertical integration of the illegal trade and the rise of powerful and well-connected drug capos. They can also set off bloody turf wars over territory and access that fundamentally threaten the security of the state.

FALSE DILEMMAS

Much of the message of this book is sobering: Aggressive counternar-cotics and counterinsurgency policies often are at odds. When implemented as a part of an effort to defeat insurgents, eradication has failed. Moreover, it has failed to reduce drug production and consumption on any significant scale. However, there is good news as well. The analysis shows that in fighting insurgencies involved in illicit economies, governments need not choose between winning the population's hearts and minds and cutting off the flow of resources to the belligerents through aggressive suppression. The dilemma is only apparent, not real. Since eradication has demonstrably failed at bankrupting insurgents, governments can forgo eradication at little cost. Moreover, as some of the cases have shown, governments may have other policy options, such as interdiction or licensing, that can more effectively reduce both the belligerents' resources and their political capital.

Similarly, the trade-off between ensuring security through counterterrorism or counterinsurgency operations and eliminating illicit economies is largely illusory. No policy can significantly and sustainably diminish an illicit economy in the absence of basic security. Therefore, whether the chosen mechanism is suppression, alternative livelihood programs, or licensing, giving priority to security represents not a trade-off but appropriate sequencing.

The true trade-off arises in balancing domestic political and bureaucratic factors, such as pressure to undertake aggressive drug suppression measures, against efforts to maximize the effectiveness of counterinsurgency and counternarcotics strategies. The United States has faced that problem in Afghanistan. Domestic pressure in the United States led to a sharp increase in the priority given to eradication and interdiction, despite the concerns of military leaders about the effect of such policies on the fight against the Taliban. But after years of the U.S. government being doggedly wedded to ineffective and counterproductive counternarcotics policies around the world, there is hope. In abandoning policies that are ineffective, even if politically popular and bureaucratically standard, the new counternarcotics strategy of the Obama administration for Afghanistan finally shows a capacity for learning at the government level. The new strategy breaks with the conventional view of the nexus of insurgency and drugs and enhances the prospects of defeating the insurgency and reducing the narcotics economy by giving priority to ensuring security and alternative development while holding back on premature eradication.

RECOMMENDATIONS FOR GOVERNMENT POLICY

Ultimately, there are no quick fixes for illicit economies and no shortcuts for defeating insurgencies and other belligerents. Governments under attack, such as those of Afghanistan and Colombia, cannot simply spray their way out of conflict. However, by heeding the following recommendations, they can increase the chances that they will ultimately prevail over both insurgent forces and the illicit economies from which the insurgents derive much of their strength.

Reducing the Strength of Belligerent Groups

—*Governments should not rely on suppression of illicit economies to defeat or even substantially weaken belligerents.* Most likely, belligerents will be able to adapt to government policy and find new sources of income. Therefore, if a government seeks to achieve a preponderance of military power, it needs to do so by beefing up its own military resources.

—*When dealing with labor-intensive illicit economies in poor countries, governments should undertake suppression efforts that affect the wider population only after military conflict has been brought to an end.* Premature suppression efforts will alienate the population and severely curtail the flow of intelligence on the belligerents from the population, causing the government to lose the competition for the hearts and minds of the population and severely hampering the military effort against the belligerents. Suppression is also unlikely to be effective because traffickers and producers will find a way to adapt, given the relative weakness of the state in contested areas. More narrowly targeted policies, such as interdiction at borders and destruction of drug labs, do not affect the population directly. Consequently, they are more compatible with counterinsurgency and counterterrorism efforts.

—*Military forces, whether domestic or international, should focus on directly defeating the belligerents and protecting the population.* They can be most effective at supporting policies to suppress illicit economies by focusing on providing basic security. Without such security, efforts to suppress illicit economies will not be effective.

—If belligerents have not yet penetrated an illicit economy, govern-ments should make every effort to prevent them from doing so. For exam-ple, they may prevent belligerents from becoming involved in narcotics cultivation in a particular region by establishing a cordon sanitaire around the region. When possible, governments should entice belligerents into suppressing the illicit economy themselves, whether through promises, threats, or an influential third party—but only if the government can dis-tance itself from such measures in the eyes of the population. By sup-pressing the illicit economy, belligerents will substantially reduce their political capital and facilitate the government's efforts to win over the population. Moreover, the government's ability to carry out this policy will depend to a large extent on the belligerents' position along the illicit economy learning curve. The belligerents are more likely to be open to suppression when their experience with the illicit economy is limited. Once they have learned the costs and benefits of involvement in the illicit economy, they will not be easily baited into such counterproductive behav-ior. Belligerents are most likely to pursue eradication when they first encounter the illicit economy. But such an opportunity could also arise as a result of a change in leadership, an increase in ideological fervor, or the need to appease an outside patron, whether foreign or domestic.

—If the belligerents themselves undertake suppression of a labor-inten-sive illicit economy, whether as the result of a government initiative or their own, the government should capitalize on the opportunity to move against them. It should immediately step in and provide economic relief to the population. It also should intensify its military effort because pop-ular support for the belligerents will be weak.

—Efforts to limit the belligerents' resources should focus on mecha-nisms that do not harm the wider population directly, such as efforts to prevent money laundering. Measures against money laundering cannot remain localized at the country level; they must be strengthened on the global level.

—Governments also should explore the possibility of licensing par-ticular illicit economies. Such measures can include converting illicit crops to legal uses or instituting a licensing system for logging or gem-stone mining.

—If the government itself undertakes efforts to suppress a labor-inten-sive illicit economy, it should soften the blow by providing immediate relief to the population in the form of humanitarian aid and alternative

livelihood programs. Alternative livelihood programs will not have a chance to really take off until military conflict has ended and security has been established. Nonetheless, in the short term, the government needs to demonstrate that it is not indifferent to the population's plight; otherwise it will push residents into the arms of the belligerents.

Reducing the Power of Criminal Groups

—*Governments should avoid treating traffickers and belligerents as a unified actor, which would strengthen the bond between them; instead, they should explore ways to pit the two actors against each other.* Far from being natural comrades in arms, traffickers and belligerents have conflicting interests. Governments can exploit that divergence of identity and interest by temporarily reducing pressure on the group that represents a lesser threat to the state and exploiting that group to acquire intelligence. At the same time, governments must be conscious of the dangers of a selective approach. Targeting only traffickers linked to belligerents, for example, may create opportunities for other traffickers to increase their control of the drug trade while building strong ties to state officials. In the long run, that may undermine the rule of law. Therefore, if policy calls for targeting only traffickers that oppose the state, plans must also be made for combating other traffickers once the threat posed by the belligerents has subsided.

—*Interdiction efforts should be designed to limit the coercive and cor- ruptive power of criminal groups.* Interdiction efforts should be designed to avoid the creation of a small number of vertically integrated, powerful criminal organizations. An illicit economy characterized by many small traders poses a much smaller threat to the state, although greater intelli- gence resources may be necessary to keep track of their activities. In addi- tion, before carrying out interdiction policies, governments should gather the resources necessary to prevent and suppress violence resulting from possible turf wars among traffickers.

Addressing Illicit Economies after Conflict Has Ended

—*Even after the conflict has ended, eradication of illicit crops should be undertaken only when the population has access to effective alternative livelihood programs.* Failure to provide such assistance will result in social instability. Under those circumstances, continued eradication will require harsh repression over many years.

—*Alternative livelihood programs need to be designed to be comprehensive programs for rural economic and social development.* They need to address all the factors that drive participation in the illicit economy.

—*Governments and their international partners need to watch the watchdogs.* Organizations and individuals charged with eradication and interdiction are in a strategic position to become top traffickers. Often they can manipulate their access to intelligence and exercise control over policy to augment their economic and political power. Consequently, there must be rigorous monitoring and auditing of top law enforcement officials and other drug policy officials in order to prevent and combat corruption.

—*Governments and their international partners must address the demand for illicit commodities and contraband.* It is especially vital that extensive and committed demand-reduction measures play a central role in counternarcotics policy. Reducing demand for illegal drugs through prevention and treatment would go a long way toward limiting the benefits that belligerents obtain from this particular illicit economy. Such efforts cannot focus only on the West; they also must encompass developing countries, many of which have emerged as large secondary markets for drugs. Demand reduction will not be equally effective across the spectrum of illicit commodities. Limitations to such an approach arise especially in the case of illicit markets in which there are only a few but highly determined buyers, as may be the case with terrorists seeking to obtain weapons of mass destruction or materials with which to make them. But demand reduction is critical for dealing effectively with a host of other illicit economies, such as the trade in narcotics and in protected wildlife.

Addressing the Balloon Effect and Other Negative Externalities

—*Governments and international organizations need to consider where the illicit economy is likely to reemerge if suppression efforts in a particular country or region are effective.* Absent a major change in global demand, suppression of production in one location will only shift production elsewhere; governments and international organizations need to consider the possibility that it could re-emerge, for example, in an area dominated by a major terrorist group. Such a shift could bring the terrorists windfall gains, both in military strength and in political capital.

—*Governments and international organizations need to consider the possibility that other illicit economies will replace the current one if suppression succeeds.* Even when suppression succeeds, criminal activity rarely disappears altogether. Frequently, it is rechanneled into the production and smuggling of other illicit commodities. Thus, in suppressing one illicit economy, governments and international actors need to take precautions to prevent the emergence of another one that could be even more pernicious and difficult to control.

—*Finally, when deciding on particular regulations and prohibitions, including international sanctions, governments and international organizations need to seriously consider whether the harm resulting from such a prohibition and its enforcement is, in fact, smaller than the harm resulting from a laissez-faire approach.* Among other things, they need to consider the nature and size of the illicit economy that such a prohibition will generate; the ease with which belligerents will be able to exploit the resulting illicit economy; and the difficulty of enforcing the new regulations. Ultimately, the best way to deal with the dangerous nexus between illicit economies and military conflict may be to ensure that the two never meet.

Involvement of Belligerent Groups with Illicit Drugs

Although the list of belligerent groups involved in illegal drugs (table A-1) is far longer than commonly assumed, it nonetheless shows that not every belligerent group is running drugs. Despite the multifaceted potential benefits of participation in illicit economies, particularly the drug trade, sometimes the constraints on participation by belligerent groups are large. In the case of cultivation of illicit crops, the most basic limitations and obstacles are natural resource endowments and the level of law enforcement. Although cannabis and opium poppy plants can grow in a variety of conditions, coca is more restricted to areas that meet specific temperature and humidity requirements; it cannot be grown outside those geographic areas unless special artificial conditions are created through the use of greenhouses, fertilizers, and other agronomic technologies.[1]

But even the cultivation of more adaptable plants, such as cannabis and opium poppies, faces the issue of comparative advantage: differences in climatic conditions in Burma and Afghanistan, for example, result in significantly greater opium yield per poppy capsule and greater potency of Afghan than of Burmese opium. Consequently, traffickers and users prefer Afghan opium. As cultivation of opium in Afghanistan has expanded, Burmese cultivation has steadily shrunk in response to the reduced demand for Burmese opium. Even if the remaining belligerents in Burma wanted to expand cultivation, they would run into the limiting market force of weak demand for their opium.

A second constraint is the level of law enforcement and government control of territory. Strong states with large, effective military and police

TABLE A-1. *Cases of Known Involvement of Belligerent Groups with Illicit Drugs*

Country/ Belligerent group	Type of narcotics	Type of involvement	Period
Afghanistan			
Mujahideen	Opium Heroin	Taxation of cultivation and trafficking; processing	1980s
Warlords	Opium Heroin	Taxation of cultivation and trafficking; processing	1990s
Taliban	Opium Heroin	Taxation of cultivation and trafficking; processing; international trafficking[a]	1995–99 2001–
Northern Alliance	Opium Heroin	Taxation of cultivation and trafficking; processing	1990s
Warlords	Opium Heroin	Taxation of cultivation and trafficking; processing; domestic trafficking	2000s
Al Qaeda[a]	Opiates	Trafficking	2000s
Armenia			
Armenian Secret Army for the Liber- ation of Armenia	Heroin	Trafficking	1970s–1980s
Britain			
British government and traders	Opium	Taxation of cultivation; trafficking	Colonial era
Burma			
Communist Party of Burma	Opiates	Taxation of cultivation; domestic trafficking; processing	1970s–1980s
KMT	Opiates	Taxation of cultivation; trafficking	1950s–1980s
Kachin Independence Organization	Opiates	Taxation of cultivation	1980s–
Shan United Army	Opiates Methamphe- tamines	Taxation of cultivation; processing; trafficking Production; trafficking	1980s–
United Wa State Army	Opiates Methamphe- tamines	Taxation of cultivation and trafficking; processing; trafficking Production; trafficking	1980s–
Ka Kwe Ye	Opiates	Taxation of cultivation; trafficking	1960s–1970s
Mong Tai Army	Opiates	Taxation of cultivation; processing; trafficking	1989– 1990s
Myanmar National Democratic Alliance Army	Opiates Methamphe- tamines	Taxation of cultivation; processing; trafficking Production; trafficking	1989–
Democratic Karen Buddhist Army	Opiates	Taxation of cultivation and trafficking	1990s

Country/ Belligerent group	Type of narcotics	Type of involvement	Period
Burma (*cont.*)			
Shan State National Army	Opiates	Taxation of cultivation and trafficking	1990s
China			
Anti-Manchu under- ground groups	Opium	Trafficking; distribution[b]	Nineteenth century
Chiang Kai Shek	Opium	Taxation of cultivation; processing; distribution	1920s–1940s
Mao	Opium	Tolerance; taxation	1930s– 1940s
Colombia			
FARC	Cocaine Marijuana Opium	Taxation of cultivation, processing, and trafficking; processing; trafficking	1980s–
AUC (paramilitaries) *Bandas criminales* and *grupos emergentes*	Cocaine Marijuana Opium	Taxation of cultivation, processing, and trafficking; processing; trafficking	1980s–
ELN	Marijuana Opium	Taxation of cultivation; protec- tion of labs	1990s–
M-19	Cocaine	Facilitation and protection of trafficking	1980s
EPL	Cocaine Marijuana	Taxation of cultivation	1980s
Cuba			
Omega 7	Cocaine Marijuana	Protection of trafficking and distribution	1980s
India			
British forces	Opium (licit cultivation)	Taxation; trafficking; distribution	Until 1940s
Sikhs (Punjab)	Opiates	Trafficking	1980s
Kashmiri insurgents	Opiates	Trafficking	1980s–
Naxalites	Opiates Marijuana	Taxation of cultivation; trafficking	1990s–
National Socialist Council of Nagaland	Opiates	Trafficking	1980s–
People's Liberation Army (Imphal Val- ley and Manipur)	Opiates	Trafficking	1980s–
United Liberation Front of Assam	Opiates	Trafficking	1980s–
Kuki National Army	Opiates	Trafficking	1980s–

TABLE A-1. *(continued)*

Country/ Belligerent group	Type of narcotics	Type of involvement	Period
Indochina			
French occupation forces	Opiates	Taxation of cultivation	Until 1950s
Hill tribes	Opium	Cultivation	Until 1970s
Independence movement	Opium	Trafficking	1945–49
Japan			
Occupation forces in China	Opium	Taxation of cultivation; distribution	1930s–1940s
Lebanon			
Palestinian, Phalangist, Druze, and Shiite factions during civil war	Hashish	Protection of trafficking; trafficking	1970s–1980s
Hezbollah	Hashish	Taxation of cultivation; trafficking	1980s
	Heroin	Taxation of cultivation; trafficking	1980s– 1990s
	Cocaine	Trafficking from Latin America to Europe	1990s–
	Methamphe-tamines[a]	Taxation of distribution in Canada and the United States[a]	1990s–
Nepal			
Maoists	Opiates	Trafficking	1990s–
Nicaragua			
Contras	Cocaine	Protection and taxation of trafficking	1980s
Northern Ireland			
Real IRA	Opiates, cocaine, and marijuana	Trafficking; distribution	1990s–
Irish People's Liberation Organisation	Opiates, cocaine, and marijuana	Trafficking; distribution	Early 1990s
Ulster Defense Association	Opiates, cocaine, and marijuana	Trafficking; distribution	1990s–
Ulster Volunteer Force	Opiates, cocaine, and marijuana	Trafficking; distribution	1990s–
Pakistan			
Kashmiri militants	Opiates	Trafficking	1990s–
Baluchi militants	Opiates	Trafficking	2000s–
Taliban	Opiates	Refining; trafficking	2000s–

Country/ Belligerent group	Type of narcotics	Type of involvement	Period
Palestinian Territory			
Hamas	Opiates Cocaine	Taxation of trafficking and distribution (tri-border region of South America)	1990s–
Peru			
Shining Path	Cocaine	Taxation of cultivation; protec- tion of trafficking; processing; money laundering	1980s–1990s
		Protection of trafficking	2000s
MRTA	Cocaine	Taxation of cultivation	1980s
Philippines			
Abu Sayyaf Group	Marijuana[a]	Production	2000s–
New People's Army	Marijuana	Taxation of cultivation; trafficking; distribution	1980s–
Moro National Liberation Front	Marijuana Methamphe- tamines	Taxation of cultivation Production	1990s
Russia			
Chechen mujahideen	Opiates	Trafficking	1990s–
Renegade Russian armed forces	Opiates	Trafficking; distribution[a]	1990s–
Spain			
ETA (Basque Father- land and Liberty)	General	Trafficking; distribution; money laundering	1980s–
Sri Lanka			
Liberation Tigers of Tamil Eelam	Heroin Cocaine Methamphe- tamines	Trafficking	1980s–
Turkey			
PKK (Kurdistan Workers Party)	Opiates	Taxation of trafficking and money laundering; processing; trafficking;	1980s–
Dev-Sol	Heroin	Trafficking	1970s–1980s
Gray Wolves	Heroin	Trafficking	1970s–1980s
Uzbekistan			
Islamic Movement of Uzbekistan	Opiates	Trafficking	1990s–

a. Widespread allegations have been made but without clear tangible evidence.

b. Trafficking refers to transportation in bulk to wholesale dealers; distribution refers to retail sale to drug users.

forces not only make it hard for belligerent groups to emerge but also inhibit the emergence and spread of a large-scale illicit economy.

Third, at least in the initial stages, belligerent groups rarely have the resources and know-how to set up a large illicit economy. In the case of drugs, they frequently do not have the contacts with criminal trafficking networks that would allow them to sell at least the basic raw materials to the traffickers, let alone the knowledge and precursor agents needed to refine raw materials into medium-stage products, such as coca paste. Although the labor intensiveness of synthetic drug production is very low, the know-how and the access to controlled precursor agents, such as pseudoephedrine for producing methamphetamines, needed to synthesize drugs frequently make it difficult for nascent belligerent groups to establish such economies from scratch. It is much more likely that belligerent groups will acquire the knowledge and contacts necessary to exploit an existing illicit economy before they attempt to set up a new one.

A fourth crucial constraint on belligerents' ability to participate in certain illicit economies is the balance of supply and demand in the market. Traffickers may not be interested in abandoning their traditional producers or protectors for new, inexperienced, untested ones, and there may not be enough demand to allow both new and traditional producers to sell the same commodity. The relative stability of international demand for narcotics for the past twenty years, for example, has resulted in the shifting of production among various countries, depending on their comparative advantage at a particular time, but rarely in large increases in total world production. The cultivation of coca has shifted among Bolivia, Colombia, and Peru at various times, allowing for production to increase in a particular country while it decreases in a competing country. But there has not been unconstrained, simultaneous expansion of production in all three countries, nor has there been the unconstrained entrance of new large-scale producers, such as Venezuela, Ecuador, or Brazil.

Only suppression of production in a particular locale due to bad weather conditions or eradication or a major new expansion of demand for narcotics, such as experienced in the West in the 1960s and 1970s, allows new entrants to penetrate the market while traditional producers continue with their customary scale of operations. For example, production of opiates in the Golden Crescent emerged in the late 1970s as a result of a large increase in demand for opiates in the West and the suppression of production in the Golden Triangle due to drought. Since the late 1990s, there has been worldwide growth in demand for cocaine in Europe and Latin America, which, while a traditional supplier, has become a significant consumer of cocaine as well (U.S. demand, on the other hand, has declined slightly as a result of the leveling off of the number of new cocaine addicts and a slight decline in use by aging long-term addicts). The use of methamphetamines also has increased significantly; consequently, opportunities for expansion of the supply market may well emerge.

The fifth constraint on belligerents' participation in a particular illicit economy is the presence of competing belligerent groups that may crowd out new entrants. Large-scale cultivation of illicit crops may well allow for the participation of several belligerent groups; however, in small-scale illicit economies or in economies strongly dominated by one belligerent group, other belligerent groups may not be able to participate.

Sixth, belligerent groups may also face ideological and religious restraints—both internal and external—on participating in the illicit economy. As the example of Northern Ireland shows, the pressure from the larger community can be much stronger in rich developed countries. In poor countries, even groups that are ideologically opposed to a particular illicit economy may not suppress it in order to avoid alienating the segment of the local population that depends on the illicit economy for economic survival, but that does not necessarily mean that they will choose to actively participate in it and materially profit from it. If the group is assured of income from other sources—other illicit economies, some legal economic activity, or foreign sponsors—and if it has other sources of political capital, it may well forgo participating in a particular form of illicit economy. That outcome is especially likely in countries that have a rich overall economy and non–labor-intensive illicit economies.

Similarly, a belligerent group may have to balance the need to satisfy its internal constituents with the need to please a powerful external sponsor. If the external sponsor for some reason disapproves of the group's participation in the illicit economy and the group is dependent on the external sponsor for financial resources or for a safe haven, the belligerent group may well choose to minimize damage to its ability to persist and expand by refraining from participating in the illicit economy. Although the population's negative response to suppression will dissuade the belligerents from attempting to destroy the illicit economy, they may choose a hands-off approach rather than positive involvement. The threat of international (or U.S.) sanctions based on drug trafficking charges and the opprobrium of the wider international community may also reinforce such inhibitions, especially in the case of groups that are highly motivated to court international opinion.

Methodology of the Study

An obvious difficulty in studying illicit economies in the context of military conflict is the limited availability of data due to the criminal nature of the activities studied, the secrecy of many insurgent and terrorist organizations, and the difficulty of doing systematic fieldwork in countries consumed by civil war and other violence.

The limited availability of good data is an acute problem in even the easiest aspect of the study to research, the size of an illicit economy. In the case of the drug economy, even the most basic step, estimating the size of the area cultivated with illicit crops, yields at best a wild guesstimate, and figures from the UN Office on Drugs and Crime, local governments, and the United States government vary dramatically. Moreover, any estimates based on the estimate of the size of the cultivated area—such as those for the amount of heroin or cocaine produced, the volume of goods trafficked, the efficacy of interdiction, farm gate or street prices of illicit goods, and the size of the belligerents' financial profits from the illicit economy— are even more difficult to make.

The official estimation process works like this: Satellite data are gathered to estimate the area cultivated with illegal crops—say, coca. Alternatively, a research team is sent to a sample area to measure the area cultivated with illicit crops, and the size of the overall cultivated area in the country is extrapolated from that measure. The physical estimation procedure, however, assumes that the sample area is representative of the overall territory, which may or may not be true. Even the satellite method is not foolproof. Satellites rarely cover the entire territory of even major drug-producing countries; moreover, they often fail to penetrate cloud cover or detect the presence of illicit crops under dense forest.[1]

A formula based on already unreliable data about the extent of cultivation is used to derive the number of kilograms of coca leaf harvested, the amount of coca paste produced from that quantity of coca leaf, and finally the amount of cocaine produced from the coca paste. Yet as the U.S. State Department admits, the size of a harvest can hinge upon "small changes in factors such as soil fertility, weather, farming techniques, disease."[2] Furthermore, productivity per plant varies with the plant's age, the number of harvests per year, and the specific variety of coca planted. At least nine different varieties of coca plant exist in Latin America, each with a different alkaloid yield, yet there is no estimate of the amount and distribution of each variety cultivated in the total area.

With each step up the processing ladder, estimates become more complicated and less reliable. Yields after refining, for example, depend on the technique used, the quality of precursor agents, and the skill of the workers and chemists involved. Thus, at each step, new uncertainties are introduced, compounding the soft character of the original input data. Estimates of flows and the effectiveness of interdiction, for example, are based on seizures. Yet, since the knowledge of the size of production is so poor, it is not clear what percentage of total output is actually being captured through interdiction. Instead, because of the inherent difficulty of catching small bulk products over thousands of miles of territory, often it is just assumed that interdiction captures about 10 to 20 percent of illicit flows. How then does one interpret a sudden dramatic jump in the amount of drugs seized? Does it mean that interdiction efforts have suddenly become more effective or that larger quantities of drugs are flowing across borders? The case of synthetic drugs is even more complicated, because production can be estimated only on the basis of seizures and number of labs busted. But again, no one knows what percentage of total output is represented by seizures and labs busted. Once again, this approach introduces the baseline problem.[3] Estimating prices, such as payoffs to traffickers, belligerents, and government officials and even the "easiest component," street prices in consumer countries, is even more of a magical process, based on interviews and undercover work in selected locales. In the highly segmented, highly imperfect markets that drug markets are, prices and payoffs vary greatly over time and even from shipment to shipment.

Estimating softer variables, such as belligerents' political capital faces even greater challenges. Measuring popular support for belligerents in the absence of frequent, reliable polling data is inherently difficult. Yet, both polling data and other systematic measures of popular support are hard to obtain in areas where violence and lawlessness are prevalent and where belligerents, traffickers, and the military repress the local population. Often even common demographic data are missing. This study therefore relies on interviews and qualitative descriptors, based on less than systematic data, of belligerents' popular support, perceived legitimacy, and overall political capital.[4] But insisting that only variables that can be and have been "measured" may be examined in a study of insurgency, terrorism, and the drug trade would eliminate large components of the subject matter and a host of topics with theoretical importance and critical practical significance in policymaking.

Interviews also are difficult to conduct since traffickers and peasant producers tend to be wary of admitting participation in the trade and disclosing information. While government officials may well be willing to give interviews, the information that they give could be significantly biased. Recognizing the inherent limitations of the data produced, I have carried out fieldwork and interviews in five countries analyzed to various degrees in the book: Peru, Colombia, Afghanistan, Burma, and India. (Unfortunately, because of constraints on the length of the book, India could not be brought in as a case study.) In each place, I interviewed producers of illicit commodities, such as *cocaleros* and poppy farmers, traffickers, and belligerents (some captured, some still at large), government officials, representatives of international organizations, and NGO workers. Between 2005 and 2009, spanning weeks to months in each place and sometimes requiring repeated trips to a location, hundreds of interviews overall were conducted in national capitals, local smuggling centers, and remote production regions characterized by lawlessness and violence, such as the Convención-Lares and Ayacucho areas in Peru; southern Afghan provinces of Helmand, Kandahar, Uruzgan, and Zabul; Nariño, Magdalena Medio, and Montes de Maria in Colombia; Shan state in Burma; and the *dacoit* area of Madhya Pradesh and poppy areas of Kashmir in India. That list is not exhaustive. Getting access to some of the locations and being able to interview the actors involved frequently required getting to know a person who knew a person who knew a person who knew a person.

Although the book draws richly on those interviews, the citations are sparse and vague since specific attribution would create great threats to the security of many of the interviewees. Since many interviewees live under conditions of war and lawlessness, the threats to them from belligerents, criminals, law enforcement officials, military forces, and abusive governments are very acute. After my room was broken into and some of my notes stolen in one of the least dangerous places, I no longer kept any written materials with names of the interviewees. Even in the case of government officials and representatives of international organizations, the politically sensitive nature of the issue led me to always cite the interviews without attribution and with only general identification. As a result, I use references to my interviews as little as possible and whenever information existed in the public domain, I preferred to use that as a citation.

Another difficulty is the very high level of *multicollinearity*. The character of a government's response to an illicit economy influences to a large extent whether or not drug traffickers are present. Legalization of the illicit economy may allow governments to eliminate all traffickers. Yet the relationship is not fully determinative, so the factor "the presence of thuggish traffickers" cannot be removed: a black market, with thuggish traffickers, may exist even within a legal economy. Similarly, there is a very strong correlation between the state of the overall economy and the presence of the drug-conflict nexus. There is, for example, not one case in which extensive cultivation of illicit crops coincides with military conflict in the context of an overall rich economy with multiple sources of alternative livelihoods. Finding critical cases in which the variables do not covary is extremely difficult in this domain of inquiry.

The *baseline problem* presents yet another potential impediment to testing the validity of the propositions. Some of the factors that influence the size and scope of the belligerents' benefits have not varied in reality, even if they can vary theoretically. Full legalization of drugs, for example, has not been tried anywhere. The best variation that the study can achieve with respect to that factor is the de facto legalization seen in some countries. Similarly, some combinations of structural and policy conditions do not exist—for example, a large-scale, labor-intensive illicit economy in a rich country in the context of military conflict. Consequently, my analysis can offer only a limited test.

Case Selection

To address potential threats to the validity of the study, it is especially important to examine in detail the relationships between illicit economies and military conflict in particular cases instead of relying on statistical regression. I examined the relationships in detail in three cases: Peru, Colombia, and Afghanistan. Northern Ireland and Burma were treated as smaller supplemental cases to provide additional useful scenarios of those relationships. Turkey, Mexico, and India were brought in as quick illustrations of other important dynamics. In addition to the three major cases, the supplemental cases and illustrations were drawn on intensively for developing the policy recommendations in the book.

The cases were selected not only because of their intrinsic importance in global and national efforts to deal with the often symbiotic relationships between illicit economies and violent conflict but also for maximum analytic variation and weighting of the contextual factors—structural conditions as well as alternative government responses to the illicit economy—on both the material and political components of the belligerents' strength. All too often, studies of the drug trade and other illicit economies neglect to consider cases with such variation.

Peru and Afghanistan are especially illustrative of the impact of change in government policy toward the illicit economy on the strength of belligerents and the course of conflict. In the case of Peru, the government policy toward drug cultivation kept switching back and forth between repressive policies and laissez-faire policies even while other variables influencing government legitimacy and intelligence provision remained constant, thus allowing for isolation of the impact of government policies. Moreover, the repressive policies covered both eradication and interdiction, which were at times adopted in isolation, thus allowing for making fine-tuned distinctions between the impact of each policy. The case of Peru also includes two nongovernment belligerent groups that interacted with both the illicit economy and the drug traffickers, thereby making it a good vehicle for analyzing the relationship between politically motivated belligerents and criminal organizations. Moreover, the types of belligerent involvement with the illicit economy covered the spectrum from negative involvement, to noninvolvement, to positive involvement.

The Afghanistan case is rich with a multiplicity of conflicts and belligerent actors with dramatically different ideologies, goals, and beliefs, including pro-Communist guerrillas, anti-Soviet mujahideen, warlords, the Taliban, and other terrorist groups—all interacting with a variety of illicit economies, including drug trafficking, and adopting a different type of involvement at various times. The case therefore allows for analysis of possible intervening variables, such as ideology, on the ability of groups to derive benefits from the illicit economy. Moreover, the Afghanistan case contains both labor-intensive and non–labor-intensive illicit economies, which generate approximately the same level of financial benefits to belligerents but which are predicted by my theory to generate vastly different levels of political capital for their sponsors.

The official policy toward drugs also varied along several dimensions in Afghanistan. First, in different regions, various ruling elites have adopted different attitudes toward drugs. Second, over time, even in the same regions, such as those controlled by the Taliban, official policy varied from stringent eradication to de facto, if not de jure, legalization, thus allowing for isolation of the impact of various government policies on the different components of the strength of belligerent groups.

The case of Colombia—the most studied case in the existing literature on the impact of illicit economies on military conflict—complements the previous cases in allowing for observation of two values of the amplifying factors with low incidence: a rich overall economy in the context of military conflict and illicit economies—exemplified in this case by the involvement of M-19 insurgents in the drug trade in Bogotá (in other drug-producing regions of Colombia, poverty was prevalent)—and the absence of traffickers. Multiple belligerent groups, covering a broad ideological spectrum, are present in the case of Colombia, and at various times they have eliminated traffickers from different parts of the country under their control. Focusing on the impact of this factor, in addition to the ability of the groups to extract various gains from the illicit economy, allowed me to take a fresh approach to this case, one that differed from those taken so far in other analyses. Moreover, I trace, in detail, the evolution of the conflict and its nexus to the drug economy since the 1960s to date.

Although the case of Colombia does not allow for evaluation of the various government responses to the illicit economy since the policy has been more or less intensive eradication, it allows for evaluating the ability of eradication to bankrupt belligerent groups. Since very intensive large-scale eradication has been applied consistently for several years in Colombia, if it can succeed in bankrupting the belligerents anywhere, it should be in Colombia.

The case of Northern Ireland provides a further opportunity to examine the rare incidence of the interaction of belligerent groups with illicit economies in a rich country. It also allows for further exploration of the effects of less labor-intensive economies on the political capital of belligerents. Finally, Burma provides an opportunity to examine the effects of varying government responses to the illicit economy, including an innovative twist on laissez-faire bordering on de facto, if not de jure, legalization of the drug trade in the country and its effects on the relationships between the population, the belligerents, and the government.

Table C-1 summarizes how the major cases achieve variation with respect to type of belligerents' involvement in the illicit economy and with respect to the four contextual factors that the theory postulates function as amplifiers of the posited relationships.

TABLE C-1. *Belligerent Groups by Type of Involvement in Illicit Economy and Contextual Factors*

Contextual factors		Type of involvement		
		Positive	Negative	No involvement
State of overall economy	Poor	Sendero; MRTA; FARC; ELN; AUC; mujahideen; Taliban; warlords	Sendero; FARC; warlords; Taliban; other terrorist groups	MRTA; muja-hideen MRTA; muja-hideen
	Rich	M-19		
Character of illi-cit economy	Labor-intensive	Sendero; MRTA; FARC; ELN; AUC; mujahideen; Taliban; warlords	Sendero; FARC; Taliban (drugs and logging)	MRTA; ELN; M-19; muja-hideen
	Non-labor-intensive	FARC; ELN; M-19; mujahideen; Taliban; warlords		
Presence of traffickers	Present	Sendero; MRTA; FARC; AUC; ELN; M-19; mujahideen; Taliban; warlords; Northern Alliance	Sendero; FARC; Taliban; other terrorist groups	MRTA; ELN; mujahideen
	Absent	FARC; AUC; Muja-hideen; Taliban; warlords	Warlords	
Government response to illicit economy	Eradication	Sendero; MRTA; FARC; AUC; ELN; Taliban; warlords; Northern Alliance; other terrorist groups	Sendero; FARC; Warlords; Taliban	MRTA; ELN
	Interdiction	SL, MRTA FARC, AUC, ELN warlords, Taliban, other terrorist groups		MRTA; ELN
	Laissez faire	SL Mujahideen, war-lords, Northern Alliance	Taliban	SL (1970s), MRTA Mujahideen
	Licensing/ Legaliza-tion	Taliban	Taliban	

NOTES

CHAPTER ONE

1. I am grateful to Sarah Chayes, an aid worker in Kandahar, for the information on the sting operation in the Kandahar village. To protect local residents, the names of the village and its inhabitants are not used. For further information on the relationship between the population and the Taliban near Kandahar, see Sarah Chayes, *The Punishment of Virtue: Inside Afghanistan after Taliban* (New York: Penguin Press, 2006).

2. See, for example, Rensselaer Lee III, *Smuggling Armageddon* (New York: St. Martin's Griffin, 1998): 47–72, and Phil Williams and Paul Woessner, "Nuclear Material Trafficking: An Interim Assessment," *Transnational Organized Crime* 1, no. 2 (Summer 1995): 206–38.

3. John Ashcroft, U.S. attorney general, "Prepared Remarks," Drug Enforcement Agency/Drug Enforcement Rollout, Washington, March 19, 2002 (www.ciponline.org/colombia/02031903.htm [May 23, 2004]).

4. Organization for Economic Cooperation and Development, Financial Action Task Force on Money Laundering, *Report* (Paris: February 7, 1990). Americans alone are estimated to spend $64 billion on illegal narcotics annually. See Steven W. Casteel, assistant administrator for intelligence, Drug Enforcement Administration, "Narco-Terrorism: International Drug Trafficking and Terrorism—a Dangerous Mix," statement before the Senate Committee on the Judiciary, May 20, 2003 (www.usdoj.gov/dea/pubs/cngrtest/ct052003p.html [August 22, 2005]).

5. U.N. International Drug Control Program, *The Social and Economic Impact of Drug Abuse and Control* (Vienna: UNDCP, 1994): 29; R. T. Naylor, *Wages of Crime: Black Markets, Illegal Finance, and the Underworld Economy* (Cornell University Press, 2002). Some current estimates put the size of the drug trade at $1 trillion. See, for example, Moises Naím, *Illicit: How Smugglers, Traffickers,*

and Copycats Are Hijacking the Global Economy (New York: Doubleday, 2005). However, as I explain in appendix B, all such numbers are at best educated guesses and sometimes are largely intended to capture public attention. To err on the conservative side, I use the lower estimates. Either way, the profits are very large, and the actual size of the revenues from illicit economies does not make any practical difference for the analysis.

6. For government analyses exemplifying the conventional view, see, for example, Rand Beers, assistant secretary for international narcotics and law enforcement affairs, *Narco-Terror: The Worldwide Connection between Drugs and Terrorism: Hearing before the U.S. Senate Judiciary Committee, Subcommittee on Technology, Terrorism, and Government Information,* March 13, 2002 (http://judiciary.senate.gov/hearing.cfm?id=196 [April 10, 2003]), and Robert Charles, "U.S. Policy and Colombia," testimony before the House Committee on Government Reform, June 17, 2004 (http://reform.house.gov/UploadedFiles/State%20-%20Charles%20Testimony.pdf [June 20, 2004]).

7. From a speech to the Organization of American States Permanent Council, Washington, March 25, 2004, cited in International Crisis Group, *War and Drugs in Colombia,* Latin America Report 11, January 27, 2005: 9 (www.crisis group.org/library/documents/latin_america/11_war_and_drugs_in_colombia.pdf [February 10, 2005]).

8. Author's interview with an official of the World Bank, Washington, Summer 2003.

9. Paul Collier and Anke Hoeffler, "Greed and Grievance in Civil Wars," October 21, 2001 (http://econ.worldbank.org/files/12205_greedgrievance_23oct. pdf [April 16, 2003]).

10. U.S. Department of State, *The 2003 International Narcotics Control Strategy Report* (www.state.gov/p/inl/rls/nrcrpt/2003/vol1/html/29828.htm [March 2, 2004]).

11. Rachel Ehrenfeld, *How Terrorism Is Financed and How to Stop It* (Chicago: Bonus Books, 2005). See also Douglas J. Davids, *Narco-terrorism* (Ardsley, N.Y.: Transnational Publishers, 2002); James Adams, *The Financing of Terror* (London: New English Library, 1986); Grant Wardlaw, "Linkages between the Illegal Drugs Traffic and Terrorism," *Conflict Quarterly* 8, no. 3 (Summer 1988): 5–26; and Stefan Leader and David Wiencek, "Drug Money: The Fuel for Global Terrorism," *Jane's Intelligence Review,* February 2000: 49–54. In her account of Peru in the 1980s, Gabriela Tarazona-Sevillano goes beyond these analyses by providing a highly detailed and nuanced view of the relationship between the drug economy and insurgency that describes some of the political benefits that belligerent groups derive from the drug trade. However, she stops short of analyzing their significance for the counterinsurgency effort. Instead, like other analysts of narcoterrorism, she focuses on the pecuniary benefits of the drug trade and advocates treating traffickers and belligerents as a unified entity. Gabriela Tarazona-

Sevillano with John B. Reuter, *Sendero Luminoso and the Threat of Narcoterrorism* (Washington: Center for Strategic and International Studies, 1990).

12. This literature reconceptualizes civil war as a new system for gaining profit and power. It identifies economic motives—greed or loot-seeking—as the principal drivers (or at a minimum, the essential enablers) of civil wars; political grievances are no longer seen as the critical factor. The conclusion, as summarized by Karen Ballentine, is that "peace can be best achieved not by long and arduous efforts to negotiate a political compromise, nor by the even more risky approach of direct intervention, but by implementing technical measures that, in the short term, will reduce both the accessibility and the profitability of lucrative economic resources to combatant groups." See Karen Ballentine, "Beyond Greed and Grievance: Reconsidering the Economic Dynamics of Armed Conflict," in *The Political Economy of Armed Conflict: Beyond Greed and Grievance*, Karen Ballentine and Jake Sherman, eds. (Boulder, Colo.: Lynne Rienner, 2003): 274. See also Collier and Hoeffler, "Greed and Grievance in Civil Wars"; Mats Berdal and David Keen, "Violence and Economic Agendas in Civil Wars: Some Policy Implications," *Millennium: Journal of International Studies* 26, no. 3 (1997): 795–818; Mats Berdal and David Malone, *Greed and Grievance: Economic Agendas in Civil War* (Boulder, Colo.: Lynne Rienner, 2000); David Keen, *The Economic Functions of Violence in Civil Wars*, Adelphi Paper 320 (IISS/Oxford University Press, 1998).

13. For example, Louise Shelley emphasizes the following links between the two phenomena: terrorists engage in criminal activity to support themselves financially; both terrorist and crime groups use network structures that sometimes intersect; both engage in money laundering and corruption; and both operate in areas where the state is weak. See Louise Shelley, "The Nexus of Organized International Criminals and Terrorism," *International Annals of Criminology* 1, no. 2 (2002): 85–93; Rollie Lal, "South Asian Organized Crime and Terrorist Networks," *Orbis* 49, no. 2 (Spring 2005): 293–304; Chris Dishman, "Terrorism, Crime, and Transformation," *Studies in Conflict and Terrorism* 42, no. 1 (2001): 43–58; Tamara Makarenko, "The Crime-Terror Continuum: Tracing the Interplay between Transnational Crime and Terrorism," *Global Crime* 1, no. 1 (2004): 129–45; and Svante Cornell, "Crime without Borders," *Axess Magazine* 6 (2004): 18–21 (www.silkroadstudies.org/pub/0408Axess_EN.htm [January 8, 2005]).

14. Also known as the coercion theory, the cost-benefit analysis of counterinsurgency emerged in the 1970s. Key theorists such as Georges Bonnet and Roger Trinquier sought to exploit an insurgency's vulnerability in its initial phase by focusing on destroying the belligerents' physical resources. See Georges Bonnet, *Les guerres insurrectionnelles et revolutionnaires* [Insurgencies and Revolutions] (Paris: Payot, 1958), and Roger Trinquier, *Modern Warfare* (London: Pall Mall Press, 1964). Similarly, Charles Wolf argued that popular support was not essential for insurgents in developing countries; rather, what mattered was the acquisition of

material supplies by the insurgents from the population: "From an operation point of view, what an insurgent movement requires for successful and expanding operations is not popular support, in the sense of attitudes of identification and allegiance, but rather a supply of certain inputs . . . at a reasonable cost, interpreting cost to include expenditure of coercion as well as money." See Charles Wolf Jr., *Insurgency and Counterinsurgency: New Myths and Old Realities*, Document No. P-3132-1 (Santa Monica, Calif.: Rand, 1965): 5.

15. For works that focus on the failure of the war on drugs in consuming nations, see Peter Reuter, "The Limits of Drug Control," *Foreign Service Journal* 79, no. 1 (January 2002): 18–23; Robert MacCoun and Peter Reuter, *Drug War Heresies* (Cambridge University Press, 2001); Eva Bertram and others, *Drug War Politics: The Price of Denial* (University of California Press, 1996); Ethan Nadelmann, "Drug Prohibition in the United States: Costs, Consequences, and Alternatives," *Science* 245 (September 1989): 939–47; Ethan Nadelmann, "Commonsense Drug Policy," *Foreign Affairs* 77, no. 1 (January–February 1998): 111–26; Ted Galen Carpenter, *Bad Neighbor Policy* (New York: Palgrave Macmillan, 2003); and C. Peter Rydell and Susan S. Everingham, *Controlling Cocaine: Supply versus Demand Programs* (Santa Monica, Calif.: Rand, 1994). For analyses of its effect on producing countries see Rensselaer W. Lee III, *The White Labyrinth: Cocaine and Political Power* (New Brunswick, N.J.: Transaction Publishers, 1989); Cynthia McClintock, "The War on Drugs: The Peruvian Case," *Journal of Interamerican Studies and World Affairs* 30, nos. 2 and 3 (Summer/Fall 1988): 127–42; Richard Clutterbuck, *Drugs, Crime, and Corruption* (New York University Press, 1995); Edgardo Buscaglia and William Ratliff, *War and Lack of Governance in Colombia: Narcos, Guerrillas, and U.S. Policy* (Stanford: Hoover Institution on War, Revolution, and Peace, 2001); Francisco Gutiérrez Sanín, "Criminal Rebels? A Discussion of Civil War and Criminality from the Colombian Experience," *Politics and Society* 32, no. 2 (June 2004): 257–85; and Coletta A. Youngers and Eileen Rosin, *Drugs and Democracy in Latin America* (Boulder, Colo.: Lynne Rienner, 2005).

16. Hearts-and-minds theorists recommend that the government prevent insurgents from winning the legitimacy game by supplying the population with basic goods and services, improving standards of living, and reducing government abuse, brutality, and corruption. See, for example, Robert Thompson, *Defeating Communist Insurgency* (London: Chatto and Windus, 1966); Robert Thompson, *Revolutionary War in World Strategy, 1945–1969* (London: Secker & Warburg, 1970); Frank Kitson, *Low-Intensity Operations* (London: Faber and Faber, 1971); John S. Pustay, *Counterinsurgency Warfare* (New York: Free Press, 1965); David Galula, *Counterinsurgency Warfare: Theory and Practice* (New York: Praeger, 1964); John J. McCuen, *The Art of Revolutionary Warfare* (London: Faber and Faber, 1966). For recent work in this vein, see John Nagl, *Learning to Eat Soup with a Knife: Counterinsurgency Lessons from Malaya and Vietnam* (University

of Chicago Press, 2005), and David Kilcullen, *The Accidental Guerrilla: Fighting Small Wars in the Midst of a Big One* (Oxford University Press, 2009).

17. See James C. Scott, *The Moral Economy of the Peasant* (Yale University Press, 1976); Eric Wolf, *Peasant Wars of the Twentieth Century* (New York: Harper and Row, 1969); Mancur Olson, *The Logic of Collective Action: Public Goods and the Theory of Groups* (Harvard University Press, 1965); Samuel L. Popkin, *The Rational Peasant: The Political Economy of Rural Society in Vietnam* (University of California Press, 1979); Mark Lichbach, "What Makes Rational Peasants Revolutionary? Dilemma, Paradox, and Irony in Peasant Collective Action," *World Politics* 46, no. 2 (April 1994): 383–418; Theda Skocpol, "What Makes Peasants Revolutionary?" *Comparative Politics* 14, no. 3 (April 1982): 351–75; Timothy Wickham-Crowley, *Exploring Revolution: Essays on Latin American Insurgency and Revolutionary Theory* (Armonk, N.Y.: M.E. Sharpe, 1991); and T. David Mason and Dale A. Krane, "The Political Economy of Death Squads: Toward a Theory of the Impact of State-Sanctioned Terror," *International Studies Quarterly* 33, no. 2 (1989): 175–98.

18. Conor Cruise O'Brien, "Terrorism under Democratic Conditions," in *Terrorism, Legitimacy, and Power: The Consequences of Political Violence*, Martha Crenshaw, ed. (Wesleyan University Press, 1983): 91–104.

19. Richard E. Rubenstein, "The Noncauses of Modern Terrorism," in *International Terrorism: Characteristics, Causes, and Controls*, Charles W. Kegley Jr., ed. (New York: St. Martin's, 1990): 130.

20. Mónica Serrano and María Celia Toro, "From Drug Trafficking to Transnational Organized Crime in Latin America," in *Transnational Organized Crime and International Security: Business as Usual?* Mats Berdal and Mónica Serrano, eds. (Boulder, Colo.: Lynne Rienner, 2002): 141–54, and Mauricio Rubio, "Violence, Organized Crime, and the Criminal Justice System in Colombia," *Journal of Economic Issues* 32, no. 2 (1998): 605–10. It needs to be noted, however, that efforts to suppress the production of illicit drugs sometimes also lead to an increase in government human rights abuses. See, for example, Youngers and Rosin, *Drugs and Democracy in Latin America*.

21. For details on the economic effects of illicit economies, see, for example, Francisco E. Thoumi, *Illegal Drugs, Economy, and Society in the Andes* (John Hopkins University Press, 2004); Pranab Bardhan, "Corruption and Development: A Review of the Issues," *Journal of Economic Literature* 35, no. 3 (1997): 1320–65; Peter Reuter, "The Mismeasurement of Illegal Drug Markets: The Implications of Its Irrelevance," in *Exploring the Underground Economy*, Susan Pozo, ed. (Kalamazoo, Mich.: W.E. Upjohn Institute, 1996): 63–80; and Mauricio Reina, "Drug Trafficking and the National Economy," in *Violence in Colombia 1990–2000: Waging War and Negotiating Peace*, Charles Berquist, Ricardo Peñaranda, and Gonzalo Sánchez G., eds. (Wilmington, Del.: Scholarly Resources, 2001).

22. To protect the village, I do not give its name.

CHAPTER TWO

1. The words "positive" and "negative" are not meant to imply any moral judgment about the appropriateness of the behavior.

2. Cynthia McClintock, *Revolutionary Movements in Latin America: El Salvador's FMLN and Peru's Shining Path* (Washington: U.S. Institute of Peace Press, 1998): 73.

3. Level of popular support correlates with expectations of who will win a conflict and so be able to punish or reward previous cooperation or refusal to cooperate. See, for example, Stathis Kalyvas, *The Logic of Violence in Civil War* (Cambridge University Press, 2006); Robert Thompson, *Defeating Communist Insurgency* (London: Chatto and Windus, 1966); Nathan Leites and Charles Wolf Jr., *Rebellion and Authority: An Analytical Essay on Insurgent Conflicts* (Chicago: Markham Publishing, 1970); Orrin DeForest and David Chanoff, *The Rise and Bitter Fall of American Intelligence in Vietnam* (New York: Simon and Schuster, 1990); and Robert W. Komer, "The Malayan Emergency in Retrospect: Organization of a Successful Counterinsurgency Effort," Report R-957-ARPA (Stanford, Calif.: Rand, February 1972) (www.rand.org/pubs/reports/2005/R957.pdf).

4. The literature on organized crime typically assumes that criminal organizations serve one or more of the following functions: economic (by generating material profits); social (by establishing contacts and promoting social solidarity); and quasi-governmental (by regulating the economic activity not only of their members but also of other illegal economic competitors within their sphere of influence by establishing and enforcing rules of conduct). See Klaus von Lampe, "Criminally Exploitable Ties: A Network Approach to Organized Crime," in *Transnational Organized Crime: Myth, Power, and Profit,* Emilio C. Viano, Jose Magallanes, and Laurent Bridel, eds. (Durham: Carolina Academic Press, 2003); and Annelise Graebner Anderson, *The Business of Organized Crime: A Cosa Nostra Family* (Stanford, Calif.: Hoover Institution Press, 1979). However, like politically motivated belligerent actors, criminal organizations can also regulate the organization of the larger society by establishing rules and enforcing them whether they are related to an illicit or a licit economy.

5. Diego Gambetta, *The Sicilian Mafia: The Business of Private Protection* (Harvard University Press, 1993).

6. Ibid.: 17. See also Herschel I. Grossman, "Rival Kleptocrats: The Mafia versus the State," in *The Economics of Organized Crime,* Gianluca Fiorentini and Sam Peltzman, eds. (Cambridge University Press, 1995): 144, 155; Diego Gambetta and Peter Reuter, "Conspiracy among the Many: The Mafia in Legitimate Industries," in *The Economics of Organized Crime,* Fiorentini and Peltzman, eds.: 116–42.

7. Fiorentini and Peltzman, *The Economics of Organized Crime*: 1–30.

8. My work on the relationship between belligerents and criminals draws on the work of Phil Williams on strategic alliances of transitional criminal organizations,

in which he explains why such strategic alliances often are rather fragile. See Phil Williams, "Transnational Criminal Organizations: Strategic Alliances," *Washington Quarterly* 18, no. 1 (Winter 1994): 57–72. For an excellent discussion of the problems of cooperation in cartels, see Debora Spar, *The Cooperative Edge: The Internal Politics of International Cartels* (Cornell University Press, 1994).

9. The concept of alternative livelihoods evolved out of the policy of crop substitution, which encouraged farmers to grow licit crops, such as coffee and onions, instead of coca or opium poppies. The failure of crop substitution gave rise to the concept of alternative development. Alternative development was meant to encompass comprehensive rural development that addressed the larger structural factors that led farmers to choose illicit crops over licit ones, such as inadequate infrastructure, lack of established markets, instability of prices, and lack of access to credit. In practice, many alternative development efforts were limited in scope. Thailand offers a rare example of the success of alternative development projects in eliminating the cultivation of illicit crops at a countrywide level and improving the lives of the rural population.

Disappointment with alternative development led to formulation of a new concept: alternative livelihoods. In theory, the concept of alternative livelihoods refers to a wider state-building and development agenda that addresses the real drivers of illicit crop production. It becomes an integral part of a country's overall development policies, measuring success not only in the numbers of hectares of illicit crops eliminated but also in terms of overall development and improvement in the lives of the rural population. It remains to be seen whether this concept will be translated into actual policies or whether it will devolve essentially back to crop substitution combined with some limited investment in infrastructure and microfinance. David Mansfield and Adam Pain, "Alternative Livelihood: Substance or Slogan?" AREU Briefing Paper (Kabul: Afghanistan Research and Evaluation Unit, October 2005).

10. A lively academic debate exists about the elasticity of demand for illicit commodities. If demand for an illicit commodity is sufficiently elastic, liberalization of the regulatory regime will result in increases in consumption. On the other hand, if demand is inelastic, liberalization will not be associated with increases in consumption. Relatively few empirical studies make use of reliable, systematic data for illicit commodities, since, due to their illicitness, such data are not easily available. Nonetheless, the existing data suggest that demand for gambling and betting appears to be rather elastic. As far as demand for drugs is concerned, estimating demand elasticity is considerably more complicated because of the varying degrees of physical dependence associated with different drugs and with different individuals' physiological responses. While the physical dependence of old users may well result in very inelastic demand, that may not be the case for new users. Moreover, many users appear to use a variety of drugs and therefore could be responsive to changes in price for a particular drug. Therefore, while the demand for drugs may be quite inelastic if the demand market is dominated primarily by heavy long-time

users, the demand for a specific drug may still be rather elastic. See, for example, Peter Reuter, *Disorganized Crime: The Economics of the Visible Hand* (MIT Press, 1983); Fiorentini and Peltzman, *The Economics of Organized Crime*; Richard Lawrence Miller, *The Case for Legalizing Drugs* (New York: Praeger, 1991). Accordingly, economists who have explored the possibility of decriminalization or legalization suggest a price discrimination regime for users, with drugs being sold very cheaply to long-time registered users and at very high prices to new users. For a seminal analysis, see Mark H. Moore, "Policies to Achieve Discrimination on the Effective Price of Heroin," *American Economic Review* 63, no. 2 (1973): 270–77.

Until recently, most drug control economists believed that overall demand was in fact rather inelastic. New analyses, however, suggest that the price of drugs does matter. Demand for hard drugs, such as cocaine and heroin, is now considered to be somewhat elastic with respect to price, so that a 1.0 percent increase in price should reduce consumption somewhere between 0.2 to 1.0 percent. See Mark A. R. Klein, "Controlling Drug Use and Crime with Testing, Sanctions, and Treatment," in *Drug Addiction and Drug Policy: The Struggle to Control Addiction*, Philip B. Heymann and William N. Brownsberger, eds. (Harvard University Press, 2001): 168–92; Henry Saffer and Frank Chaloupka, "The Demand for Illicit Drugs," *Economic Inquiry* 37, no. 1 (1999): 401–11; and Dhaval M. Dave, "Illicit Drug Use among Arrestees and Drug Prices," National Bureau of Economic Research (2004) (www.nber.org/papers/w10648.pdf [March 19, 2004]). Jonathan Caulkins and Peter Reuter argue that prices for drugs are extremely variable over time and space and that while high prices deter use, they have ambiguous effects on drug-related crime. See Jonathan P. Caulkins and Peter Reuter, "What Price Data Tell Us about Drug Markets," *Journal of Drug Issues* 28, no. 3 (Summer 1998): 593–613. Regardless of the theoretical debate about the overall elasticity of demand for drugs, practical experience suggests that a temporary suppression of production in a particular region will at least in the short term—for up to several years—result in an increase in farm gate and downstream prices. But the time lag before the effect of suppression is felt in retail prices may in fact be substantial. At least so far, production has always managed to recover before any suppression resulted in a substantial and lasting increase in retail prices. In fact, retail prices had been falling steadily since the early 1980s until a small increase in U.S. street prices was registered in 2007.

11. Peter Reuter, "The Limits of Drug Control," *Foreign Service Journal* 79, no. 1 (January 2002): 18–23.

12. Office of National Drug Control Policy, *Supplement to the 2009 National Drug Control Strategy* (www.whitehousedrugpolicy.gov/publications/policy/ndcs09/ndcs09_data_supl/ds_drg_rltd_tbls.pdf [May 1, 2009]).

13. See, for example, Peter Reuter and Edwin M. Truman, *Chasing Dirty Money* (Washington: Peterson Institute for International Economics, 2004); Robert E. Powis, *The Money Launderers* (Chicago: Probus, 1992); and Stephen E. Flynn, "The Global Drug Trade versus the Nation-State: Why the Thugs Are

Winning," in *Beyond Sovereignty: Issues for A Global Agenda,* Maryann Cusimano Love, ed. (Toronto: Wadsworth, 2003): 167–94.

14. The term "decriminalization" is usually applied to reducing or altogether removing the sanctions against the use of drugs while maintaining sanctions against trafficking and marketing.

15. Among the major legal producers of medical opiates for export are Turkey, India, Australia, France, and Spain.

16. See, for example, Greg Campbell, *Blood Diamonds* (Boulder, Colo.: Westview Press, 2002); Douglas Farah, *Blood from Stones* (New York: Broadway, 2004); Jeffrey S. Morton, "The Legal Regulation of Conflict Diamonds," *Politics and Policy* 33, no. 3 (September 2005): 389–414; E. Ablorh-Odjidja, "Conflict Diamonds: The Kimberley Process for Corruption," *New African* (August-September 2003): 40–41; and Ana M. Perez-Katz, "The Role of Conflict Diamonds in Fueling Wars in Africa: the Case of Sierra Leone," *International Affairs Review* 11, no. 1 (Winter-Spring 2002): 60–75.

17. In the drug certification process, enacted by Congress in 1986, the State Department conducts an annual review of the efforts of the world's major drug-producing and drug-transit countries to comply with international counternarcotics regulations and U.S. counternarcotics efforts and the president determines whether compliance is taking place. The law gives the president three choices: to certify fully, to deny certification, or to grant a waiver on the basis of "vital national interests." If certification is denied, the decertified country automatically faces economic sanctions, such as the withholding of at least half of most U.S. government assistance. The process is frequently criticized as both lacking objectivity and being driven by other political considerations as well as limiting the effectiveness of a variety of U.S. policies. See, for example, Bill Spencer with Gina Amatangelo, "Drug Certification," *Foreign Policy in Focus* 6, no. 5 (February 2001) (www.irc-online.org/fpif/briefs/vol6/v6n05drugs.html [April 24, 2005]). Proponents of the certification process, however, argue that it is a key factor in reducing global drug production. Former secretary of state Madeleine Albright, for example, commented that while the certification law "certainly can be refined, it has produced amazing results in the fight against illegal narcotics." See Eric Green, "Drug Control" (www.usembassy.org.uk/drugs33.html [April 24, 2005]).

18. Frequently, even when the government carries out eradication, corrupt elements within the government may nonetheless participate in the drug trade.

CHAPTER THREE

1. The area devoted to coca cultivation peaked at 130,000 hectares in 1992.

2. Patrick L. Clawson and Rensselaer W. Lee III, *The Andean Cocaine Industry* (New York: St. Martin's, 1996): 161.

3. David Scott Palmer, "Peru's Persistent Problems," *Current History* 89, no. 543 (January 1990): 6–7.

210 / Notes to Pages 36–38

4. Douglas J. Davids, *Narco-terrorism* (Ardsley, N.Y.: Transnational Publishers, 2002): 23.

5. David Scott Palmer, *Shining Path of Peru* (New York: St. Martin's, 1994), and Gustavo Gorriti, *The Shining Path: A History of the Millenarian War in Peru,* Robin Kirk, trans. (University of North Carolina Press, 1999).

6. Carlos Iván Degregori, *Sendero Luminoso: lucha armada y utopia autoritaria* [Shining Path: Armed Struggle and Authoritarian Utopia] (Lima: Instituto de Estudios Peruanos, 1986).

7. Richard Clutterbuck, *Drugs, Crime, and Corruption* (New York University Press, 1995).

8. Gordon H. McCormick, *From the Sierra to the Cities: The Urban Campaign of the Shining Path* (Santa Monica, Calif.: Rand, 1992): 22.

9. Clutterbuck, *Drugs, Crime and Corruption*: 19.

10. Cynthia McClintock, "Peru's Sendero Luminoso Rebellion: Origins and Trajectory," in *Power and Popular Protest,* Susan Eckstein, ed. (University of California Press, 2001): 78–79.

11. Otto Guibovich, *Shining Path: Birth, Life, and Death* (Camberley, England: Staff College, 1993): 18.

12. Enrique Obando, "Subversion and Anti-Subversion in Peru 1980–82," *Low-Intensity Conflict and Law Enforcement* 2, no. 2 (Autumn 1993): 323. See also LaMond Tullis, *Unintended Consequences: Illegal Drugs and Drug Policies in Nine Countries* (Boulder, Colo.: Lynne Rienner, 1995): 96.

13. "Los Intis de la Coca [Coca Intis]," *Perú Económico,* September 1987. "Coca Intis" refers to a type of currency.

14. Gabriela Tarazona-Sevillano, with John B. Reuter, *Sendero Luminoso and the Threat of Narcoterrorism* (Washington: Center for Strategic and International Studies, 1990): 113. Tarazona-Sevillano suggests that local traffickers earned perhaps as much as $7.5 billion annually, but that number would put in-Peru drug trade earnings close to 43 percent of GDP in 1985, when Peru's GDP was 17.2 billion, and 29 percent in 1986, when it was 25.8 billion (www.indexmundi.com/peru/gdp_(official_exchange_rate).html). While possible, those numbers considerably exceed the average estimates of Peru's cocaine business in the 1980s. Once again, they reveal the extraordinary difficulties in assessing drug revenues. Clearly, however, far greater profits, perhaps 80 percent or more, accrued to traffickers outside the border and to consumer country distributors.

15. Tarazona-Sevillano, *Sendero Luminoso and the Threat of Narcoterrorism*: 116.

16. "U.S. AID Project Wins Few Friends and Fails to Match the Drug Industry's Complete Package," *Andean Report* (December 1985): 244.

17. David Whynes, "Illicit Drugs Policy in Asia and Latin America," *Development and Change* 22 (1991): 475–96.

18. Rensselaer W. Lee III, *The White Labyrinth: Cocaine and Political Power* (New Brunswick, N.J.: Transaction Publishers, 1989): 46. For a comparison with

Bolivia, see Kevin Healy, "The Boom within the Crisis: Some Recent Effects of Foreign Cocaine Markets on Bolivia's Rural Society and Economy," in *Coca and Cocaine: Effects on People and Policy in Latin America,* Deborah Pacini and Christine Franquemont, eds., Cultural Survival Report Series 23 (1986): 101–45.

19. Raúl González, "Coca y subversión en el Huallaga [Coca and Subversion in Huallaga]," *Quehacer* 48 (September–October 1987): 58–72.

20. David Scott Palmer, "Peru, the Drug Business, and Shining Path: Between Scylla and Charybdis?" *Journal of Interamerican Studies and World Affairs* 34, no. 3 (Autumn 1992): 68.

21. Edmundo Morales, *New Trends in Coca and Cocaine Economy in the Andes of Peru* (New York: Narcotics and Drug Research, 1985): 7–14.

22. Edmundo Morales, *Cocaine: White Gold Rush in Peru* (University of Arizona Press, 1989).

23. Lester Grinspoon and James B. Bakalar, *Cocaine: A Drug and Its Social Evolution* (New York: Basic Books, 1985): 12.

24. Lee, *The White Labyrinth*: 60.

25. Tarazona-Sevillano, *Sendero Luminoso and the Threat of Narcoterrorism*: 109.

26. Cynthia McClintock, "The War on Drugs: The Peruvian Case," *Journal of Interamerican Studies and World Affairs* 30, no. 2-3 (Summer–Autumn 1988): 133.

27. Cynthia McClintock and Fabian Vallas, *The United States and Peru: Cooperation at a Cost* (New York: Routledge, 2003): 113.

28. Author's interview with a prominent Peruvian journalist, Lima, Peru, summer 2005.

29. Author's interviews with academics and *cocaleros* in Ayacucho, Peru, summer 2005.

30. Clyde B. Taylor, "International Insurgency and Drug Trafficking: Present Trends in Terrorist Activity," Joint Hearings before the Committee on Foreign Relations and the Committee on the Judiciary, U.S. Senate, May 1985 (Government Printing Office, 1986): 133.

31. Lee, *The White Labyrinth*: 62–64 and 86.

32. Jo Ann Kawell, "The Cocaine Economy," in *The Peru Reader: History, Culture, Politics,* Orin Starn, Carlos Iván Degregori, and Robin Kirk, eds. (Duke University Press, 1995): 408–09.

33. U.S. Department of State, *International Narcotics Control Strategy Report* (Washington, 1988): 78, 92, 109.

34. "Los Intis de la Coca."

35. Clutterbuck, *Drugs, Crime, and Corruption*: 46.

36. Enrique Obando, "El Narcotráfico en el Perú: Una Aproximación Histórica [Narcotics Trafficking in Peru: A Historical Estimate]," *Análisis Internacional* 2 (1993): 85.

37. González, "Coca y subversión en el Huallaga,": 70; Tarazona-Sevillano, *Sendero Luminoso and the Threat of Narcoterrorism*: 121.

38. Cynthia McClintock, *Revolutionary Movements in Latin America: El Salvador's FMLN and Peru's Shining Path* (Washington: U.S. Institute of Peace Press, 1998): 163.

39. Palmer, "Peru, the Drug Business, and Shining Path: Between Scylla and Charybdis?": 66. See also Hernando de Soto, *The Other Path* (London: Taurus, 1989).

40. In McCormick, *From the Sierra to the Cities,* the estimate is $20 to $30 million (p. 22). José Gonzales estimates an income of $20 to $100 million. See José E. Gonzales, "Peru: Sendero Luminoso en el Valle de la Coca [Peru: Sendero Luminoso in the Valley of Coca]," in *Coca, cocaine, y narcotrafico: Laberinto en los Andes* [Coca, Cocaine, and Narcotics Trafficking: Labyrinth in the Andes], Diego García Sayan, ed. (Lima: Comision Andina de Jurista, 1989): 217. The $550 million figure was an estimate by a Peruvian admiral, based on his knowledge of the airstrip fees in the Upper Huallaga Valley, in his testimony to the Peruvian congress. See *Latin American Weekly Report,* January 24, 1991: 1.

41. McClintock, *Revolutionary Movements in Latin America*: 73, and Tom Marks, "Making Revolution with Shining Path," in *Shining Path of Peru,* Palmer, ed.: 218.

42. McClintock, *Revolutionary Movements in Latin America*: 292.

43. Ibid.

44. Cynthia McClintock, "The Evolution of Internal War in Peru: The Conjunction of Need, Creed, and Organizational Finance," in *Rethinking the Economics of War: The Intersection of Need, Creed, and Greed,* Cynthia J. Arnson and I. William Zartman, eds. (Washington: Woodrow Wilson Center Press, 2005): 63.

45. Palmer, "Peru, the Drug Business, and Shining Path: Between Scylla and Charybdis?": 70.

46. Lee, *The White Labyrinth*: 175–76.

47. Palmer, "Peru, the Drug Business and Shining Path: Between Scylla and Charybdis?": 77. See also Gabriela Tarazona-Sevillano, "The Organization of Shining Path," in *Shining Path of Peru,* Palmer, ed.: 203.

48. A top Peruvian military official quoted in Marks, "Making Revolution with Shining Path": 218.

49. Author's interviews with former Peruvian defense and intelligence officials, Peru, summer 2005. See McCormick, *From the Sierra to the Cities*: 20–32.

50. David Scott Palmer, "National Security," in *Peru: A Country Study,* Rex A. Hudson, ed., Area Handbook Series, 4th ed. (Washington: Federal Research Division, Library of Congress, 1993): 289–92.

51. McCormick, *From the Sierra to the Cities*: 38.

52. Elena Alvarez, "Illegal Export-Led Growth in the Andes: A Preliminary Economic and Socio-Political Assessment for Peru," draft of January 25, 1993, quoted in Tullis, *Unintended Consequences: Illegal Drugs and Drug Policies in Nine Countries*: 98.

53. Lawrence Jay Speer, "Legal, Illegal firms Share Peru Jungle," *Washington Times,* July 13, 1993.

54. McClintock, "The Evolution of Internal War in Peru: The Conjunction of Need, Creed, and Organizational Finance": 65.

55. Félix Cóndor quoted in Simon Strong, *Shining Path: Terror and Revolution in Peru* (New York: Times Books, 1992): 263.

56. Alan Riding, "Rebels Disrupting Coca Eradication in Peru," *New York Times,* January 26, 1989.

57. Proclamation of the Sendero Luminoso, quoted in Gustavo Gorriti, "Shining Path's Stalin and Trotsky," in *Shining Path of Peru,* Palmer, ed.: 186.

58. Sandra Woy-Hazleton and William A. Hazleton, "Shining Path and the Marxist Left," in *Shining Path of Peru,* Palmer, ed.: 233. See interview with Luis Arce Borja, "There Is No Other Way," by Anita Fokkema, in "Fatal Attraction: Peru's Shining Path," *NACLA Report on Americas* (December-January 1990–91): 25.

59. Reproduced in Lee, *The White Labyrinth*: 85.

60. Waltrud Queiser Morales, "The War on Drugs: A New U.S. National Security Doctrine?" *Third World Quarterly* 11, no. 3 (July 1989): 147–69.

61. González, "Coca y subversión en el Huallaga": 67.

62. Interview reproduced by Tarazona-Sevillano, *Sendero Luminoso and the Threat of Narcoterrorism*: 124.

63. Richard Craig, "Illicit Drug Traffic: Implications for South American Source Countries," *Journal of Interamerican Studies and World Affairs* 29, no. 2 (Summer 1987): 21.

64. Tullis, *Unintended Consequences: Illegal Drugs and Drug Policies in Nine Countries*: 22.

65. Cyrus Ernesto Zikarzadeh, *Social Movements in Politics: A Comparative Study* (New York: Longman, 1997): 213, and Merrill Collett, "Maoist Guerrilla Band Complicated Anti-Drug War in Peru," *Washington Post,* June 4, 1988.

66. José E. Gonzales, "Guerrillas and Coca in the Upper Huallaga Valley," in *Shining Path of Peru,* Palmer, ed.: 129.

67. David Scott Palmer, "The Revolutionary Terrorism of Peru's Shining Path," in *Terrorism in Context,* Martha Crenshaw, ed. (Pennsylvania State University Press, 1995): 270.

68. Created in late 1983, the MRTA, headed by Víctor Polay Campos, rejected Maoism and exhibited a pro-Cuba, pro-Soviet orientation. It criticized Sendero as both ideologically misguided and excessively brutal and liked to present itself as kinder and gentler than Sendero. Approximately 1,000 militants strong at its peak, the MRTA was responsible for about 10 percent of all political attacks and about 5 percent of all deaths from violence (McClintock and Vallas, *The United States and Peru: Cooperation at a Cost*: 69).

69. McClintock, *Revolutionary Movements in Latin America*: 138

70. González, "Coca y subversión en el Huallaga": 69.

71. Peter Andreas, "The U.S. War on Drugs in Peru," *The Nation,* August 13–20, 1988.

72. Tarazona-Sevillano, *Sendero Luminoso and the Threat of Narcoterrorism*: 117.

73. Lee, *The White Labyrinth*: 164.

74. See, for example, Billie Jean Isbell, "Shining Path and Peasant Responses in Rural Ayacucho," in *Shining Path of Peru,* Palmer, ed.: 79–86.

75. Carlos Iván Degregori, "Harvesting Storms: Peasant *Rondas* and the Defeat of Sendero Luminoso in Ayacucho," in *Shining and Other Paths: War and Society in Peru, 1980–1995,* Steve J. Stern, ed. (Durham: Duke University Press, 1998): 137.

76. McClintock, *Revolutionary Movements in Latin America*: 69.

77. William Montalbano, "Coca Valley: Peru Jungle Surrealism," *Los Angeles Times,* December 2, 1985.

78. Gonzales, "Guerrillas and Coca in the Upper Huallaga Valley": 125. Clutterbuck, *Drugs, Crime, and Corruption*: 45–46.

79. See Lee, *The White Labyrinth*: 89.

80. McClintock and Vallas, *The United States and Peru: Cooperation at a Cost*: 115.

81. "Counterinsurgency and Anti-Narcotics Measures Become Intertwined in Upper Huallaga," *Andean Report* 14, no. 6 (June 1987): 102–06.

82. Gonzales, "Guerrillas and Coca in the Upper Huallaga Valley": 125.

83. McClintock and Vallas, *The United States and Peru: Cooperation at a Cost*: 115.

84. Tarazona-Sevillano, *Sendero Luminoso and the Threat of Narcoterrorism*: 129.

85. For details, see McClintock, "The War on Drugs: The Peruvian Case": 133–34.

86. Quoted in James F. Rochlin, *Vanguard Revolutionaries in Latin America* (Boulder, Colo.: Lynne Rienner, 2003): 62.

87. Gonzales, "Guerrillas and Coca in the Upper Huallaga Valley": 130.

88. Author's interviews with academics and journalists in Lima, Peru, summer 2005; McClintock, *Revolutionary Movements in Latin America*: 66. See also Carlos Tapia, *Del "Equilibrio Estrategico" a la derrota de Sendero Luminoso* [From "Strategic Equilibrium" to the Defeat of Sendero Luminoso] (Lima: Instituto de Estudios Peruanos, 1996).

89. McClintock, *Revolutionary Movements in Latin America*: 92.

90. Enrique Obando, "La subversión: Situación interna y consecuencias internacionales [Subversion: Internal Situation and International Consequences]," *Analísis Internacional* 1 (January–March 1993): 45–62.

91. Carlos Iván Degregori, "After the Fall of Abimael Guzmán: The Limits of Sendero Luminoso," in *The Peruvian Labyrinth: Polity, Society, and Economy,*

Maxwell A. Cameron and Philip Mauceri, eds. (Pennsylvania State University Press, 1997): 179–91.

92. Quoted by Raúl González, "Las armas de un general [A General's Weapons]," *Quehacer* 62, December 1989–January 1990: 38–43. Even under Arciniega's rule, however, there were allegations that the army still carried out human rights abuses and harassed the farmers and that the number of disappearances increased.

93. Gonzales, "Guerrillas and Coca in the Upper Huallaga Valley": 134–36.

94. Mark R. Day, "Peru Balks at U.S. Military-Aid Offer," *Christian Science Monitor,* May 3, 1990. Many U.S. analysts had a similar reaction. One U.S. analyst, for example, commented that the U.S. request that Peru wage an all-out war against drugs is like "asking a country that's fighting the Civil War and going through the Great Depression to take on Prohibition as well." Quoted in Peter Andreas, "Peru's Addiction to Coca Dollars," *The Nation,* April 16, 1990: 515.

95. David Scott Palmer, "'Terror in the Name of Mao': Revolution and Response in Peru," in *Democracy and Counterterrorism: Lessons from the Past,* Robert J. Art and Louise Richardson, eds. (Washington: U.S. Institute of Peace Press, 2006): 195–220.

96. Orin Starn, "Villagers at Arms: War and Counterrevolution in the Central-South Andes," in *Shining and Other Paths,* Stern, ed.: 245.

97. Author's interview with a former Ministry of Defense official, Lima, Peru, summer 2005.

98. For details, see James Jones, "La Experiencia del PNUFID [PNUFID's Experience]," in *Desarrollo Alternativo y Desallorro Rural: Debate sobre sus Límites y Posibilidades* [Alternative Development and Rural Development: The Debate on Their Limits and Possibilities], Hugo Cabienses and Eduardo Musso, eds. (Lima: Centro Regional Andino and IICA, 1999).

99. Melvyn Levitsky, "Testimony of the Director of the Bureau of International Narcotics Matters, U.S. Department of State," Hearings before the U.S. Senate, Committee on Governmental Affairs, Permanent Subcommittee on Investigation, September 26–29, 1989, 101 Cong., 1st sess.

100. Fujimori also denied Arciniega military protection, a move that de facto invited the Shining Path to assassinate the general, and Arciniega was forced to leave Peru for exile abroad. Author's interview with a prominent Peruvian journalist who covered the war, Lima, summer 2005. See, for example, Washington Office on Latin America (WOLA), "Drug War Paradoxes: The U.S. Government and Peru's Vladimiro Montesinos," *Drug War Monitor,* July 2004: 6; and Isaías Rojas, "Peru: Drug Control Policy, Human Rights, and Democracy," in *Drugs and Democracy in Latin America: The Impact of U.S. Policy,* Coletta A. Youngers and Eileen Rosin, eds. (Boulder, Colo.: Lynne Rienner, 2005): 194. See also Pablo G. Dreyfus, "When All the Evils Come Together: Cocaine, Corruption, and Shining

Path in Peru's Upper Huallaga Valley, 1980 to 1995," *Journal of Contemporary Criminal Justice* 15, no. 4 (1999): 370–96.

101. Andreas, "The U.S. War on Drugs in Peru"; "Political Report," *Peru Report* 2, no. 11 (November 1988): 71–78.

102. Gonzales, "Guerrillas and Coca in the Upper Huallaga Valley": 137.

103. Quoted in ibid.: 138.

104. Ibid.

105. Ibid.

106. Quoted by Clawson and Lee, *The Andean Cocaine Industry*: 218.

107. Quoted by Michael Isikoff, "Bush, Latin Leaders Agree to Stepped-Up Drug Fight," *Washington Post*, February 28, 1992.

108. McClintock and Vallas, *The United States and Peru: Cooperation at a Cost*: 120–21.

109. The United States came to consider Montesinos a close Peruvian ally and someone who could guarantee the success of counternarcotics operations in Peru. However, he manipulated the interdiction effort to obtain money and increase his power over the drug trade in Peru, ordering interdiction operations against certain traffickers while shielding others for a considerable payoff. Evidence also emerged that Montesinos was involved in money laundering and cocaine trafficking, including the use of army helicopters to transport cocaine. After Fujimori's departure from Peru in 2000 and the reestablishment of democracy in the country, Montesinos, along with eighteen generals and more than fifty high-ranking civilian and military officials, was arrested on drug corruption charges. He ultimately was indicted on a variety of trafficking and laundering charges, including selling AK-47s worth $8 million to Colombia's FARC guerrillas. Apparently, he also was directly connected to several Mexican cartels, including the Tijuana cartel. For a comprehensive list of the various charges, accusations, and evidence, see WOLA, "Drug War Paradoxes: The U.S. Government and Peru's Vladimiro Montesinos."

110. McClintock, *Revolutionary Movements in Latin America*: 293.

111. Susan C. Stokes, *Cultures in Conflict: Social Movements and the State in Peru* (University of California Press, 1995): 61–83.

112. Palmer, "'Terror in the Name of Mao': Revolution and Response in Peru."

113. Jo-Marie Burt, "*Barriadas*: The Case of Villa El Salvador," in *Shining and Other Paths*, Stern, ed.: 271.

114. Author's interview with Enrique Obando, Lima, June 2005.

115. Anthony Faiola, "As Coca Market Goes, So Shall They Reap," *Washington Post*, November 18, 1997.

116. Experts continue to debate the cause of the drop in coca leaf prices. The U.S. government and some counternarcotics experts attribute the drop to the combination of interdiction and eradication. General Barry McCaffrey, the director of the Office of National Drug Control Policy at the time, called the counternarcotics efforts in Peru "revolutionary," "without historic precedent," and "absolutely astounding"; see McClintock and Vallas, *The United States and Peru: Coopera-*

tion at a Cost: 125. Other counternarcotics experts and human rights advocates point to the aging of coca plants, their reduced productivity, and the damage caused by a fungus (*Fusarium exysporum*) that infected coca plants in Peru between 1991 and 1993. See Tullis, *Unintended Consequences: Illegal Drugs and Drug Policies in Nine Countries*: 98; Rojas, "Peru: Drug Control Policy, Human Rights, and Democracy": 205; and WOLA, "Drug War Paradoxes: The U.S. Government and Peru's Vladimiro Montesinos": 8–9. Allegations have been made that the fungus did not occur naturally but was released by the CIA. See, for example, Jeremy Bigwood, "The Drug War's Fungal 'Solution' in Latin America,"Andean Seminar Lecture Series, sponsored by George Washington University and WOLA, December 8, 2000 (http://jeremybigwood.net/Lectures/GWU-WOLA-JB/GWUNov2000.htm [May 5, 2004]). According to information I obtained in interviews with U.S., U.K., and Afghan counternarcotic officials in Washington in summer 2004 and winter 2005, the use of a fungus was under consideration for dealing with the opium poppy problem in Afghanistan. Still others suggest that the emergence of a new market structure in Colombia, which was driven by the destruction of the big Medellín and Cali cartels, was the cause of the drop in coca prices. The new and considerably smaller cartels, they argue, could not operate well across borders and had to stimulate new production in Colombia, thus displacing the Peruvian coca leaf (from author's interviews with Peruvian counternarcotics officials and academics specializing on the drug trade, Lima, in summer 2005). See also McClintock and Vallas, *The United States and Peru: Cooperation at a Cost*: 127; and Rojas, "Peru: Drug Control Policy, Human Rights, and Democracy": 211.

While there may be some truth to all of those explanations, it would be wrong to dismiss the importance of the interdiction operations. First, although earlier interdiction efforts that had been effective in disrupting traffic and lowering prices were done on a smaller scale, it is unlikely that interdiction would have no effect when adopted on a much larger scale after 1995. Second, the fact that old plants were not replaced with new ones is a result, not a cause, of the decline in demand for Peru's coca leaves. Had there been sufficient demand, farmers would have invested in replanting. Third, although the new boutique Colombian cartels found it easier to operate from a production base in Colombia, it is not at all obvious that they would have been deterred from procuring coca in Peru without the great hazards imposed by Air Bridge Denial. Expanding production is a costly and risky activity, and profit-maximizing and risk-minimizing organizations undertake it only if no better alternatives are available. Moreover, other small trafficking organizations, such as in Burma and Pakistan, and even individual traffickers, such as in Afghanistan, have managed to operate across borders.

117. McClintock and Vallas, *The United States and Peru: Cooperation at a Cost*: 126. See also Theo Ronken and others, *The Drug War in the Skies: The U.S. "Air Bridge Denial" Strategy: The Success of a Failure* (Cochabamba, Bolivia: Acción Andina, Transnational Institute, 1999); Enrique Obando "U.S. Policy

toward Perú: At Odds for Twenty Years," in *Addicted to Failure: U.S. Security Policy in Latin America,* Brian Loveman, ed. (Lanham, Md.: Rowman and Littlefield, 2006): 169–98.

118. United Nations Office on Drugs and Crime, *Coca Cultivation in the Andean Region: A Survey of Bolivia, Colombia, and Peru,* June 2005 (www.unodc.org/pdf/andean/Part1_executive_summary.pdf [May 5, 2006]). These numbers were disputed both by Peruvian counternarcotics officials and some Peruvian scholars (from author's interviews with Peruvian counternarcotics officials and academics, Lima, summer 2005).

119. U.S. Department of State, *International Narcotics Control Strategy Report,* annual reports, 1997–2000.

120. Clawson and Lee, *The Andean Cocaine Industry*: 181.

121. Meanwhile, the illicit economy is threatening a fragile but rich and highly biodiverse ecosystem in the Peruvian Amazon. For details, see, for example, Chris Fagan and Diego Shoobridge, "An Investigation of Illegal Mahagony Logging in Peru's Alto Púrus National Park and Its Surroundings," *Parks Watch,* January 2005 (www.parkswatch.org/spec_reports/logging_apnp_eng.pdf [September 15, 2005]), and Kenneth R. Young, "Environment and Social Consequences of Coca/Cocaine in Peru: Policy Alternatives and Research Agenda," in *Dangerous Harvest: Drug Plants and the Transformation of Indigenous Landscapes,* Michael K. Steinberg, Joseph J. Hobbs, and Kent Mathewson, eds. (Oxford University Press, 2004): 249–73.

122. United Nations Office on Drugs and Crime, *Coca Cultivation in the Andean Region: A Survey of Bolivia, Colombia, and Peru,* June 2008 (www.unodc.org/documents/crop-monitoring/Andean_report_2008.pdf [August 15, 2008]).

123. United Nations Office on Drugs and Crime, *Peru Coca Cultivation Survey,* June 2004 (www.unodc.org/pdf/peru/peru_coca_survey_2003.pdf [May 5, 2005]).

124. Author's interviews with academics specializing in the drug trade in Peru, Lima, summer 2005.

125. Obando, "U.S. Policy toward Perú," and United Nations Office on Drugs and Crime, *Coca Cultivation in the Andean Region.* The United States attributed the rise in prices to the slow speed of eradication while the Peruvian government has attributed it to the suppression of production in Colombia and the suspension of interdiction in Peru. See Isaías Rojas, "The Push for Zero Coca: Democratic Transition and Counternarcotics Policy in Peru," *Drug War Monitor,* WOLA Briefing Series, Washington, February 2003 (www.wola.org/media/Old%20publications/2003_Feb-DWM_Peru_The_Push_for_Zero_Coca_in_Peru.pdf [April 18, 2005]).

126. United Nations Office on Drugs and Crime, *Coca Cultivation in the Andean Region.*

127. International Crisis Group, *Coca, Drugs and Social Protest in Bolivia and Peru,* Latin America Report 12, March 3, 2005 (www.crisisgroup.org/library/documents/latin_america/12_coca_drugs_and_social_protest_in_bolivia_and_peru_amended.pdf [March 17, 2005]).

128. McClintock and Vallas, *The United States and Peru: Cooperation at a Cost*: 128.

129. Based on U.S. Department of State annual reports, *International Narcotics Control Strategy Reports, 1999–2005*.

130. Quoted by Nicole Bonnet, "Special Report—The Apurímac River Valley," *The Peru Report and Peru Business Digest,* February 19, 1998: 29.

131. See Rojas, "The Push for Zero Coca: Democratic Transition and Counternarcotics Policy in Peru": 7.

132. For details, see International Crisis Group, *Latin American Drugs II: Improving Policy and Reducing Harm,* Latin America Report 26, March 14, 2008 (www.crisisgroup.org/library/documents/latin_america/_latin_american_drugs_ii__improving_policy_and_reducing_harm_final.pdf [March 20, 2008]). For a detailed discussion of the *cocalero* mobilization after the defeat of Sendero, see Mirella Van Dun, *Cocaleros: Violence, Drugs, and Social Mobilization in the Post-Conflict Upper Huallaga Valley, Peru* (Amsterdam: Rozenberg Publishers, 2009).

133. The following section draws on my article "Trouble Ahead: The *Cocaleros* of Peru," *Current History* 105, no. 688 (February 2006): 79–83.

134. The membership of the MAS party has become considerably broader than simply *cocaleros,* but they still are an important, powerful faction.

135. Michael Shifter, "Breakdown in the Andes," *Foreign Affairs* 83, no. 5 (September-October 2004): 126–39.

136. Author's interviews with Peruvian academics and NGO representatives, Ayacucho, Peru, summer 2005.

137. Joshua Partlow, "In Peru, a Rebellion Reborn," *Washington Post,* November 12, 2008: 12.

138. "New 'Ultimatum' from Sendero Leader," *Latin American Weekly Report* 16, April 27, 2004: 5.

139. Palmer, "'Terror in the Name of Mao': Revolution and Response in Peru."

140. Author's interviews with *cocaleros* in Ayacucho, Peru, during the 2005 strikes, July 2005. During the 2004 strikes, government offices were set afire and 10,000 court files at the attorney general's office—mainly on terrorism and drug trafficking—were destroyed. Drug traffickers, independent of Sendero, played an important role in that incident.

141. Quoted in Partlow, "In Peru, a Rebellion Reborn."

142. Simon Romero, "Cocaine Trade Helps Rebels Reignite War in Peru," *New York Times,* March 18, 2009.

143. Author's interviews with Peruvian counternarcotics officials, Lima, summer 2005.

CHAPTER FOUR

1. U.S. Department of State, Bureau for International Narcotics and Law Enforcement Affairs, *International Narcotics Control Strategy Report (INCSR)* (Government Printing Office, 2000).

2. Roberto Steiner Sampedro, "Los Ingresos de Colombia Producto de la Exportación de La Drogas Illícitas [Colombia's Income from the Exportation of Illicit Drugs]" *Coyuntura Economíca* 16, no. 4 (December 1996): 73–106, and United Nations Office on Drugs and Crime, *Coca Cultivation in the Andean Region: A Survey of Bolivia, Colombia, and Peru,* June 2008 (www.unodc.org/documents/crop-monitoring/Andean_report_2008.pdf [June 16, 2008]).

3. Jorge Restrepo, Michael Spagat, and Juan F. Vargas, "The Dynamics of the Colombian Civil Conflict: A New Data Set," *Homo Oeconomicus* 21 (2004): 396–429 (www.rhul.ac.uk/economics/Research/WorkingPapers/pdf/dpe0410.pdf [May 18, 2006]). Colombia's income distribution is the world's ninth most unequal, with two-thirds of Colombians living on less than $3 a day. In the rural areas, the poverty level can climb to more than 85 percent. See Contraloría General de la República de Colombia, *Evaluación de la política social 2003* [Evaluation of Social Policy 2003] (Bogotá: CGR, July 2004): 43 (www.contraloria gen.gov.co:8081/internet/html/publicaciones/detalles.jsp?id=81 [June 03, 2005]).

4. Lewis Tambs, the U.S. ambassador to Colombia between 1983 and 1985, is widely credited with coining the term *narcoguerrilla.*

5. Luis Alberto Moreno, "Aiding Colombia's War on Terrorism," *New York Times,* May 2, 2003.

6. From a speech to the Organization of American States Permanent Council, Washington, D.C., March 25, 2004, cited in International Crisis Group, *War and Drugs in Colombia,* Latin America Report 11, January 27, 2005: 9 (www.crisisgroup.org/library/documents/latin_america/11_war_and_drugs_in_colombia.pdf [February 10, 2005]).

7. Cited by Gabriel Marcella, *The United States and Colombia: The Journey from Ambiguity to Strategic Clarity* (Carlisle, Pa.: U.S. Army War College, 2003): 49.

8. Andrés López Restrepo and Álvaro Camacho Guizado, "From Smugglers to Drug-Lords to "Traquetos": Changes in the Colombian Illicit Drug Organizations," University of Notre Dame Kellogg Institute, 2001 (www.nd.edu/~kellogg/pdfs/LopeCama.pdf [October 28, 2005]).

9. For details, see Howard Abadinsky, *Organized Crime* (Chicago: Nelson-Hall Publishers, 1997), and Elaine Shannon, *Desperados: Latin Drug Lords, U.S. Lawmen, and the War America Can't Win* (New York: Viking Press, 1988).

10. One of the reasons why eradication was undertaken was the widespread perception that the Colombian police in charge of internal interdiction were too corrupt for interdiction to make any significant impact on production in Colombia. See Richard B. Craig, "Illicit Drug Trade and U.S.-Latin American Relations," *Washington Quarterly* 8, no. 4 (Fall 1985): 105–24.

11. Ricardo Vargas Meza, "The Revolutionary Armed Forces of Colombia (FARC) and the Illicit Drug Trade," 1999 (www.tni.org/archives/vargas/farc.htm [April 28, 2006]): 5. Ricardo Rocha estimates that between 1988 and 1993, the second coca boom attracted 578,000 people into the southeast. See Ricardo

Rocha, *La Economía Colombiana tras 25 Años de Narcotráfico* [The Colombian Economy over Twenty-Five Years of the Drug Trade] (Bogotá: United States Drug Control Program and Siglo de Hombre Editores, 2000): 150, and Rensselaer W. Lee III, *The White Labyrinth: Cocaine and Political Power* (New Brunswick, N.J.: Transaction Publishers, 1989): 43.

12. U.S. Department of State, *International Narcotics Control Strategy Report (INCSR)*, March 2008 (www.state.gov/documents/organization/102583.pdf [March 9, 2008]): 129.

13. Although the Cali and Medellín cartels have come to epitomize the quintessential criminal organization as tightly controlled and hierarchically organized, criminal organizations vary widely in their internal structure, including tightness of the hierarchy, formality, durability of internal and external links, and other characteristics. Yet even the Cali and Medellín cartels relied on layers of subcontractors and freelancers. See, for example, Patrick L. Clawson and Rensselaer W. Lee III, *The Andean Cocaine Industry* (New York: St. Martin's, 1996): 40–41. Nor, despite the use of the term *cartel*, did they have the power to set the price for cocaine. Nonetheless, for convenience sake, I stick with the commonly used term to identify them.

14. The most notorious of the labs was Escobar's immense complex Tranquilandia, the largest cocaine lab ever found. When the Colombian police raided it in 1984, they found 13.8 metric tons of cocaine, worth at least $34 million. For colorful and often gory details on Tranquilandia and Escobar's other ventures, see Robin Kirk, *More Terrible Than Death* (New York: Public Affairs, 2003): 71–91.

15. The Cali cartel, for example, reportedly bought parts of several prominent Colombian banks to facilitate money laundering. See Paul B. Stares, *Global Habit: The Drug Problem in a Borderless World* (Brookings, 1996): 59. Such direct capture of the financial institutions by the traffickers was aided by Colombia's lax money laundering laws during the 1980s.

16. Francisco Thoumi, *Economía, Política, y Narcotráfico* [Economy, Politics, and Drug Trade] (Bogotá: Tercer Mundo, 1994): 148–49.

17. The decision to diversify was made by the Cali cartel at the end of the 1980s. Facing saturation of the U.S. market for cocaine, the Cali cartel also decided to diversify distribution to Europe, engaging in a business partnership with Italy's Cosa Nostra and other criminal organizations.

18. Lee, *The White Labyrinth*: 3. Many of the main Medellín *narco-jefes* had experience with other illicit economies and smuggling. Gonzalo Rodríguez Gacha, for example, trafficked in smuggled emeralds and enthusiastically participated in violence associated with the trade. Carlos Lehder stole cars and sold marijuana in New York before becoming one of the narco chiefs. Beginning his criminal career in his teens, Pablo Escobar stole headstones from local graveyards, filed off the inscriptions, and resold the headstones. See Francisco Thoumi, *Political Economy and Illegal Drugs in Colombia* (Boulder, Colo.: Lynne Rienner, 1994): 153–54.

Their Cali counterparts began their criminal careers in counterfeiting and kidnapping. See also Stares, *Global Habit*: 33; and Andrés López Restrepo, "Conflicto interno y narcotráfico entre 1970 y 2005 [Internal Conflict and the Drug Trade between 1970 and 2005]" in *Narcotráfico en Colombia: Economía y Violencia* [The Drug Trade in Colombia: Economy and Violence], Alfredo Rangel Suárez, ed. (Bogotá: Fundación Seguridad y Democracia: 2005): 87–144.

19. Francisco Thoumi, "The Economic Impact of Narcotics in Colombia," in *Drug Policy in the Americas,* Peter Smith, ed. (Boulder, Colo.: Westview Press, 1992): 68–70.

20. Lee, *The White Labyrinth*: 36.

21. For an excellent discussion of the socioeconomic and cultural dimensions of the cocaine trade in Medellín during the 1980s and early 1990s, see Mary Roldán, "Colombia: Cocaine and the 'Miracle' of Modernity," in *Cocaine: Global Histories,* Paul Gootenberg, ed. (London: Routledge, 1999): 165–82.

22. Ibid.: 174.

23. Clawson and Lee, *The Andean Cocaine Industry*: 112. See also Bruce M. Bagley, "Dateline Drug Wars: Colombia: The Wrong Strategy," *Foreign Policy* 77 (Winter 1989): 160–61.

24. Clawson and Lee, *The Andean Cocaine Industry*: 5.

25. Jenny Pearce, *Colombia: Inside the Labyrinth* (London: Latin American Bureau, 1990): 247. See also Carlos Medina Gallego, *Autodefensas, paramilitares, y narcotráfico en Colombia: Origen, desarrollo y consolidación: El Caso de Puerto Boyacá* [Self-Defense Groups, Paramilitaries, and the Drug Trade in Colombia: Origin, Development, and Consolidation: The Puerto Boyacá Case] (Bogotá: Documentos Periodísticos, 1990).

26. Richard Clutterbuck, *Drugs, Crime and Corruption* (New York University Press, 1995): 60.

27. Lee, *The White Labyrinth*: 136–37. See also Jorge Eliecer Orozco, *Lehder: El Hombre* [Lehder: The Man] (Bogotá: Plaza y Janes, 1987): 57–60, 162–85.

28. Lee, *The White Labyrinth*: 137.

29. Ibid.: 116.

30. The traffickers' anger over Colombia's extradition treaty first erupted in the mid-1980s, when in exchange for amnesty from prosecution, the traffickers offered to pay Colombia's external debt, dismantle their cocaine factories and trafficking networks, and repatriate their off-shore assets, thereby injecting $3 billion a year into the Colombian economy. Their proposal was rejected by the Colombian government, resulting in the traffickers' unleashing of the first wave of terror. For details, see Scott B. MacDonald, *Mountain High, White Avalanche* (New York: Praeger, 1989): 40–43, and Craig, "Illicit Drug Trade and U.S.-Latin American Relations": 117. In 1987, Lehder became the first to be extradited to the United States.

31. Between 1981 and 1991, 242 judges were killed, and many were forced into exile abroad to avoid assassination. See, for example, Marcella, *The United States and Colombia*: 14–15, and "Colombia's Court Reform," *The Economist,* January 8, 2005.

32. Phillip McLean, "Colombia: Failed, Failing, or Just Weak?" *Washington Quarterly* 25, no. 3 (Summer 2002): 128.

33. The Medellín cartel also attempted to buy 120 Stinger missiles in Florida in April 1990, but its effort was foiled by the FBI.

34. Clawson and Lee, *The Andean Cocaine Industry*: 99.

35. In addition to equipping his jail with various luxuries, Escobar also participated in the selection of his own prison guards.

36. The Cali cartel and specifically its *narco-jefe,* José "Chepe" Santacruz Londoño, had already attempted to kill Escobar during the 1980s. Between 1992 and 1993, the Cali cartel hired as informers scores of Escobar's subordinates as well Japanese communications experts to track Escobar down. For a detailed account of law enforcement operations against Escobar, see Mark Bowden, *Killing Pablo: The Hunt for the World's Greatest Outlaw* (New York: Atlantic Monthly Press, 2001).

37. Gabriel García-Marquez, *News of a Kidnapping* (New York: Penguin Books, 1998). For a while after his escape from *La Catedral,* Escobar arranged for the provision of false information, having about a hundred people call in different information on his location every day.

38. Roldán, "Colombia: Cocaine and the 'Miracle' of Modernity": 175.

39. For details on U.S. decisionmaking on Colombia during that period, see Russell Crandall, *Driven by Drugs: U.S. Policy toward Colombia* (Boulder, Colo.: Lynne Rienner, 2002). On March 31, 1997, the U.S. government formally decertified Colombia for failing to cooperate with U.S. counternarcotics efforts.

40. See Francisco Thoumi, *Illegal Drugs, Economy, and Society in the Andes* (John Hopkins University Press, 2003): 210–25.

41. Gilberto Rodríguez Orejuela was extradited to the United States in 2004.

42. Diego Montoya was arrested in 2007 and subsequently extradited to the United States, and Wilber Varela was assassinated in Venezuela in February 2008.

43. Some of these operators, such as Chupeta and El Gordo, have been arrested, but their "boutique cartels" continue operating and transforming themselves.

44. About three-quarters of the population were peasants, while 3 percent of landowners controlled more than half of the agricultural land, including the best land. See Harvey F. Kline, *Colombia: Democracy under Assault* (Boulder, Colo.: Westview Press, 1995): 43.

45. Jenny Pearce aptly characterized Colombia's political system as a "democracy without people." See Pearce, *Colombia: Inside the Labyrinth*: 207. During the 1980s, the political system underwent a process of decentralization and political opening, culminating in the adoption of a new, more inclusive constitution in

1991. See, for example, Harvey F. Kline, *State Building and Conflict Resolution in Colombia, 1986–1994* (University of Alabama Press, 1999). Nonetheless, the party system still does not offer representation to the majority of the population, and its delegitimation has steadily increased. The most recent manifestation was the victory in the 2006 presidential elections of Álvaro Uribe, who ran as a candidate outside the two traditional parties. Uribe, who presented himself as an essentially independent candidate, created a new political party used only as a temporary electoral vehicle. That mirrors the trend toward a legitimacy crisis among traditional parties across Latin America in the 2000s.

46. Nazih Richani, *Systems of Violence: The Political Economy of War and Peace in Colombia* (State University of New York Press, 2002): 63. As much as 40 percent of FARC's members are women, and perhaps one-third are under the age of eighteen. See Adam Isacson, "Was Failure Avoidable? Learning from Colombia's 1998–2002 Peace Process," Paper 14, Dante B. Fascell North–South Center Working Paper Series, University of Miami, March 2003 (www.miami.edu/nsc/publications/NSCPublicationsIndex.html#WP [August 20, 2004]). The youth of the rank-and-file soldiers increased in the 2000s, reflecting the forcible recruitment of children.

47. FARC members sign up for life, and there are few exit opportunities. Individual desertions became frequent only after the military achieved important victories over the FARC in 2005. FARC members can only rarely see their families, and women members need to argue hard to be allowed to have a child; even then, they must put the child in the care of relatives. See, for example, Francisco Gutiérrez Sanín, "Criminal Rebels? A Discussion of Civil War and Criminality from the Colombian Experience," *Politics and Society* 32, no. 2 (June 2004): 268–71.

48. After the demise of the Soviet Union, the FARC shed its Marxist–Leninist rhetoric and orthodoxy and replaced it with a new ideological concept, labeled Bolivarianism. In addition to soft-peddling its socialist ideas, the new ideological package explicitly embraced nationalism. FARC's declarations during the 1990s included the following goals: principal but not total state ownership of the energy, communications, public services, and natural resources sectors; land redistribution; confiscation of assets from or renegotiation of contracts with multinational companies in Colombia; guaranteed stable and profitable prices for agricultural products; and the allocation of 50 percent of the national budget for social welfare and 10 percent for scientific research. Instead of altogether overthrowing the political system, FARC in essence advocated making the state more interventionist and concerned with regard to the poor sectors and regions. See, for example, Cecilia López Montaño and Arturo García Durán, "Hidden Costs of Peace in Colombia," in *Colombia: Essays on Conflict, Peace, and Development* (Washington: World Bank, 2000): 152–53. Its political message has become progressively weaker in the 2000s.

49. Alfredo Rangel Suárez, *Colombia: guerra en el fin de siglo* [Colombia: War at the End of the Century] (Bogotá: Tercer Mundo Editores, 1998): 12.

50. Román D. Ortiz, "Insurgent Strategies in the Post–Cold War: The Case of the Revolutionary Armed Forces of Colombia," *Studies in Conflict and Terrorism* 25 (2002): 136.

51. Walter Broderick, *El guerrillero invisible* [The Invisible Guerrilla] (Bogotá: Indermedio, 2000).

52. Kirk, *More Terrible Than Death*: 99–103.

53. Ortiz, "Insurgent Strategies in the Post–Cold War": 133.

54. Mark Chernick, "Economic Resources and Internal Armed Conflicts: Lessons from the Colombian Case," in *Rethinking the Economics of War: The Intersection of Need, Creed, and Greed,* Cynthia J. Arnson, and I. William Zartman, eds. (Washington: Woodrow Wilson Center Press, 2005): 190.

55. Author's interviews with Colombian academics who did research in the Caguán area, Bogotá, fall 2005. See Henry Salgado, "Conflicto agrario y expansión de los cultivos de uso ilícito en Colombia [Agrarian Conflict and Expansion of Illicit Crops in Colombia]" *Controversia* 182 (June 2004); Juan Guillermo Ferro, "Las FARC y su relación con la economía de la coca en el sur de Colombia: Testimonios de Colonos y Guerrilleros [The FARC and Its Relationship to the Coca Economy in Southern Colombia: Testimonies of Settlers and Guerrillas]" in *Violencias y estrategias colectivas en la región andina* [Violence and Collective Strategies in the Andean Region], Gonzalo Sánchez G. and Eric Lair, eds. (Bogotá: Editorial Norma, 2004); José Jairo González, "Cultívos ilícitos, colonización, y revuelta de raspachines [Illicit Crops, Colonization, and the Revolt of the Coca Pickers]" *Revista Foro,* September 1998; and Juan Guillermo Ferro and Graciela Uribe, *El orden de la guerra: LAS FARC-EP: entre la organización y la política* [The Order of War: The FARC-EP: Between Organization and Politics] (Bogotá: CEJA, 2002).

56. Presentation by José Olarte, mayor of Calamar, Guaviare, at "Local Government Amidst the Armed Conflict: The Experience of Colombian Mayors," Georgetown University and National Endowment for Democracy Conference, Georgetown University, Washington, September 27, 2000. Quoted in Angel Rabasa and Peter Chalk, *Colombian Labyrinth: The Synergy of Drugs and Insurgency and Its Implications for Regional Stability* (Santa Monica: Rand, 2001): 26.

57. Rabasa and Chalk, *Colombian Labyrinth:* 26.

58. Mark Chernick, "Negotiating Peace amid Multiple Forms of Violence," in *Comparative Peace Processes in Latin America,* Cynthia J. Arson, ed. (Washington: Woodrow Wilson Center Press, 1999): 166. The FARC's overall taxation system is progressive, and the poorest peasants are exempted from at least some taxation. See Richani, *Systems of Violence*: 70.

59. Vargas Meza, "The Revolutionary Armed Forces of Colombia (FARC) and the Illicit Drug Trade."

60. Mark S. Steinitz, "The Terrorism and Drug Connection in Latin America's Andean Region," Policy Papers on the Americas XIII, Study 5 (Washington: CSIS, July 2002). After his arrest, a Brazilian top trafficker who was one of the FARC's

international connections claimed that considerably higher fees were charged by the FARC: $500 per kilo of cocaine to be shipped and $15,000 per flight. See Marcella, *The United States and Colombia*: 27.

61. Camilo Echandía Castilla, "La amapola en el arco de las economicas del ciclo corto [The Poppy in the Arc of Short-Cycle Economics]" *Analisís Politico* 27 (January-April 1996). After the military successes against the FARC since 2002, described below, opium poppy cultivation declined and the FARC lost control of many of the poppy areas, such as in southern Nariño. Author's fieldwork in Colombia, summer and fall 2008.

62. Author's interviews with Colombian academics and NGOs operating in the drug regions, Bogotá, fall 2005. See International Crisis Group, *War and Drugs in Colombia*: 9.

63. Donnie Marshall, chief of operations, Drug Enforcement Administration, "Cooperative Efforts of the Colombian National Police and Military in Anti-Narcotics Efforts and Current DEA Initiatives in Colombia," testimony before the Subcommittee on National Security, International Affairs, and Criminal Justice, July 9, 1997 (U.S. Government Printing Office, 1997): 6.

64. See, for example, International Crisis Group, *War and Drugs in Colombia*: 9. The extent of the FARC's penetration of international smuggling networks and its distribution capacity in source countries continues to be hotly debated among experts on the FARC and drug trafficking. Having contacts with smuggling organizations is, of course, not the same as having the know-how and the will to carry such activities on its own. In March 2002, U.S. courts indicted FARC members for the first time on drug trafficking charges and requested their extradition. In March 2006, a federal grand jury in Washington indicted fifty top FARC commanders. Simón Trinidad, one of the top leaders, has been extradited to the United States. Information about FARC's connections to Mexican drug trafficking organizations and the Italian mafia is based on author's interviews with U.S. and Colombia government officials, Bogotá, fall 2008, and Washington, spring 2009.

65. See, for example, Vargas Meza, "The Revolutionary Armed Forces of Colombia (FARC) and the Illicit Drug Trade": 7.

66. It is important to note that the Colombian drug dealers have an intimate relationship not only with the insurgents and paramilitaries but also with many Colombian politicians and members of the armed forces. Although major cleanup of political and state corruption has taken place, corruption of the political system and the military and law enforcement apparatus remains significant. Revelations of widespread corruption among Colombian air force officers in 1998, for example, gave rise to the expression "the Blue Cartel," referring to the color of the air force uniforms. For details on the evolution of drug-related corruption in Colombia, see, for example, Mauricio Vargas, Jorge Lesmes, and Edgar Téllez, *El presidente que se iba a caer* [The President Who Was Going to Fall] (Bogotá: Editorial Planeta, 1996), and Ted Galen Carpenter, *Bad Neighbor Policy* (New York: Palgrave Macmillan, 2003): 125–130.

67. Daniel García-Peña Jaramillo, "Light Weapons and Internal Conflict in Colombia," in *Lethal Commerce: The Global Trade in Small Arms and Light Weapons,* Jeffrey Boutwell, Michael T. Klare, and Laura W. Reed, eds. (Cambridge: American Academy of Arts and Sciences, 1995): 100.

68. Author's interviews with Colombian economists specializing on the drug trade, Bogotá, fall 2005 and summer 2008.

69. Mark S. Steinitz, "Insurgents, Terrorists, and the Drug Trade," *Washington Quarterly* 8, no. 4 (Fall 1985): 142.

70. Richani, *Systems of Violence*: 75. A study by the Colombian police put the FARC's and the AUC's income at a high of $105 million a month. Colombia National Police Internal Document A-4523, Government of Colombia, December 2000, cited in Edgardo Buscaglia and William Ratliff, *War and Lack of Governance in Colombia: Narcos, Guerrillas, and U.S. Policy* (Stanford: Hoover Institution on War, Revolution, and Peace, 2001): 26. Other intelligence sources placed the total income of the guerrillas in 1995 at as high as $800 million. See Mark Chernick, "Colombia's Escalating Violence," *Strategic Comments* 3, no. 4 (May 1997). However, given the size of the Colombian economy and its known difficulties in absorbing illicit monies, that figure is likely inflated.

71. The Colombian government estimates that kidnapping brought $1.2 billion to the FARC and the ELN between 1991 and 1998. See Pax Christi Netherlands, *The Kidnapping Industry in Colombia* (Utrecht, Belgium: 2001): 35. The majority of kidnapping today is carried out by leftist guerrillas, especially the FARC. Until 2005, guerrillas kidnapped an average of 1,500 people a year, and Colombia had one of the highest kidnapping rates in the world. Since 2005 and the implementation of President Álvaro Uribe's Democratic Security Policy, kidnapping rates have declined dramatically.

72. Alfredo Rangel Suárez, "Parasites and Predators: Guerrillas and the Insurrection Economy of Colombia," *Journal of International Affairs* 53, no. 2 (Spring 2000): 585.

73. Presentation by Gilberto Toro, executive secretary, Federación Colombiana de Municipios (Colombian Federation of Municipalities), at "Government Amidst the Armed Conflict: The Experience of Colombian Mayors," Georgetown University and National Endowment for Democracy Conference, Georgetown University, Washington, September 27, 2000, cited in Rabasa and Chalk, *Colombian Labyrinth*: 50.

74. Pearce, *Colombia: Inside the Labyrinth*: 173.

75. In 1989, the FARC estimated that it needed about $56 million to increase the number of combatants from the existing 13,200 to 18,000. See Richani, *Systems of Violence*: 76.

76. Rangel Suárez, *Colombia: guerra en el fin de siglo*: 12.

77. Eduardo Pizarro Leongómez, *Insurgencia sin revolución* [Insurgency without Revolution] (Bogotá: Tercer Mundo 1996): 99.

78. Ibid: 126–27.

79. Simon Romero, "Venezuela Still Aids Colombia Rebels, New Material Shows," *New York Times,* August 3, 2009. The apparently still persisting material and logistical support for the FARC by the Venezuelan government of Hugo Chávez has been a source of major contention and tension between Colombia and Venezuela. Colombia's rebels as well as traffickers also use Venezuela as a safe haven, as they do northern Ecuador.

80. See LaVerle Berry and others, *A Global Overview of Narcotics-Funded Terrorist and Other Extremist Groups,* Federal Research Division, Library of Congress, May 2002 (www.loc.gov/rr/frd/pdffiles/NarcsFundedTerrs_Extrems.pdf [August 05, 2004]).

81. Douglas Farah, "Colombia Rebels' Arsenal Grows as Cocaine Sales Increase in E. Europe," *Washington Post,* November 4, 1999.

82. Berry and others, *A Global Overview of Narcotics-Funded Terrorist and Other Extremist Groups:* 65.

83. Author's interviews with U.S. government officials, Washington, summer 2004, and Colombian government officials from the Ministry of Defense, Bogotá, summer 2008.

84. Richani, *Systems of Violence:* 89.

85. Pearce, *Colombia: Inside the Labyrinth:* 173. See also Ricardo Vargas Meza, "Cultivos ilícitos en Colombia: elementos para un balance [Illicit Crops in Colombia: Factors for a Balance]" in *Narcotráfico en Colombia: Economía y Violencia,* Rangel Suárez, ed.: 87-144.

86. Ferro, "Las FARC y su relación con la economía de la coca." Author's interviews with Colombian government officials and academics, Bogotá, fall 2005. See also Camilo Echandía Castilla, *El Conflicto Armado y las Manifestaciones de la Violencia en las Regiones de Colombia* [Armed Conflict and Manifestations of Violence in the Regions of Colombia] (Bogotá: Presidencia de la República de Colombia, Oficina del Alto Comisionado para la Paz, 2000): 79.

87. Author's interviews with experts on paramilitaries, Bogotá, fall 2005. See also Richani, *Systems of Violence* : 70-1.

88. U.S. Department of State, Bureau of International Narcotics Matters, *International Narcotics Control Strategy Report (INCSR)* (Government Printing Office, 1986): 90.

89. Vargas Meza, "The Revolutionary Armed Forces of Colombia (FARC) and the Illicit Drug Trade."

90. Pearce, *Colombia: Inside the Labyrinth:* 173.

91. Jaime E. Jaramillo, Mora Leonidad, and Fernando Cubides, *Colonización, Coca, y Guerrilla* [Colonization, Coca, and Guerrilla] (Bogotá: Universidad Nacional de Colombia, 1986): 135–57.

92. Based on author's interviews with Peruvian and Colombian officials charged with alternative development in Lima, summer 2005, and Nariño and Bogotá, fall 2005 and fall 2008.

93. In addition to exploiting the illicit narcotics economy, the FARC also has funded the provision of social services through other illicit economic activities, such as blackmailing major international companies and forcing them to invest in local schools, vocational training, and so forth. See Ricardo Vargas Meza, ed., *Drogas, Poder y Región en Colombia: Impactos Locales y Conflictos* [Drugs, Power, and Region in Colombia: Local Impacts and Conflicts] (Bogotá: CINEP, 1994). It has also sought to control who runs local administrations, both by nominating its candidates for elections and physically threatening their opponents. The FARC places great importance on infiltrating local politics and exercising power at the local level.

94. Buscaglia and Ratliff, *War and Lack of Governance in Colombia*: 8–9. See also James Dao, "The War on Terrorism Takes Aim at Crime," *New York Times*, April 7, 2002.

95. Daniel Lazare, "A Battle against Reason, Democracy, and Drugs: The Drug War Deciphered," *NACLA's Report on the Americas* XXXV, no. 1 (July-August 2001): 17.

96. See, for example, World Wildlife Fund, "Comments on Glyphosate," October 30, 1999 (www.ciponline.org/colombia/103001.htm [May 01, 2003]), and "Report on Verification Mission 'Impacts in Ecuador of Fumigations in Putumayo as Part of Plan Colombia,'" October 2002 (www.ciponline.org/colombia/02121301.htm [May 01, 2003]). The United States government denies that glyphosate has any negative effects, and several U.S. government-sponsored studies have failed to find any negative side effects of using glyphosate. Environmental groups point out, however, that because the FARC shoots at spray planes, spraying is frequently conducted from a height at which dispersion of the chemicals to non-coca areas cannot be controlled; that the substance is mixed with other chemicals to ensure that it sticks to coca leaves for as long as possible and hence it becomes dangerous to both humans and the environment; and that according to the label, it is not supposed to be used near water sources, which obviously cannot be avoided in the southern and southeastern jungles of Colombia where coca is grown.

97. Author's interviews with NGO representatives operating in Colombia's drug regions, Bogotá, fall 2005, and Magdalena Medio region, summer 2008.

98. Ibid. Author's interviews with *cocaleros* in Magdalena Medio and Nariño and with non-coca farmers in Montes de Maria, summer and fall 2008. See also James F. Rochlin, *Vanguard Revolutionaries in Latin America* (Boulder, Colo.: Lynne Rienner, 2003): 100.

99. Richani, *Systems of Violence*: 49, and "You Do the Maths," *The Economist*, January 10, 2004.

100. Rabasa and Chalk, *Colombian Labyrinth*: 50; Caroline Moser, "Building Sustainable Peace and Social Capital," in *Colombia: Essays on Conflict, Peace, and Development*, Andres Solimano, ed. (Washington: Word Bank, December 2000): 14.

101. Richani, *Systems of Violence*: 44.

102. The Colombian military has stayed out of political disputes, preserving its independence from both the executive and legislative branches. At least until the presidency of Álvaro Uribe, it exercised close to absolute autonomy over national security and matters of public order, including its budgets. At the same time, it was not shy about letting its preferences on policies be known and undertook actions contradictory to the interests and goals of the government. It opposed, for example, President Belisario Betancur's peace negotiations with the M-19 during the 1980s and President Andrés Pastrána's peace negotiations with the FARC during the late 1990s. See, for example, Richani, *Systems of Violence*: 37–42.

103. Interview with Molina in *El Tiempo* cited by Lee, *The White Labyrinth*: 215.

104. Kirk, *More Terrible Than Death*: 188.

105. See Lee, *The White Labyrinth* (1989): 217–18; and Clawson and Lee, *The Andean Cocaine Industry*: 187.

106. Kirk, *More Terrible Than Death*: 181.

107. See Richani, *Systems of Violence*: 55; Pearce, *Colombia: Inside the Labyrinth*: 195, 240; and Human Rights Watch, *Colombia's Killer Networks: The Military-Paramilitary Partnership and the United States* (New York: 1996).

108. Author's interviews with Colombian military officers and academic experts on paramilitaries and Colombian military forces, Bogotá, fall 2005. To reciprocate, the army has provided intelligence to the paramilitaries. Other security agencies also cooperated with the paramilitaries on intelligence. In October 2005, for example, information emerged that Colombia's law enforcement and intelligence agency, DAS, was deeply penetrated by spies of the paramilitaries and that various high officials were selling information to the paramilitaries. See Juan Forero, "Two Top Directors Leave Colombia's Secret Police as Scandal Mounts," *New York Times,* October 28, 2005.

109. For details, see María Clemencia Ramírez Lemus, Kimberly Stanton, and John Walsh, "Colombia: A Vicious Circle of Drugs and War," in *Drugs and Democracy in Latin America,* Coletta A. Youngers and Eileen Rosin, eds. (Boulder, Colo.: Lynne Rienner, 2005): 107. See also Crandall, *Driven by Drugs.*

110. James Brooke, "U.S. Copters are a Target in Colombia," *New York Times,* March 27, 1995.

111. U.S. Department of State, *International Narcotics Control Strategy Report (INCSR)* (Government Printing Office, 1996): 83 and 88.

112. Reprinted in Clawson and Lee, *The Andean Cocaine Industry*: 184.

113. Underfunded, mismanaged, and complicated by the distance of Colombia's illicit crop–growing areas from licit markets, alternative development efforts were overall a dismal failure during the 1990s. PLANTE (Plan Nacional de Desarrollo Alternativo [National Alternative Development Plan]), the Colombian alternative development agency, frequently did not coordinate with the police and the

military, making agreements with *cocalero* communities only a few days before the army or the police sprayed the coca crops and thereby making the *campesinos* believe that the government deceived them. Projects were chronically unfunded, and frequently their design was inappropriate for the economic conditions in their areas. Of four projects examined by Thoumi, only one resulted in a substantial reduction of coca cultivation, achieving 75 percent of the project's goals in decreasing cultivation. The successes of the remaining three hovered around 10 percent of their goals, while failing to substantially improve the economic conditions of the farmers. As various Colombian government agencies and NGOs came to understand that there was money for them to be made if they participated in "alternative development," alternative development money was also diverted to projects only very remotely related to rural or overall economic development. For details, see Thoumi, *Illegal Drugs, Economy, and Society in the Andes*: 311–51. For challenges of alternative livelihood policies and their failures in Colombia, see, for example, Adam Isacson, "The Tragedy of Alternative Development in Colombia," December 3, 2001 (www.colombiareport.org/colombia92.htm [November 3, 2003], and Adam Isacson, "Plan Colombia: Six Years Later," Center for International Policy Report, November 2006 (www.ciponline.org/colombia/0611ipr.pdf [January 2, 2007]). Nonetheless, many important improvements have taken place in the design of alternative livelihood programs since the mid-2000s. See USAID, *Assessment of the Implementation of the United States Government's Support Plan for Colombia's Illicit Crop Reduction Components*, prepared by Vanda Felbab-Brown and others, Management Systems International, April 2009 (http://pdf.usaid.gov/pdf_docs/PDACN233.pdf [August 27, 2009]).

114. Clawson and Lee, *The Andean Cocaine Industry*: 219–20.

115. Christopher Torchia, "Colombian Coca Farmers Vent Rage," *Washington Times*, September 3, 1996.

116. Clawson and Lee, *The Andean Cocaine Industry*: 220.

117. Kirk, *More Terrible Than Death*: 243; and Vargas Meza, "The Revolutionary Armed Forces of Colombia (FARC) and the Illicit Drug Trade."

118. Mary Matheson, "Colombian Leader Tries to Please U.S. on Drugs, but Ignites Peasant Revolt," *Christian Science Monitor*, August 12, 1997.

119. For details, see Rabasa and Chalk, *Colombian Labyrinth*: 42.

120. Author's interviews with Colombian Ministry of Defense officials and officials of the U.S. embassy in Colombia, Bogotá, fall 2005 and summer 2008.

121. Richani, *Systems of Violence*: 45.

122. According to State Department estimates, in Colombia 50,900 hectares were planted with coca in 1995 and 136,000 hectares were planted in 2000. See *International Narcotics Control Strategy Report* 1996, 2000, and 2001. The State Department data have been disputed. Sergio Uribe, for example, maintains that the area under cultivation during the mid-1990s was already substantially higher, at around 100,000 hectares, than the roughly 60,000 hectares indicated by the

International Narcotics Control Strategy Report. See Sergio Uribe, "Los cultivos ilícitos en Colombia [Illicit Crops in Colombia]" in *Drogas ilícitas en Colombia: su impacto económico, politico, y social* [Illicit Drugs in Colombia: Their Economic, Political, and Social Impact], Francisco Thoumi, ed. (Bogotá: PNUD-DNE, 1997): 35–133.

123. The FARC's fears were fueled by the paramilitaries' attacks on members of the Unión Patriótica [Patriotic Union], a leftist party founded by the FARC in the 1980s.

124. See, for example, Isacson, "Was Failure Avoidable?" and Thoumi, *Illegal Drugs, Economy, and Society in the Andes*: 229.

125. Alejandro Reyes, "La Violencia Política [Political Violence]" in *Prevención de conflictos y alerta temprana: El caso de Colombia* [Conflict Prevention and Early Warning: The Case of Colombia], Marc Chernick, ed. (Washington and Bogotá: United Nations Development Program, Georgetown University, and Universidad de los Andes, 2005). Author's interview in Bogotá, fall 2005.

126. For a general overview of the group's origins and goals, see Kline, *State Building and Conflict Resolution in Colombia*: 19–21.

127. Pearce, *Colombia: Inside the Labyrinth*: 171.

128. Kirk, *More Terrible Than Death*: 104.

129. Ibid.

130. María Jimena Duzán, *Death Beat: A Colombian Journalist's Life inside the Cocaine Wars,* Peter Eisner, trans. (New York: Harper Collins, 1994): 4. Apparently some police officers on the payroll of the traffickers caught M-19 members and handed them over to MAS to be tortured, actively cooperating with the cleansing campaign.

131. Kirk, *More Terrible Than Death*: 107.

132. The M-19 agreed to the deal not only because of its own experience with MAS but also because of the systematic and effective effort of the MAS to eliminate the FARC's political party, Unión Patriótica (UP), during the guerrillas' peace negotiations with the administration of President Belisario Betancur in the early 1980s. See Alonso Salazar, *La Parábola de Pablo: Auge y Caída de Un Gran Capo del Narcotráfico* [The Parable of Pablo: The Rise and Fall of a Great Drug Capo] (Bogotá: Planeta, 2001): 102–05, 135–45, 160–61.

133. Rex A. Hudson, "Colombia's Palace of Justice Tragedy Revisited: A Critique of the Conspiracy Theory," *Terrorism and Political Violence* 7, no. 3 (Summer 1995): 100–21.

134. MacDonald, *Mountain High, White Avalanche*: 42–43. Former M-19 members subsequently admitted to later receiving general assistance from Escobar (see Salazar, *La Parábola de Pablo*), and in 1988 the group reportedly was hired by the Medellín cartel to murder Attorney General Carlos Mauro Hoyos. See Scott B. MacDonald, *Dancing on a Volcano: The Latin American Drug Trade* (New Praeger, 1988): 35.

135. Author's interviews with Colombian academics, Bogotá, fall 2005.

136. Quoted in Kline, *State Building and Conflict Resolution in Colombia*: 6.

137. Kirk, *More Terrible Than Death*: 138.

138. Pearce, *Colombia: Inside the Labyrinth*: 283.

139. Rabasa and Chalk, *Colombian Labyrinth*: 30; Gutiérrez Sanín, "Criminal Rebels?": 263. For a good overview, see Carlos Medina Gallego, *El ELN: Una historia contada a dos voces* [The ELN: A Story Told in Two Voices] (Bogotá: Rodríguez Quito, 1996).

140. Richani, *Systems of Violence*: 86.

141. Ibid: 85; Rabasa and Chalk, *Colombian Labyrinth*: 30-33.

142. Rangel Suárez, *Colombia: guerra en el fin de siglo*: 12.

143. The FARC has also blown up the oil pipelines. In 2001 alone, the two groups staged 170 attacks against the Caño-Limón pipeline. See Alexandra Guáqueta, "The Colombian Conflict: Political and Economic Dimensions," in *The Political Economy of Armed Conflict: Beyond Greed and Grievance*, Karen Ballentine and Jake Sherman, eds. (Boulder, Colo.: Lynne Rienner, 2003): 85.

144. Steve Wienberg, *Armand Hammer: The Untold Story* (New York: 1989): 264-68.

145. Guáqueta, "The Colombian Conflict": 84–85.

146. Rangel Suárez, *Colombia: guerra en el fin de siglo*: 12, 61–63.

147. Gonzalo Sánchez G., "Introduction: Problems of Violence, Prospects for Peace," in *Violence in Colombia 1990–2000: Waging War and Negotiating Peace*, Charles Berquist, Ricardo Peñaranda, and Gonzalo Sánchez, eds. (Wilmington: Scholarly Resources, 2001): 24. See also Eduardo Pizarro Leongómez, *Una democracia asediada* [A Democracy Besieged] (Bogotá: Norma, 2004): 185.

148. Thoumi, *Illegal Drugs, Economy, and Society in the Andes*: 283.

149. Rochlin, *Vanguard Revolutionaries in Latin America*: 127.

150. The term "self-defense groups" is also used for community-based militias, which are distinct from the mobile hit squads hired by drug dealers and large land owners. In practice, the two groups frequently overlapped, and after 1989 all the remaining self-defense groups became paramilitaries. Some of the groups were legal; some were not. Almost all were tolerated by the government. The state itself promoted the creation of some of the groups—such as CONVIVIR, an umbrella organization of vigilante groups—during the government of Ernesto Samper (1994–98). Under the command of the Directorate of Security and Surveillance of the Ministry of Defense, the vigilante groups were to provide logistical support and intelligence to the military forces. Even after CONVIVIR was legally banned in 1999, some of them continued providing protection to land owners and drug traffickers—some independently, others by joining the AUC, the umbrella paramilitary organization. For details, see Fernando Cubides, "From Private to Public Violence: The Paramilitaries," in *Violence in Colombia 1990–2000,* Berquist, Peñaranda, and Sánchez, eds.: 127–50, and Gustavo Duncan, "Narcotraficantes,

mafiosos, y guerreros. Historia de una subordinación [Drug Traffickers, Mafiosos, and Fighters: History of a Subordination]" in *Narcotráfico en Colombia,* Rangel Suárez, ed.: 19–87. See also Carlos Medina Gallego, *La Violencia parainstitucional, paramilitary, y parapoliticial en Colombia* [Parainstitutional, Paramilitary, and Parapolitical Violence in Colombia] (Bogotá: Rodríguez Quito Editores, 1994).

151. Richani, *Systems of Violence:* 90. Author's interviews with Colombian experts on paramilitaries, Bogotá, fall 2005.

152. Rangel Suárez, *Colombia: guerra en el fin de siglo:* 50. Author's fieldwork in Colombia, fall 2008.

153. The leading commander of the AUC and its public face for nearly two decades, Carlos Castaño was killed in 2003 after suggesting to members of the Norte del Valle cartel that they strike a deal with the government of Colombia and the United States to stop the drug business in exchange for immunity from extradition. A power struggle exploded inside the cartel, and the faction that wanted to continue with the drug trade—including Don Berna and Vicente Castaño, Carlos Castaño's own brother—is believed to have killed Carlos Castaño. Salvatore Mancuso, a top pro–drug business figure in the AUC, took leadership of the group.

154. See López Montaño and García Durán, "Hidden Costs of Peace in Colombia: 153–54; and a compilation of FARC, ELN, and AUC documents and statements published in *Violence in Colombia 1990–2000,* Berquist, Peñaranda, and Sánchez, eds.: 243–55.

155. Adam Isacson, "Peace or Paramilitarization?" July 2005 (http://ciponline.org/colombia/0507ipr.pdf [August 4, 2005]).

156. For details, see Marshall, "Cooperative Efforts of the Colombian National Police and Military in Anti-Narcotics Efforts and Current DEA Initiatives in Colombia."

157. Ambassador William Wood, quoted in International Crisis Group, *War and Drugs in Colombia:* 16.

158. Echandía Castilla, *El Conflicto Armado y las Manifestaciones de la Violencia en las Regiones de Colombia.*

159. Steven W. Casteel, assistant administrator for intelligence, DEA, "Narco-Terrorism: International Drug Trafficking and Terrorism: A Dangerous Mix," testimony before the Senate Committee on the Judiciary, Mary 20, 2003 (www.google.com/search?sourceid=navclient-ff&ie=UTF-8&rlz=1B2GGGL_enUS 177&q=Casteel+ %22Narco-Terrorism %22, [August 13, 2004]). Author's interviews with U.S. government officials, Washington, summer and fall 2004.

160. Isacson, "Peace or Paramilitarization?" See also "Lording It Over Colombia: Colombia's Paramilitaries and Drug Lords," *The Economist,* October 23, 2004.

161. International Crisis Group, *War and Drugs in Colombia:* 15.

162. Isacson, "Peace or Paramilitarization?"

163. According to police estimates, as cited by Richani, *Systems of Violence*: 109.

164. Richani, *Systems of Violence*: 123.

165. Adam Isacson, *Peace Talks with Paramilitaries: Four Conditions for U.S. Support,* December 10, 2002 (www.ciponline.org/colombia/02121001.htm [August 04, 2003]). Author's interviews with Colombian academics, Bogotá, fall 2005.

166. Isacson, "Peace or Paramilitarization?": 4.

167. Richani, *Systems of Violence*: 124.

168. Gutiérrez Sanín, "Criminal Rebels?": 268.

169. Richani, *Systems of Violence*: 148, and Kirk, *More Terrible Than Death*: 276.

170. In a frequently cited episode in the 1980s, some of the paramilitary groups hired private Israeli and British security firms for training. For details, see, for example, Nazih Richani, "Multinational Corporations, Rentier Capitalism, and the War System in Colombia," *Latin American Politics and Society* 47, no. 3 (Fall 2005): 113–44.

171. Massacres committed by the paramilitaries peaked in the 1997–2002 period. See Jorge Restrepo and Michael Spagat, "Civilian Casualties in the Colombian Conflict: A New Approach to Human Security," CERP Davidson Institute, October 27, 2004 (http://personal.rhul.ac.uk/uhte/014/HS %20in %20Colombia %20Civil %20Conflict.pdf [December 02, 1004]. For an excellent discussion of the paramilitaries as "entrepreneurs of coercion," see Mauricio Romero, *Paramilitares y autodefensas 1982–2003* [Paramilitaries and Self-Defense Groups 1982–2003] (Bogotá: IEPRI, 2003).

172. Richani, *Systems of Violence*: 112.

173. Ibid.

174. Author's interviews with Colombian experts on paramilitaries, Bogotá, fall 2005.

175. International Crisis Group, *War and Drugs in Colombia*: 13. See also Carlos Castaño's memoirs in Alberto Aranguren, *Mi confesión* [My Confession] (Bogotá: Oveja Negra, 2002).

176. Guáqueta, "The Colombian Conflict: Political and Economic Dimensions": 82.

177. Apparently the paramilitaries also have used social services, such as health clinics known as ARS (Administradoras del Regimen Subsidiado [Administrators of the Subsidized Regime]) to launder money. Presentation by Representative Luis Fernando Velasco Chávez of Cauca at a WOLA conference in Washington, April 19, 2005, summarized in Kimberly Stanton, "The Colombian Conflict: Regional Impact and Policy Responses," WOLA Conference Report, August 2005: 13.

178. Pearce, *Colombia: Inside the Labyrinth*: 247. See also Medina Gallego, *Autodefensas, paramilitares, y narcotráfico en Colombia.*

179. Guáqueta, "The Colombian Conflict: Political and Economic Dimensions": 78.

180. Author's interviews with experts on paramilitaries, Bogotá, fall 2005. See also Romero, *Paramilitares y autodefensas 1982–2003,* and Duncan, "Narcotraficantes, mafiosos y guerreros": 19–87.

181. Author's interviews with representatives of NGOs operating in drug regions and Colombian academics who had conducted research among the *cocaleros,* Bogotá, fall 2005. See also Thoumi, *Illegal Drugs, Economy, and Society in the Andes*: 238, and "The World Geopolitics of Drugs, 1998–1999: Annual Report," *Geopolitical Drug Observer,* April 2000: 143 (www.ogd.org [February 15, 2003]).

182. Uribe, "Los cultivos ilícitos en Colombia.

183. See International Crisis Group, *Latin American Drugs I: Losing the Fight,* Latin America Report 25, March 14, 2008 (www.crisisgroup.org/library/documents/latin_america/25_latin_american_drugs_i_losing_the_fight_final.pdf: 8-9 [April 3, 2008]).

184. Uribe, "Los cultivos ilícitos en Colombia."

185. Until at least the mid-1990s, such evidence was lacking. See, for example, Richani, *Systems of Violence*: 99. Author's interviews with *campesinos* and representatives of alternative development NGOs in the poppy-growing areas of Nariño, fall 2008.

186. International Crisis Group, *War and Drugs in Colombia.*

187. See, for example, Juan Forero, "Colombian Conflict Spills into Indians' Perfect World," *New York Times,* May 2, 2005, and Indira Lakshmanan, "Still Battling for Survival," *Boston Globe,* November 16, 2004.

188. In fact, Colombian experts maintain that in the case of indigenous groups, for example, there is great variation in the groups' attitudes toward the cultivation of illicit crops, and many do so voluntarily, since coca represents the most reliable subsistence crop. Author's interviews with Colombian academics who have conducted research on indigenous groups and drugs, Bogotá, fall 2005. Author's interviews with *cocaleros,* Montes de Maria and Nariño, summer and fall 2008.

189. Francisco Gutiérrez Sanín, "Diverging Paths: Comparing Responses to Insurgent Challenges in Colombia and Perú," paper prepared for the Crisis States Centre, London School of Economics, 2006, author's copy.

190. Marcella, *The United States and Colombia*: 22-5, and Kirk, *More Terrible Than Death*: 68-9.

191. Restrepo, Spagat, and Vargas, "The Dynamics of the Colombian Civil Conflict."

192. Author's interviews with Colombian academics and government officials, Bogotá, fall 2005. See also International Crisis Group, *War and Drugs in Colombia*: 20.

193. Isacson, "Peace or Paramilitarization?": 4.

194. Author's interviews with Colombian government officials, Bogotá, fall 2005. Similarly, although rivals, the Medellín and Cali cartels frequently shared transportation to minimize transportation costs and distribute the risk and costs of seizure.

195. Author's interviews in Magdalena Medio, Montes de Maria, and Bogotá, summer 2008. See also Gutiérrez Sanín, "Criminal Rebels?": 270.

196. International Crisis Group, *War and Drugs in Colombia*: 12.

197. On February 4, 2008, more than 4 million marched against the FARC, and many left-leaning parties, such as Polo Democratico, have distanced themselves from the group. Under pressure from the international community and publicly shamed by revelations in captured FARC computers of tacit support for the guerrillas, President Hugo Chávez of Venezuela also sought to distance himself from the FARC during the latter part of 2008 and early part of 2009 and to clamp down at least somewhat on FARC sanctuaries in Venezuela. However, evidence that surfaced later in 2009 shows that the Venezuelan government continues to support the FARC.

198. Peter DeShazo, Tanya Primiani, and Phillip McLean, "Back from the Brink: Evaluating Progress in Colombia, 1999–2007" (Washington: CSIS, November 2007): 7; and Centro Nacional de Datos, Fondelibertad, Ministrio de Defensa Nacional, República de Colombia, "Cifras Extorcion [Extortion Figures]," June 20, 2007 (www.antisecuestro.gov.co/documentos/7_16_2007_4_58_07_PM_CifrasHistorias.pdf {May 17, 2008]).

199. Air Bridge Denial was restarted in Colombia in 2003, although it remained suspended elsewhere in Latin America. It was accompanied by Operation Firewall, a new interdiction effort.

200. Colleen Cook, *Colombia: Issues for Congress*, CRS Report for Congress, Congressional Research Service, February 26, 2008: 34.

201. Throughout most of the Bush administration, 80 percent of Plan Colombia funds supported military operations and eradication and interdiction efforts and 20 percent supported efforts to provide alternative livelihoods and bring about socioeconomic improvements. In 2008, the ratio shifted from 80:20 to 55:45. Since then the Obama administration has supported further cuts in funding for military and eradication programs.

202. U.S. Department of State, *International Narcotics Control Strategy Report (INCSR)*, March 2008 (www.state.gov/documents/organization/102583.pdf [March 18, 2008]): 129.

203. Ibid.

204. Robert B. Charles, assistant secretary of state for international narcotics and law enforcement affairs, "U.S. Policy and Colombia," testimony before the House Committee on Government Reform, June 17, 2004 (http://reform.house.gov/UploadedFiles/State %20- %20Charles %20Testimony.pdf [September 19, 2004]), and International Crisis Group, *War and Drugs in Colombia*.

205. U.S. Department of State, *International Narcotics Control Strategy Report (INCSR)*, March 2009 (www.state.gov/documents/organization/120054.pdf [March 3, 2009]): 208.

206. *International Narcotics Control Strategy Report*, March 2008: 129. In contrast, the goal of a 50 percent cut has essentially been achieved in poppy cultivation and heroin production. In 2000, 5,010 hectares of poppy were cultivated in Colombia, with the potential to produce 8.7 metric tons of heroin, while in 2006 only 2,400 hectares were cultivated, amounting to 4.6 metric tons of heroin. However, it is not clear to what extent the decline can be attributed to counternarcotics policies. Poppy cultivation has always been a marginal activity, and several factors appear to have contributed to its decline, including the expansion of the state presence (which can be credited to Plan Colombia), the relatively small difference between the prices of poppy and legal crops, the relatively well-developed roads in the area of poppy cultivation in Nariño, and its proximity to major regional markets. Those factors have encouraged farmers to turn to legal activities, such as dairy farming. However, some former poppy cultivators appear to be struggling economically and have resorted to smuggling gasoline and other legal products from Ecuador. (Author's interviews with ex–poppy farmers and government officials in Nariño, October 2008.)

207. The 2007 cocaine potential was estimated at 535 metric tons, a number positively lower than the 580 metric tons estimated for 2000. In 2006, 157,200 hectares of coca were cultivated in Colombia, with the potential to produce 610 metric tons of cocaine. See *International Narcotics Control Strategy Report*, March 2009, and Office of National Drug Control Policy, press release, September 10, 2008 (www.whitehousedrugpolicy.gov/news/press08/091008.html [September 22, 2008]).

208. This section draws heavily on the author's fieldwork in Colombia in the summer and fall of 2008. For details, see USAID, *Assessment of the Implementation of the United States Government's Support Plan for Colombia's Illicit Crop Reduction Components*.

209. So far, 600 such peasant squadrons have been established. Uribe also increased the number of soldiers to 200,000, paid for with a one-time tax increase. International Crisis Group, *Colombia: Presidential Politics and Peace Prospects*, Latin America Report 14, June 16, 2005 (www.crisisgroup.org/library/documents/latin_america/14_colombia_presidential_politics_and_political_prospects.pdf [September 9, 2005]). The Democratic Security Policy also included constrictions on human rights and civil liberties. See, for example, Vinay Jawahar, "Turning Point in Colombia: Rapporteur's Report," Colombia Working Group, Interamerican Dialogue, June 2004 (www.thedialogue.org/publications/2005/spring/2004AnnualReport.pdf [March 27, 2005]): 4–5.

210. Ministerio de Defensa, República de Colombia, "Logros de la Política de Consolidacíon Seguridad Democrática [Achievements of the Democratic Security Consolidation Policy]," Bogotá, September 2007: 67.

211. These numbers do not include the allocation for alternative development and other social and justice programs.

212. Author's interviews with officials of the U.S. embassy in Bogotá and officials of the Ministry of Defense, Bogotá, summer and fall 2008. See also International Crisis Group, *Colombia: Making Military Progress Pay Off,* Latin America Policy Briefing 17, April 29, 2008: 8.

213. During the Clinton administration, the U.S. military was prohibited from providing intelligence on the guerrillas to the Colombian military. Since 2002, the U.S. military has been allowed to provide real-time intelligence to the Colombians for counterinsurgency operations, a development that has dramatically enhanced the ability of the Colombian forces to strike against the FARC since it frequently lacks critical human intelligence.

214. General Bantz J. Craddock, *Posture Statement before the Senate Armed Services Committee,* March 14, 2006 (http://ciponline.org/colombia/050309crad.pdf [March 18, 2006]). They included Simón Trinidad, "Rodrigo Granda" (the FARC's "foreign minister," who was arrested in Caracas), and "Sonia."

215. Guillermo Sáenz Vargas, a.k.a. "Alfonso Cano," the group's second-in-command, replaced Marín as the new leader.

216. Author's interviews with Colombian government officials and independent analysts who interviewed captured FARC members, summer and fall 2008. For more information on the cache of sixty-six pounds of low-grade uranium that the FARC apparently tried to sell, see Frances Robles, "Uranium Cache Linked to FARC Rebels," *Miami Herald,* March 27, 2008.

217. U.S. Government Accounting Office (GAO), "Plan Colombia: Drug Reduction Goals Were Not Fully Met, but Security Has Improved; U.S. Agencies Need More Detailed Plans for Reducing Assistance," October 2008: 25.

218. ONDCP study cited by Juan Forero, "Colombia's Low-Tech Coca Assault," *Washington Post,* July 7, 2007.

219. Author's interviews with Colombian military officers in the war zones and officials of the Ministry of Defense, Bogotá, summer 2008. Although since the mid-1990s individual *frentes* were supposed to be more or less independently financed, there was nonetheless resource reallocation among the *frentes,* with supplies from *frentes* operating in drug regions going to *frentes* operating in nonproducing regions.

220. Author's interviews with *cocaleros* in Magdalena Medio, summer 2008.

221. Author's interviews with Colombian officials of the Ministry of Defense, Bogotá, summer 2008, and with academics who conducted research in Macarena, in the department of Meta (a former FARC stronghold and a high-priority area of counterinsurgency operations), Washington, fall 2008.

222. Author's interviews in Montes de Maria, summer 2008. In fact, the author witnessed spontaneous intelligence provision by the local population to the local military commander in Montes de Maria during her fieldwork.

223. Author's interviews with Colombian intelligence and security experts, officials of the Ministry of Defense, and U.S. embassy officials in Bogotá, summer 2008.

224. Given that the number of the demobilized members significantly increased previous estimates of the size of the paramilitaries, critics have charged that the paramilitaries hired any local available men to "demobilize" in order to be seen to be in compliance with the law. As membership between the FARC and the paras has been extraordinarily fluid in some highly contested areas, such as in central Colombia, it is also likely that some FARC members defected to the AUC in the early 2000s when the AUC took over some former FARC territories or switched to the AUC after 2005 to take advantage of the demobilization deal.

225. Ministerio de Defensa, República de Colombia, "Logros de la Política de Consolidacíion Seguridad Democrática": 29.

226. Ibid.: 17–18.

227. DeShazo, Primiani, and McLean, "Back from the Brink": 18.

228. Ibid.

229. Author's interviews with Colombian officials of the Ministry of Defense, Bogotá, summer 2008.

230. Isacson, "Peace or Paramilitarization?": 7; and Duncan, "Narcotraficantes, mafiosos, y guerreros." In 2004 Salvatore Mancuso, one of the AUC's chiefs, boasted that the paramilitaries controlled 30 percent of the national congress.

231. Presentation by Claudia López, investigative journalist for Colombia's *El Tiempo,* InterAmerican Dialogue, Washington, December 9, 2008.

232. "Politics, Drugs, and the Gun," *The Economist,* April 30, 2005.

233. See, for example, International Crisis Group, *Colombia's New Armed Groups,* Latin America Report 20, May 10, 2007.

234. The government of Colombia gives the lower number; independent research groups in Colombia state the higher one.

235. To fund its stepped-up military offensive, the government passed a special "tax on the rich," scheduled to expire in 2010.

236. GAO, "Plan Colombia: Drug Reduction Goals Were Not Fully Met, but Security Has Improved": 70. DeShazo, Primiani, and McLean, "Back from the Brink": 38. Nonetheless, many regions, including the coca areas, suffer greater unemployment rates, as high as 20 to 30 percent.

237. UN Economic Commission for Latin America and the Caribbean (CEPAL), "Estadísticas Sociales [Social Statistics]," *Anuario estadístico de America Latina y el Caribe 2006* [Statistical Yearbook for Latin America and the Caribbean] (Santiago, Chile: CEPAL, Marzo 2007): 74. The GINI coefficient of inequality fell slightly from 0.59 in 2003 to 0.54 in 2006. UN Development Program, "Human Development Report 2007/2008" (http://hdr.undp.org/en/media/HDR_20072008_EN_Complete.pdf [December 1, 2008]): 282, and DeShazo, Primiani, and McLean, "Back from the Brink": 45.

238. The lack of development in the rural areas is more than simply a matter of time. To a large extent, the failure of the robust macroeconomic growth to trickle down to the marginalized population of the rural areas is a function of the political economy in Colombia, which favors capital and large landowners but taxes labor very heavily and puts small farmers at a disadvantage.

CHAPTER FIVE

1. United Nations Office on Drugs and Crime (UNODC), *Afghanistan Opium Survey 2007,* October 2007 (www.unodc.org/pdf/research/Afghanistan_ Opium_Survey_2007.pdf); UNODC, *Afghanistan Opium Survey 2008: Executive Summary,* August 2008 (www.unodc.org/documents/data-and-analysis/ExSum25 August-standard.pdf); UNODC, *Afghanistan Opium Winter Rapid Assessment Survey* (www.unodc.org/documents/crop-monitoring/Afghan-winter-survey- Feb08-short.pdf); and UNODC, *Afghanistan Opium Survey 2009: Summary Findings,* September 2009 (www.unodc.org/documents/crop-monitoring/ Afghanistan/Afghanistan_opium_survey_2009_summary.pdf).

2. UNODC, "Opium Amounts to Half of Afghanistan's GDP in 2007, Reports UNODC," November 16, 2007 (www.unodc.org/unodc/en/press/releases/opium- amounts-to-half-of-afghanistans-gdp-in-2007,-reports-unodc.html [November 16, 2007). Since 2002, the percentage of GDP attributed to the drug trade has oscil- lated between 60 and 30 percent, not because the illicit economy has been reduced, but because some sectors of the legal economy, such as telecommunications, have expanded.

3. Kirk Semple, "Cannabis Replacing Opium Poppies in Afghanistan," *International Herald Tribune,* November 4, 2007.

4. For details on the main mujahideen factions, see Larry Goodson, *Afghanistan's Endless War* (University of Washington Press, 2001): 61–64.

5. J. Bruce Amstutz, *Afghanistan: The First Five Years of Soviet Occupation* (Washington: National Defense University, 1986): 133; David Isby, *Russia's War in Afghanistan* (London: Osprey, 1986): 8.

6. The consumption, production, and cultivation of opiates have all been deemed *haram* by different authorities. Typically the breadth of the prohibition in force has depended on the interests of local powerbrokers and international stake- holders, as well as their ability to mobilize local mullahs behind their preferred interpretation.

7. U.S. Department of State, Bureau of International Narcotics Matters, *International Narcotics Control Strategy Report* (INCSR) (Government Printing Office, 1984): 4. The opium was smuggled across the border to Pakistan and sold to heroin refiners operating under the protection of General Fazle Haq, governor of the North West Frontier Province. By 1988, there were an estimated 100 to 200 heroin refineries in the province's Khyber Agency (an administrative subunit)

alone. Alfred W. McCoy, *The Politics of Heroin: CIA Complicity in the Global Drug Trade,* rev. ed. (New York: Lawrence Hill Books, 2003): 478.

8. Hezb-i-Islami was 75 percent Pashtun and drew most of its members from the Ghilzai and smaller tribes. Its strongest bases of support were in northeastern Afghanistan and among Afghan refugees in Pakistan.

9. Barnett Rubin, *Fragmentation of Afghanistan* (Yale University Press, 1995): 199.

10. Ibid.: 183.

11. For details, see Antonio Giustozzi and Noor Ullah, "'Tribes' and Warlords in Southern Afghanistan, 1980–2005," Crisis States Research Centre, Working Paper 7, September 2006 (www.crisisstates.com/download/wp/wpSeries2/wp7.2.pdf [December 15, 2006]).

12. Alain Labrousse, *Afghanistan: Opium de guerre, opium de paix* [Afghanistan: Opium of War, Opium of Peace] (Paris: Fayard, 2005): 109.

13. McCoy, *The Politics of Heroin*: 484–85.

14. Rubin, *Fragmentation of Afghanistan*: 263.

15. For details, see Guistozzi and Ullah, "'Tribes' and Warlords in Southern Afghanistan."

16. For details, see Rubin, *Fragmentation of Afghanistan*: 159.

17. Pir Sayed Ahmad Gillani was the fourth major mujahideen warlord suspected of extensive participation in the illicit economy. He too operated in an area of traditional opium poppy cultivation, but unlike Hekmatyar, Nasim, and Ismat, he came from the eastern province of Nangarhar. He was high on the Soviet Union's list of drug suspects, and the Soviet intelligence report on Gillani's National Islamic Front of Afghanistan, which operated in Nangarhar, concluded that "the militia makes profits on selling drugs and exacting taxes from the population." See Lieutenant Colonel Yury Shvedov, *War in Afghanistan,* trans. by Natalie Kovalenko (Moscow: Ministry of Defense, Institute of Military History, 1991): 131–32.

18. Scott B. MacDonald, "Afghanistan," in *International Handbook on Drug Control,* Scott B. MacDonald and Bruce Zagaris, eds. (Westport, Conn.: Greenwood Press, 1992): 319.

19. Some of the mujahideen supported their families by selling captured weapons in Pakistan.

20. Ali Ahmad Jalali and Lester W. Grau, *Afghan Guerrilla Warfare: In the Words of the Mujahideen Fighters* (St. Paul, Minn.: MBI Publishing Company, 2001): 65–66.

21. Barnett Rubin, *The Search for Peace in Afghanistan* (Yale University Press, 1995): 117.

22. Olivier Roy, *Islam and Resistance in Afghanistan* (Cambridge University Press, 1990): 23.

23. Quoted in Rubin, *Fragmentation of Afghanistan*: 245.

24. Olivier Roy, *Afghanistan: From Holy War to Civil War* (Princeton: Darwin Press, 1995): 107.

25. Ikramul Haq, "Pak-Afghan Drug Trade in Historical Perspective," *Asian Survey* 36, no. 10 (October 1996): 954; and Michael Griffin, *Reaping the Whirlwind* (London: Pluto Press, 2001): 145. High officials of the Pakistani government were involved in the drug trade. By the mid-1980s, the drug trade had created an illicit economy in Pakistan of, by some accounts, as much as $8 billion, or half the size of the official economy. See, for example, McCoy, *The Politics of Heroin*. Among high-ranking officials directly incriminated in the drug trade were Lieutenant General Fazle Haq, governor of North West Frontier Province and a confidant of General Zia; Hamid Hasnain, another personal friend of Zia's and vice president of the state-owned Habib Bank; and Haji Ayub Afridi, the National Assembly member for Khyber Agency, an important coordinator of Pakistan's Afghanistan policy and, according to many reports, Pakistan's largest drug baron. For details, see Sumita Kumar, *Drug Trafficking in Pakistan* (New Dehli Institute for Defense Studies and Analyses, 1995). For a history of the drug trade in Pakistan, see Pierre-Arnaud Chouvy, *Opium: Uncovering the Politics of Poppy* (London: I.B. Tauris, 2009).

26. For details, see Goodson, *Afghanistan's Endless War*: 73–76; and Ahmed Rashid, *Taliban* (Yale University Press, 2001): 21.

27. Jonathan Goodhand, "From Holy War to Opium War? A Case Study of the Opium Economy in North East Afghanistan," *Central Asian Survey* 19, no. 2 (June 2000): 265–80; Martin Cooke, "Afghanistan: Drugs and Jewels Help Pay for War," *Daily Telegraph* (Australia), July 31, 1999.

28. Kanai Manayev, "Drug-Fuelled Crime in Central Asia," *Times of Central Asia,* January 4, 2001. Similarly, Rashid Dostum became progressively enmeshed in the narcotics trade as new trafficking routes developed from his base in northwestern Afghanistan through Uzbekistan to Russia and onward to Europe. John Cooley, *Unholy Wars: Afghanistan, America, and International Terrorism* (London: Pluto Press, 2002): 130. At the same time, poppy cultivation was taking off in Central Asia, especially in Tajikistan, which soon became embroiled in a civil war. For details on the poppy economy there, see Letizia Paoli, Victoria A. Greenfield, and Peter Reuter, *The World Heroin Market: Can Supply Be Cut?* (Oxford University Press, 2009): 118–200.

29. McCoy, *The Politics of Heroin*: 485.

30. Ibid.

31. Barnett Rubin, "The Political Economy of War and Peace in Afghanistan," *World Development* 28, no. 10 (2000): 1789–803 (http://institute-for-afghan-studies.org/ECONOMY/political_economy_of_war_peace.htm [April 14, 2004]).

32. William Maley, *The Afghanistan Wars* (New York: Palgrave Macmillan, 2002): 223–26, 232.

33. Anthony Davis, "How the Taliban Became a Fighting Force," in *Fundamentalism Reborn: Afghanistan and the Taliban*, William Maley, ed. (New York University Press, 1998): 46.

34. For details on the extent of Pakistan's involvement, see ibid.: 43–71; and Ahmed Rashid, "Pakistan and the Taliban," in *Fundamentalism Reborn*, Maley, ed.: 85–86.

35. Jobin Goodarzi, "Washington and the Taliban, Strange Bedfellows," *Middle East International,* October 25, 1996.

36. For details, see Rashid, "Pakistan and the Taliban," and Davis, "How the Taliban Became a Fighting Force."

37. Frederik Balfour, "Dark Days for a Black Market: Afghanistan and Pakistan Rely Heavily on Smuggling," *Business Week,* October 15, 2001 (http://business week.com/magazine/content/01_42/b3753016.htm [May 14, 2004]).

38. Rashid, *Taliban:* 29. Previously, Pakistani truckers could enter Afghanistan, but Afghan truckers could not enter Pakistan. This one-sided arrangement has been revived in the post-Taliban era.

39. Ahmed Rashid, "Nothing to Declare," *Far Eastern Economic Review,* May 11, 1995.

40. Griffin, *Reaping the Whirlwind:* 41.

41. Roy, *Afghanistan: From Holy War to Civil War.*

42. Davis, "How the Taliban Became a Fighting Force": 51.

43. Common punishments included imprisonment, beatings, and immersion in cold water for several hours at a time. Rashid, *Taliban:* 119.

44. "Afghanistan: The Taliban Face an Opium Dilemma," *Geopolitical Drug Dispatch* 63 (January 1997): 1, 3–5.

45. Griffin, *Reaping the Whirlwind:* 147.

46. Ironically Qadir's own efforts to suppress illicit activity—by eradicating a reported 5,000 hectares of poppy in 1995—had contributed to his downfall by stirring up local resentment. David Mansfield, *Resurgence and Reductions: Explanations for Changing Levels of Opium Poppy Cultivation in Nangarhar and Ghor in 2006–07* (Kabul: Afghanistan Research and Evaluation Unit [AREU], May 2008) (www.areu.org.af/index2.php?option=com_docman&task=doc_view&gid= 577&Itemid=26 [August 17, 2009]).

47. Quoted in Griffin, *Reaping the Whirlwind:* 153.

48. "Afghanistan: The Taliban Face an Opium Dilemma."

49. The Transnational Institute's Briefing Paper Series gives a much lower estimate, between $30 and $45 million a year, than Barnett Rubin, for example, who puts the Taliban's yearly earnings from drugs at $100 to $200 million. See Transnational Institute (TNI), *Afghanistan, Drugs, and Terrorism: Merging Wars,* TNI Briefing Paper 3, December 2001; and Rubin, "The Political Economy of War and Peace in Afghanistan." As explained in chapter 2, estimating the size and profits of illicit economies is more magic than science, and despite the large discrepancy both numbers are plausible. However, given the World Bank and UNODC estimates of the size of the illicit economy and traffickers' profits after the fall of the Taliban, which were produced under much greater transparency, Rubin's estimates seem more likely.

50. Jeffrey Bartholet and Steve LeVine, "The Holy Men of Heroin," *Newsweek* 134, no. 23 (December 6, 1999): 40–43.

51. UNODC, "Presentation to the International Crisis Group on Afghanistan," Brussels, July 5, 2004, author's copy.

52. Unlike many of the former mujahideen and Afghan and Pakistani traffickers, the Taliban leaders themselves continued to live extremely frugal lives.

53. Zareen Naqvi, *Afghanistan-Pakistan Trade Relations* (Islamabad: World Bank, 1999).

54. UNODC, "Access to Labour: The Role of Opium in the Livelihood Strategies of Itinerant Harvesters Working in Helmand Province, Afghanistan," Strategic Study 4, June 1999 (www.undcp.org/pakistan/report_1999-06-30 [March 18, 2004]).

55. The profits of small farmers from growing poppy are very small (about 2 percent of total profits from the drug trade) compared with those of traffickers and players higher up the chain.

56. UNODC, "Presentation to the International Crisis Group on Afghanistan."

57. In Thailand, for example, substituting flowers for the retail market for opium poppy has led to a profit increase of as much as 50 times the poppy profit per square meter. In Pakistan, growing onions has proven more profitable than growing opium poppies. See Michael Smith and others, *Why People Grow Drugs: Narcotics and Development in the Third World* (London: Panos, 1989), and David Mansfield, "The Economic Superiority of Illicit Drug Production: Myth and Reality—Opium Poppy Cultivation in Afghanistan," paper prepared for the International Conference on Alternative Development in Drug Control and Cooperation, Feldafing, Germany, September 7–12, 2002 (www.davidmansfield.org/all.php [September 2, 2009]). In Afghanistan itself, vegetables such as okra, artichoke, and onion and fruits could fetch more than opium.

58. Goodhand, "From Holy War to Opium War?"

59. Rashid, *Taliban*: 118.

60. Quoted in ibid.: 117.

61. Rashid, *Taliban*: 118. See also Ahmed Rashid, "Drug the Infidels," *Far Eastern Economic Review*, May 1997.

62. Kenneth J. Cooper, "Afghans Cultivate Islamic State, but Ignore Illicit Harvest," *Washington Post*, May 11, 1997.

63. Nigel J. R. Allan, "Opium Production in Afghanistan and Pakistan," in *Dangerous Harvest: Drug Plants and the Transformation of Indigenous Landscapes*, Michael K. Steinberg, Joseph J. Hobbs, and Kent Mathewson, eds. (Oxford University Press, 2004): 138.

64. UNODC, "The Role of Women in Opium Poppy Cultivation in Afghanistan," June 2000 (www.unodc.org/unodc/alternative_development_studies_6.html [May 14, 2004]). Pecuniary motives on the part of the Taliban cannot explain the decision to allow women to participate in opium cultivation and production. The participation of female members frequently made a crucial difference in a family's ability to achieve food security for the coming year, and although the increase in tax income thereby obtained by the Taliban was negligible, the political costs of further interfering with the rural population's food security would have been high.

65. "Heroin," *Jane's Intelligence Review*, June 1, 1998; Andrew Meier, "Afghanistan's Drug Trade," *Muslim Politics Report* 11, 1997: 3–4; and Ahmed

Rashid, "The Taliban: Exporting Extremism," *Foreign Affairs* 78, no. 6 (November–December 1999): 22–36.

66. David Mansfield, "Coping Strategies, Accumulated Wealth, and Shifting Markets: The Story of Opium Poppy Cultivation in Badakhshan 2000–2003," a report for the Agha Khan Development Network, January 2004: 4 (www.david-mansfield.org/all.php [September 2, 2009]).

67. Barbara Crossette, "The Taliban's Ban on Growing Opium Poppies Is Called a Success," *New York Times,* May 18, 2001.

68. One among many similar stories in David Mansfield, "What Is Driving Opium Poppy Cultivation? Decision Making amongst Opium Poppy Cultivators in Afghanistan in the 2003/4 Growing Season," paper for the UNODC/UNDCP Second Technical Conference on Drug Control Research, July 19–21, 2004 (www.davidmansfield.org/all.php [September 2, 2009]).

69. UNODC, "Presentation to the International Crisis Group on Afghanistan." Farm gate opium prices jumped from $28 per kilogram in 2000 to $301 per kilogram in 2001. See UNODC, *Summary Findings of Opium Trends in Afghanistan,* September 12, 2005 (www.unodc.org/pdf/afghanistan_2005/annex_opium-afghanistan-2005-09-09.pdf: 16 [September 18, 2005]).

70. According to some estimates, 3,000 metric tons of opium and 220 metric tons of heroin were stockpiled in Afghanistan, many under Taliban control. International Crisis Group, *Central Asia: Drugs and Conflict,* Report No. 26, November 26, 2001 (www.crisisgroup.org/library/documents/report_archive/A400495_26112001-2.pdf [August 16, 2004]).

71. Quoted in Mary Jacoby, "War's New Target: Drugs," *St. Petersburg Times,* February 11, 2002. See also LaVerle Berry and others, *A Global Overview of Narcotics-Funded Terrorist and Other Extremist Groups,* report prepared by the Federal Research Division, Library of Congress, May 2002 (www.loc.gov/rr/frd/pdf-files/NarcsFundedTerrs_Extrems.pdf: 6 [August 05, 2004]).

72. Christian Caryl, "The New Silk Road of Death," *Newsweek* 113, no. 12 (September 17, 2001): 27. Other sources put the level of stockpiles considerably lower, at about two years' worth. The fact that the Taliban had stockpiles, however, did not mean that the population had such stockpiles.

73. This possibility highlights the difficulty of predicting how belligerents will be affected by antinarcotics policies such as eradication. Rather than drive them into bankruptcy, as the conventional narcoguerrilla wisdom predicts, such policies may actually increase their profits, as in this case.

74. Barnett R. Rubin, "Road to Ruin: Afghanistan's Booming Opium Industry," October 7, 2004 (www.cic.nyu.edu [November 1, 2004]).

75. David Mansfield and Adam Pain, *Counternarcotics in Afghanistan: The Failure of Success?* AREU Briefing Paper Series, December 2008: 7.

76. Ibid.

77. Caryl, "The New Silk Road of Death."

78. See, for example, Bertil Lintner, "Taliban Turns to Drugs," *Far Eastern Economic Review,* October 11, 2001.

79. Stephen Tanner, *Afghanistan: A Military History from Alexander the Great to the Fall of the Taliban* (Cambridge: Da Capo Press, 2002): 308–09.

80. Carlotta Gall, "Seven-Year Drought Puts Afghanistan on the Brink," *New York Times,* December 12, 2004.

81. UNODC, *Afghanistan: Farmers' Intentions Survey 2003–2004* (www.unodc.org/pdf/afg/afg_fis_report_2003-2004.pdf [August 08, 2005]).

82. Mansfield, "What Is Driving Opium Poppy Cultivation?"

83. UNODC, *Afghanistan: Farmers' Intentions Survey 2003–2004*: 35; and UNODC, "Presentation to the International Crisis Group on Afghanistan." UNODC estimates an average yield of thirty kilograms of dried opium from one hectare of land.

84. Adam Pain, "Opium Trading Systems in Helmand and Ghor," Afghan Research and Evaluation Unit, *Issue Paper Series,* January 2006 (www.areu.org.af/publications/Opium%20Trading%20Systems.pdf [January 27, 2006]): 1, 19.

85. Jim Lobe, "Afghanistan: Concerns Grow over Taliban Resurgence, Opium," *Global Information Network,* January 29, 2004 (http://proquest.umi.com/pqdweb?did=533932931&sid=8&Fmt=3&clientId=5482&RQT=309&VName=PQD [August 03, 2004]).

86. Stephane Allix, *La Petite Cuillère De Schéhérazade* [Schéhérazade's Little Spoon] (Paris: Ramsay, 1998): 48–52.

87. UNODC, *Afghanistan Opium Survey 2008,* August 2008: 5, 7, and 13.

88. UNODC, *Afghanistan Opium Survey 2006,* September 2006 (www.unodc.org/unodc/index.html [September 16, 2006]).

89. Rubin, "Road to Ruin: Afghanistan's Booming Opium Industry." It also needs to be mentioned that such large-scale unmitigated illicit economic activity carries some serious negative economic effects. So far, in Afghanistan, it has been contributing to inflation, pushing up the price of food, consumer goods, and real estate. It also has led to real estate speculation and currency destabilization. Furthermore, the size of the illicit economy in Afghanistan's case frequently dwarfs government revenues, which in 2005, for example, were only 4.5 percent of GDP, one of the lowest rates in the world. See "Creeping towards the Marketplace," *The Economist,* February 4, 2006. Extensive cultivation of illicit crops, easy access to drugs, and the return of refugees from Pakistan, a country that has a major drug addiction problem, also contributed to a substantial rise in the number of opiate addicts in Afghanistan, perhaps as much as 4 percent of the population. "Asia: Demand-Driven—Drug Addiction in Afghanistan," *The Economist,* January 17, 2004.

90. See, for example, Pankaj Mishra, "The Real Afghanistan," *New York Review of Books* 52, no. 4 (March 10, 2005): 46.

91. Transnational Institute, *Downward Spiral: Banning Opium in Afghanistan and Burma,* TNI Briefing Paper 12, June 2005 (www.tni.org/reports/drugs/

debate12.pdf: 11 [June 29, 2005]). In a much publicized event, Noorzai was later arrested again in 2005 and extradited to the United States. Other prominent traffickers arrested in Afghanistan and extradited to the United States include Mohammad Essa and Haji Baz Mohammad.

92. Eric Schmitt, "U.S. to Add to Forces in Horn of Africa," *New York Times,* October 30, 2002.

93. Tim McGirk, "Drugs? What Drugs?" *Time,* August 18, 2003.

94. Ibid.

95. I am not arguing that the U.S. military actively encouraged the participation or entrenchment of the warlords in the drug trade, but a direct consequence of the minimalist approach of the United States was its inability and early unwillingness to prevent the warlords from consolidating their power vis-à-vis the Kabul government, including by becoming entrenched in the drug trade. See Pierre-Arnaud Chouvy, "Narco-Terrorism in Afghanistan," *Terrorism Monitor* 2, no. 6 (March 25, 2004). See also Chouvy, *Opium: Uncovering the Politics of Poppy.*

96. Quoted in Anne Barnard and Farah Stockman, "U.S. Weighs Role in Heroin War in Afghanistan," *Boston Globe,* October 20, 2004.

97. Mishra, "The Real Afghanistan": 47. See also Philippe Grangereau, "Afghanistan: Dans le Nangarhar, la mafia de l'opium regne en maitre [Afghanistan: In Nangarhar, the Opium Mafia Reigns Supreme]," *Liberation,* October 9, 2004.

98. Ron Moreau and Sami Yousafzai, "Flowers of Destruction," *Newsweek* 142, no. 2 (July 14, 2003): 29.

99. Mishra, "The Real Afghanistan": 47.

100. Ibid. Gul Agha Sherazai was replaced as the governor of Kandahar by Haji Assadulah Khalid in 2005; Sherazai was appointed the governor of Nangarhar.

101. UNODC, "Presentation to the International Crisis Group on Afghanistan."

102. UNODC, *Afghanistan: Farmers' Intentions Survey 2003–2004*: 36.

103. See, for example, Mishra, "The Real Afghanistan"; Larry Goodson, "Afghanistan's Long Road to Reconstruction," *Journal of Democracy* 14, no. 1 (January 2003): 82–99; and Kathy Gannon, "Afghanistan Unbound," *Foreign Affairs* 83, no. 3 (May-June 2004): 35–46.

104. Even the presence of U.S. Drug Enforcement Administration personnel was limited to two agents who rarely left Kabul. See Moreau and Yousafzai, "Flowers of Destruction": 33.

105. UNAMA was created in March 2002 to assist Afghanistan in state-building. Under UNAMA, the United States was charged with training Afghanistan's new army; Germany with establishing Afghanistan's police; Japan with disarming and reintegrating militias; and Italy with establishing the rule of law and reforming the judiciary.

106. Pain, "Opium Trading Systems in Helmand and Ghor."

107. John F. Burns, "Afghan Warlords Squeeze Profits from the War on Drugs, Critics Say," *New York Times,* May 5, 2002.

108. Anthony Fitzherbert, "The Impact of Afghan Transition Authority's Poppy Eradication Programme on Rural Farmers," Mercy Corps Mission Report, September-October 2003.

109. Peter Oborne and Lucy Morgan Edwards, "A Victory for Drug-Pushers," *Spectator* 292, no. 9121 (May 31, 2003): 26–27.

110. Burns, "Afghan Warlords Squeeze Profits from the War on Drugs, Critics Say."

111. Indira R. A. Lakshmanan, "Afghan Announce Victories in a New War against Opium," *Boston Globe,* April 21, 2002.

112. "Asia: Poppies Bloom Again; Drugs in Afghanistan," *The Economist,* April 22, 2002: 66.

113. Institute for War and Peace Reporting, *Farmers Enraged by Poppy Crackdown,* April 11, 2002 (www.iwpr.net/?p=rca&s=f&o=176816&apc_state=henirca200204 [March 23, 2004]).

114. Transnational Institute, *Downward Spiral: Banning Opium in Afghanistan and Burma*: 10.

115. See, for example, Christopher Blanchard, *Afghanistan: Narcotics and U.S. Policy,* CRS Report for Congress (Washington: Congressional Research Service, December 7, 2004).

116. Antonio Maria Costa, UNODC, "Letter of 11 November 2004" (www.colombo-plan.org/www/images/pubs/pdf/unodcnov2004.pdf [November 23, 2004]).

117. Jim Hoagland, "A New Afghan Policy," *Washington Post,* August 8, 2004. Author's interviews with U.S. officials at the Departments of State and Defense and at the National Security Council, Washington, summer 2004.

118. Thom Shanker, "Pentagon Sees Antidrug Effort in Afghanistan," *New York Times,* March 25, 2005. Author's interviews with U.S. government officials, Washington, spring 2006.

119. Eric Schmitt, "Afghans' Gains Face Big Threat in Drug Traffic," *New York Times,* December 11, 2004.

120. Jason Burke, "British Troops Wage War on Afghan Drugs," *Observer,* December 5, 2004.

121. Robert B. Charles, "Are British Counternarcotics Efforts Going Wobbly?" testimony before the House Committee on Government Reform Subcommittee on Criminal Justice, Drug Policy, and Human Resources, April 1, 2004 (www.useu.be/Article.asp?ID=90CBBA80-50B2-4939-8E76-FC1C3C041D2B [August 08, 2004]).

122. Robert B. Charles, "Counternarcotics Initiatives for Afghanistan," On-The-Record Briefing, Washington, D.C., November 17, 2004 (www.state.gov/p/inl/rls/prsrl/spbr/38352.htm, downloaded November 28, 2004).

123. Transnational Institute, *Plan Afghanistan,* Drug Policy Briefing 10, January 2005 (www.tni.org/policybriefings/brief10.pdf [June 13, 2005]).

124. Costa, "Letter of 11 November 2004."

125. John Lancaster, "Karzai Vows to Combat Flourishing Afghan Opium Trade," *Boston Globe,* December 10, 2004.

126. Ashraf Ghani, "Where Democracy's Greatest Enemy Is a Flower," *New York Times,* December 11, 2004.

127. A U.S. public relations company, Rendon Group, was hired to help Karzai with the anti-drug campaign under a contract for $1.4 million; it was renewed in 2005 by another $3.9 million funded through the U.S. Department of Defense.

128. As mentioned earlier, Karzai's government included many prominent politicians and warlords with ties to the drug trade. Allegations of drug trafficking have also been made against Karzai's brother in Kandahar, Ahmed Wali Karzai. See, for example, James Risen, "Reports Link Karzai's Brother to Afghanistan Heroin Trade," *New York Times,* October 4, 2008. Both Ahmed Wali Karzai and President Hamid Karzai have strongly denied the allegations, arguing that they are politically motivated. Although the allegations are widely believed around Kandahar province, no material evidence clearly establishing the allegations has surfaced. Author's interviews with Afghans in Kandahar City and ISAF officials, Kandahar City, spring 2009.

The various politicians and government appointees believed to have links to the drug trade had accumulated so much military power and political capital that Karzai did not feel that he could avoid making deals with them. Apart from giving them positions of power, in January 2005 Karzai announced an amnesty for drug traffickers who come clean, end their participation in the drug trade, and invest their illicit earnings in local development. As Deputy Minister Lieutenant General Daoud explained, under the amnesty program, "[w]e would ask them [politicians prominently connected to the drug trade] to join the government and use their influence and capital to help eliminate poppy and to support the economy." See Stephen Graham, "Afghanistan May Pardon Drug Dealers," *Associated Press,* January 10, 2005.

129. Bill Rammell, "Afghanistan Counter Narcotics Implementation Plan," Ministerial Statement, Parliamentary Under Secretary of State for Foreign and Commonwealth Affairs," London, March 10, 2005.

130. The Central Poppy Eradication Force efforts ended up costing at least $100,000 per hectare eradicated. See "After Victory, Defeat," *The Economist,* July 16, 2005.

131. David S. Cloud and Carlotta Gall, "U.S. Memo Faults Afghan Leader on Heroin Fight," *New York Times,* May 22, 2005.

132. UNODC, *Afghanistan Opium Survey 2006,* September 2006 (www.unodc.org/unodc/index.html [September 16, 2006]).

133. UNODC, *The Opium Situation in Afghanistan,* August 29, 2005.

134. Pain, "Opium Trading Systems in Helmand and Ghor."

135. Ibid.: 19–21.

136. Ibid.: 21. See also Burns, "Afghan Warlords Squeeze Profits from the War on Drugs, Critics Say."

137. Moreover, because of the slow rebuilding of the judiciary, it is not clear whether, even if indicted, such prominent traffickers could in fact be tried and sentenced. See, for example, Larry P. Goodson, "Bullets, Ballots, and Poppies in Afghanistan," *Journal of Democracy* 16, no. 1 (January 2005): 25–38.

138. Christopher Ward and others, *Afghanistan: Economic Incentives to Reduce Opium Production,* Department for International Development and the World Bank, December 20, 2007 (www.dfid.gov.uk/pubs/files/incentives-opium-prod-red-afghan.pdf [January 8, 2008]).

139. Rajiv Chandrasekaran, "U.S. Pursues a New Way to Rebuild in Afghanistan," *Washington Post,* June 19, 2009. For challenges regarding the alternative livelihood efforts in southern Afghanistan, see Joel Hafvenstein, *Opium Season* (Guilford, Conn.: Lyons Press, 2007).

140. The U.S. firm Chemonics has been administering the vast majority of USAID agricultural contracts in Afghanistan.

141. For an excellent analysis of the economic drivers of cultivation, see David Mansfield, "Water Management, Livestock, and the Opium Economy—Resurgence and Reductions: Explanations for Changing Levels of Opium Poppy Cultivation in Nangarhar and Ghor in 2006–07," AREU (May 2008).

142. Author's interviews with advisers and counternarcotics officials from ISAF and from the Provincial Reconstruction Teams (created to provide economic development in insecure areas) in Kandahar, Zabul, Helmand, and Uruzgan, spring 2009, and with counternarcotics contractors for Afghanistan, Washington, spring 2009.

143. Baitullah Mehsud was killed by a U.S. Predator strike in Pakistan in August 2009.

144. See, for example, Nicholas Schmidle, "Next-Gen Taliban," *New York Times Magazine,* January 6, 2008; Thomas H. Johnson and M. Chris Mason, "Understanding the Taliban and Insurgency in Afghanistan," *Orbis* 51, no. 1 (winter 2007): 71–89; and Seth Jones, "Averting Failure in Afghanistan," *Survival* 48, no. 1 (spring 2006): 111–28.

145. Ali Jalali, "The Future of Afghanistan," *Parameters* 36, no. 1 (spring 2006).

146. Kirk Semple, "Citing Taliban Threat, Afghan Ex-Militia Leaders Hoard Illegal Arms," *New York Times,* October 28, 2007.

147. Under the Afghan electoral law, former Taliban who had given up their links to armed groups and did not have a criminal record could even participate in the parliamentary elections. However, according to Afghan officials, only a few fighters took advantage of the amnesty; many others did not trust the terms and

feared being sent to Guantanamo or Bagram. Author's interviews with Afghan officials who had interrogated some of the captured Taliban fighters, Cambridge, Massaschusetts, winter 2005.

148. So far, the Taliban has managed to close down 200 schools.

149. Cited in Thomas Schweich, "Is Afghanistan a Narco-State?" *New York Times,* July 27, 2008. That was not the first time that pressure to undertake aerial spraying mounted. The United States seriously considered the policy as early as late 2004. In late 2007, despite opposition from NATO partners in Afghanistan, the Bush National Security Council authorized spraying with the goal of cutting the Taliban's profits and thus weakening the insurgency. But although President Bush declared himself a strong supporter of spraying, President Karzai persuaded him to shelf the policy. See, for example, Rajiv Chandrasekaran, "Administration Is Keeping Ally at Arm's Length," *Washington Post,* May 6, 2009.

150. Elizabeth Rubin, "In the Land of the Taliban," *New York Times Magazine,* October 22, 2006: 86–99 and 173; Sami Yousafzai and Ron Moreau, "For the Taliban, A Crime That Pays," *Newsweek,* September 15, 2008 (www.newsweek.com/id/157549/output/print [September 27, 2008]); Pir Zubair Shah and Jane Perlez, "Pakistan Marble Helps Taliban Stay in Business," *New York Times,* July 14, 2008.

151. Seth G. Jones, "Pakistan's Dangerous Game," *Survival* 49, no. 1 (spring 2007): 15–32.

152. "Five Afghan Officers Die in Opium Area Attacks," *Boston Globe,* March 12, 2006. Hekmatyar's and the Haqqanis' forces, the other component of the insurgent forces in the south and east, have also attacked counternarcotics officials.

153. I am grateful to Sarah Chayes for this information. Because of possible threats to local Afghans, both the names of the village and its inhabitants are not used.

154. Ali, allegedly a major trafficker himself, was widely believed to be cutting profits on traffic in the north of Afghanistan while eradicating in the east. Author's interviews with think tank and NGO representatives, Kabul, September 2005.

155. David Mansfield, "Pariah or Poverty? The Opium Ban in the Province Nangarhar in 2004/05 Growing Season and Its Impact on Rural Livelihood Strategies." GTZ Policy Brief No. 1, September 2005 (www.gtz.de/de/dokumente/en-FinalCopingReportStudyPAL20.7.pdf [October 1, 2005]).

156. Ibid.

157. Mansfield and Pain, *Counternarcotics in Afghanistan: The Failure of Success?*: 5–7.

158. N. C. Aizenman, "Afghans Report Decline of Poppy Crop, Officials Credit Karzai's Appeals, but Warn Aid Is Needed to Ensure Success," *Washington Post,* February 6, 2005.

159. Interview reproduced in Jan Koehler and Christoph Zürcher, *Conflict Processing and the Opium Poppy Economy in Afghanistan,* PAL Internal Document 5, May 2005 (www.gtz.de/de/dokumente/en-DrugsandConflictAfghanistan PAL.pdf [June 2005]): 16.

160. See, for example, Farah Stockman, "Women Pay a Price in War on Afghan Drug Trade," *Boston Globe,* September 28, 2005, and Transnational Institute, *Losing Ground: Drug Control and War in Afghanistan,* TNI Briefing Paper 15, December 2006 (www.tni.org/docs/200702281633543041.pdf [January 13, 2007]): 13.

161. This escape valve for indebted farmers has now been closed as Pakistan (as well Iran) shut down refugee camps and forced Afghan refugees to return to Afghanistan. About 5 million people have returned. In addition to compounding the opium indebtedness problem, the closing of the camps has further fueled both drug cultivation and the insurgency. It has resulted in income losses for many Afghan families by reducing remittances and chances of seasonal employment. Many returnees do not own land, and cultivating opium is frequently the only way to rent land. Those trying to reclaim previous family ownership of lands frequently trigger clan and tribal disputes that the Taliban is cleverly exploiting. In fact, local tribe-on-tribe conflict is an important component of the instability.

162. UNODC, *Afghanistan Opium Survey 2006* and *Afghanistan Opium Survey 2007.*

163. Sherzai, a former commander, was alleged to have deep connections to the drug trade in Kandahar province, where he was governor in the post-Taliban period.

164. For details, see Mansfield and Pain, *Counternarcotics in Afghanistan: The Failure of Success?:* 12.

165. Ibid.

166. Presentation by David Mansfield based on his fieldwork in Nangarhar in 2008, World Bank, Washington, June 24, 2008.

167. Interviews conducted by David Mansfield in Afghanistan in 2006 and 2007 and published in David Mansfield, *Beyond Metrics: Understanding the Nature of Change in the Rural Livelihoods of Opium Growing Households in the 2006–07 Growing Season,* a report for the Afghan Drugs Interdepartmental Unit of the U.K. government, May 2007 (www.davidmansfield.org/data/Field_Work/UK/FinalDrivers0607.pdf [June 27, 2008]).

168. See, for example, Christian Parenti, "Afghanistan: The Other War," *The Nation* 282, no. 12 (March 27, 2006): 11–17; Pamela Constable, "Afghan Villagers Greet U.S. Hunt for Insurgents with Polite Silence," *Boston Globe,* April 20, 2006; Declan Walsh, "Afghan Civilians Accuse U.S.-Led Soldiers of Abuse," *Boston Globe,* June 25, 2006.

169. Author's interviews with U.S. and NATO military officers, Washington, winter 2006, and Kandahar, spring 2009.

170. Schweich, "Is Afghanistan a Narco-State?"

171. Author's interviews with ISAF military officers and their civilian counterparts, Kandahar, Helmand, Zabul, and Uruzgan, spring 2009.

172. Cited in Chandrasekaran, "U.S. Pursues a New Way to Rebuild in Afghanistan."

173. In June 2009, Congress agreed to add $100 million for agricultural reconstruction on top of existing aid, and the Obama administration requested an additional $235 million for fiscal year 2010, thus increasing rural development funding several times.

CHAPTER SIX

1. John Horgan and Max Taylor, "Playing the Green Card: Financing Provisional IRA—Part 1," *Terrorism and Political Violence* 11, no. 2 (Summer 1999): 1–38.

2. Eamon Collins with Mick McGovern, *Killing Rage* (London: Granta, 1997): 29.

3. Andrew Silke, "Drink, Drugs, and Rock 'n' Roll: Financing Loyalist Terrorism in Northern Ireland—Part Two," *Studies in Conflict and Terrorism* 23, no. 2 (April-June 2000): 112.

4. Ibid.: 108.

5. See, for example, Anna-Marie McFaul, "Godfathers 'Now Control Illegal Drug Trade,'" *Irish News*, August 30, 1995.

6. Ibid.

7. Silke, "Drink, Drugs, and Rock 'n' Roll": 117.

8. See, for example, Martin Smith, *Burma and the Politics of Insurgency* (New York: Zed Books, 1999).

9. Bertil Lintner, *Burma in Revolt: Opium and Insurgency since 1948* (Bangkok: Silkworm Press, 1999).

10. To improve its image, the State Law and Order Restoration Council (SLORC) was renamed the State Peace and Development Council (SPDC) in the mid-1990s.

11. At the same time, the junta made a major push to modernize the armed forces and improve their counterinsurgency skills and force structure. Military reform significantly enhanced the efficacy of the government's counterinsurgency operations by improving logistics and mobility and increasing the government's presence throughout the country. Frank S. Jannuzi, "The New Burma Road (Paved by Polytechnologies?)," in *Burma: Prospects for a Democratic Future,* Robert I. Rotberg, ed. (Brookings, 1998): 197–208.

12. Robert S. Gelbard, "Burma: The Booming Drug Trade," in *Burma: Prospects for a Democratic Future,* Rotberg, ed.: 185–97.

13. Jake Sherman, "Burma: Lessons from the Cease-fires," in *The Political Economy of Armed Conflict: Beyond Greed and Grievance,* Karen Ballentine and Jake Sherman, eds. (Boulder, Colo.: Lynne Rienner, 2003): 225–55.

14. For example, Khun Sa came to operate several major companies, including Good Shan Brothers, Lo Asia World, Asia Wealth, and Kokang Import-Export Company. As the country's economy continued to crumble as a result of decades

of mismanagement and the economic sanctions imposed on Burma by the United States and Europe, the significance of illicit profits for the overall economy continued to grow and such profits became more and more officially sanctioned. The government de facto agreed to absorb the illicit money to keep the overall economy afloat. For details see Robert S. Gelbard, "SLOCR's Drug Links," *Far Eastern Economic Review,* November 21, 1996; Anthony Davis and Bruce Hawke, "Burma—The Country That Won't Kick the Habit," *Jane's Intelligence Review,* March 1998; and Bertil Linter, "Drugs and Economic Growth: Ethnicity and Exports," in *Burma: Prospects for a Democratic Future,* Rotberg, ed.: 165–83.

15. These roads facilitated not only the spread of the state's presence and the increase of overall economic activity but also the efficiency of drug trafficking. Author's fieldwork and interviews with licit and illicit goods traders in Kentung, Shan state, and Pyin U Lwin, Mandalay Division, December 2005 and January 2006.

16. Author's interviews with representatives of the UN Office on Drugs and Crime (UNODC) in Yangon, Burma, December 2006, and independent local authorities in Special Region Number 4 of Shan state, January 2006.

17. Thomas Fuller, "Ethnic Groups in Myanmar Hope for Peace, but Gird for Fight," *New York Times,* May 11, 2009. Threats to their autonomy, such as those triggered by the new constitution that the junta has been seeking to adopt in 2010, may trigger new active conflicts with some of the groups. In summer 2009, after conflict reignited with several of these opposition groups, including Karen and Kokang insurgents near the border with Thailand and China, the junta successfully defeated them, exploiting both its overwhelming force and the rifts within and among the groups.

18. See U.S. Department of State, *International Control Strategy Reports,* for the years 1984–2006 .

19. Author's interviews with UNODC officials, Yangon, Burma, December 2005.

20. Displaying a good sense of humor, Sai Lin, once one of the world's biggest drug traffickers, opened a large drug eradication museum in Mong La, the "capital" of his autonomous region near the border with China, where local law enforcement officers were eager to describe their suppression efforts to the author.

21. UN Office on Drugs and Crime, *Myanmar: Opium Survey 2005* (www. unodc.org/pdf/Myanmar_opium-survey-2005.pdf [September 10, 2006]); UN Office on Drugs and Crime, *Opium Poppy Cultivation in Southeast Asia: Lao PDR, Myanmar, and Thailand,* December 2008 (www.unodc.org/documents/crop-monitoring/East_Asia_Opium_report_2008.pdf [January 13, 2009]).

22. The groups that control these regions, such as the United Wa State Army, are themselves engaged in forcible relocation of the population from the agriculturally unproductive hill regions into more productive lower-altitude regions within the territory that they control to maintain eradication. See, for example, Transnational Institute, *Downward Spiral: Banning Opium in Afghanistan and Burma,* TNI Briefing Paper 12, June 2005 (www.tni.org/reports/drugs/debate12. pdf [June 29, 2005]).

23. Author's interviews with poppy farmers and ex–poppy farmers in the hill regions of Shan state, Burma, January 2006.

24. Sherman, "Burma: Lessons from the Ceasefires," in Ballentine and Sherman, *The Political Economy of Armed Conflict:* 251. For details on Burma's and Asia's methamphetamine trade, see Pierre-Arnaud Chouvy and Joël Meissonier, *Production, Traffic, and Consumption of Methamphetamine in Mainland Southeast Asia* (Singapore University Press–IRASEC, 2004).

25. Paradoxically, unless laundered through a bank or business, money can be more perishable than the actual drug. For example, in the 1980s Colombian drug traffickers made so much money that they were unable to launder it quickly through the Colombian economy and had to resort to burying barrels of dollars in the jungle. Because they had so much cash coming in, they rarely had to dig up the barrels, and on occasion the money would simply rot, eaten away by tropical fungi.

26. Kevin Jack Riley, *Snow Job?* (New Brunswick: Transaction Publishers, 1996): 93.

27. Peter Reuter, "Eternal Hope: America's Quest for Narcotics Control," *Public Interest* 79 (Spring 1985): 79–95.

28. UN Office on Drugs and Crime, *2006 World Drug Report* (www.unodc. org/pdf/WDR_2006/wdr2006_volume1.pdf [September 24, 2006]).

29. See, for example, Tom Kramer, Martin Jelsma, and Tom Blickman, *Withdrawal Symptoms in the Golden Triangle: A Drugs Market in Disarray* (Amsterdam: Transnational Institute, January 2009).

30. Office of National Drug Control Policy, *Supplement to the 2009 National Drug Control Strategy* (www.whitehousedrugpolicy.gov/publications/policy/ ndcs09/ndcs09_data_supl/ds_drg_rltd_tbls.pdf [May 1, 2009]). For a debate about how to interpret temporary increases in prices, see Office of National Drug Control Policy, "White House Drug Czar, DEA Administrator Release New Data Showing Significant Disruptions in U.S. Cocaine and Methamphetamine Markets," press release, November 8, 2007 (www.usdoj.gov/dea/pubs/pressrel/pr11 0807a.html [November 10, 2007]), and John Walsh, "Lowering Expectations: Supply Control and the Resilient Cocaine Market," Washington Office on Latin America, April 14, 2009 (www.wola.org/media/Lowering%20Expectations% 20April%202009.pdf [May 1, 2009]).

31. In the 1960s and 1970s, under the rule of the PRI (Partido Revolucionario Institucional [Institutional Revolutionary Party]), the former DFS (Dirección Federal de Seguridad [Federal Security Directorate]) and the PJF (Policía Judicial Federal [Federal Judicial Police]), regulated, mediated disputes between, and protected drug trafficking organizations in Mexico. The DFS developed especially strong ties to drug traffickers during the 1970s, when it tolerated their activities in exchanges for assistance with paramilitary operations against a leftist urban terrorist group, the 23rd of September Communist League. Later in the 1970s, DFS personnel went into business with the traffickers. See Luis Astorga, "El Tráfico de fármacos

ilícitos en México: Organizaciones de traficantes, corrupción, y violencia [Traffic in Illicit Drugs: Trafficking Organizations, Corruption, and Violence]," paper presented at a WOLA conference, *Drogas y Democracia en Mexico: El Impacto de Narcotráfico y de las Políticas Antidrogas* [Drugs and Democracy in Mexico: The Impact of the Drug Trade and of Anti-Drug Policies], Mexico City, June 21, 2005, cited in Laurie Freeman, "State of Siege: Drug-Related Violence and Corruption in Mexico: Unintended Consequences of the War on Drugs," WOLA Special Report, June 2006; Peter Reuter and David Ronfeldt, "Quest for Integrity: The Mexican-U.S. Drug Issues in the 1980s," *Journal of Interamerican Studies and World Affairs* 34, no. 3 (Autumn 1992): 102–03; Sergio Aguayo, "Los usos, abusos, y retos de la seguridad nacional Mexicana: 1946–1990 [The Uses, Abuses, and Challenges of Mexico's National Security]," in *En busca de la seguridad pérdida: aproximaciones a la seguridad nacional Mexicana* [In Search of Lost Security: Approaches to Mexico's National Security], Sergio Aguayo and Bruce Bagley, eds. (Mexico: Singlo Venturo Editores, 1990):107–45.

By the late 1980s, all the major political parties, including the PRI, the PRD (Partido de la Revolución Democrática [Party of the Democratic Revolution]), and the PAN (Partido Acción Nacional [National Action Party]), had been accused of ties to the drug trade. By the mid-1990s Mexico's entire law enforcement apparatus was deeply penetrated and systematically corrupted by drug trafficking organizations. See, for example, Sergio Mastretta, "Tierra caliente: La cuenca cardenista [Hot Land: The Cardenas Basin]," *Nexos* 154 (October): 47–64.

32. Associated Press, "Mexico Prez Hoped to Quell Drug Violence by 2012," *New York Times,* February 27, 2009. In private, some Mexican officials give a number as high as 9,000 deaths. The vast majority of deaths have been of people either linked to the drug trade or in the police or military.

33. For details on Calderón's policy and on challenges ahead, see Vanda Felbab-Brown, "The Violent Drug Market in Mexico and Lessons from Colombia," FPS Policy Paper 12, Brookings, Foreign Policy Studies, March 2009 (www.brookings. edu/~/media/Files/rc/papers/2009/03_mexico_drug_market_felbabbrown/03_mexico_drug_market_felbabbrown.pdf [April 30, 2009]).

34. Al Qaeda here is used only as an illustration. There is no indication that al Qaeda has any distribution networks in the United States or Europe. The best available evidence suggests that it has contacts with drug traffickers operating in Pakistan and Afghanistan.

35. U.S. Department of the Treasury, *The National Money Laundering Strategy for 2003* (2003): footnote 50; Peter Reuter and Edwin M. Truman, *Chasing Dirty Money* (Washington: Peterson Institute for International Economics, 2004): 143.

36. The logistical, leadership, and training demands of such operations are far more challenging than obtaining the financing.

37. See, for example, Francisco Thoumi, *Illegal Drugs, Economy, and Society in the Andes* (John Hopkins University Press, 2003); Kevin Healy, "The Coca-Cocaine Issue in Bolivia: A Political Resource for All Seasons," in *Coca, Cocaine,*

and the Bolivian Reality, Madeline Barbara Léons and Harry Sanabria, eds. (State University of New York Press, 1997): 227–42; Eduardo A. Gamarra, "Fighting Drugs in Bolivia: United States and Bolivian Perceptions at Odds," in *Coca, Cocaine, and the Bolivian Reality,* Léons and Sanabria, eds.: 243–52; Madeline Barbara Léons, "After the Boom: Income Decline, Eradication, and Alternative Development in the Yungas," in *Coca, Cocaine, and the Bolivian Reality,* Léons and Sanabria, eds.: 139–68; Kathryn Ledebur, "Bolivia: Clear Consequences," in *Drugs and Democracy in Latin America,* Coletta A. Youngers and Eileen Rosin, eds. (Boulder, Colo.: Lynne Rienner, 2005): 143–82; and Michael Painter, "Institutional Analysis of the Chapare Regional Development Project (CRDP)," Working Paper 59 (Binghamton, N.Y.: Institute for Development Anthropology, April 1990).

38. See, for example, Thoumi, *Illegal Drugs, Economy, and Society in the Andes.*

39. For a good overview, see Ronald D. Renard, *Opium Reduction in Thailand, 1970–2000: A Thirty-Year Journey* (Bangkok: UNDCP and Silkworm Books, 2001).

40. Ibid.: 36; and UNODC, *Opium Poppy Cultivation in Southeast Asia,* December 2008: 1.

41. Pierre-Arnaud Chouvy, "Drugs and War Destabilize Thai-Myanmar Border Region," *Jane's Intelligence Review,* April 1, 2002.

42. For a discussion of a licensing system to limit illicit logging, see "Down in the Woods," *The Economist* 378 (8470), March 25, 2006: 73–75.

43. For a first-rate comparative analysis of the impact of various domestic counternarcotics policies on drug consumption, see Robert J. MacCoun and Peter Reuter, *Drug War Heresies: Learning from Other Vices, Times, and Places* (Cambridge University Press, 2001).

44. For analysis of licensing efficacy in India and Turkey, see David Mansfield, "An Analysis of Licit Opium Poppy Cultivation: India and Turkey" (www.pachouvy.org/Mansfield2001AnalysisLicitOpiumPoppyCultivation.pdf [December 12, 2005]).

45. For a detailed analysis, see Vanda Felbab-Brown, "Opium Licensing in Afghanistan: Its Desirability and Feasibility," FPS Policy Paper 1, Brookings, Foreign Policy Studies, August 2007 (www3.brookings.edu/fp/research/felbab-brown200708.pdf [August 31, 2007]).

APPENDIX A

1. Although mainly associated with the Andean region, coca has also been grown in Asia, notably in Indonesia, Japan, and Taiwan. Parts of Africa also would be suitable for its cultivation.

APPENDIX B

1. The wild jumps in estimates of Mexican marijuana cultivation during the mid-1980s illustrate the softness of the data. The estimates of net production (after eradication) by the National Narcotics Intelligence Consumers Committee (NNICC), an interagency group chaired by the Drug Enforcement Administration (DEA), rose from 4,125 metric tons in 1985 to 5,460 metric tons in 1986. However, the State Department estimates, released in the annual *International Narcotics Control Strategy Report,* showed a substantially smaller increase from a considerably different base, with production estimated at 2,700 metric tons in 1985 and 2,800 in 1986. In 1987, the State Department showed a slight decrease in net cultivation in Mexico, while the NNICC showed a one-third increase in production. The International Narcotics Matters Bureau of the State Department justified its data as follows: "The Department of State considers its country estimates more reliable because the data were derived principally from aerial surveys. There are, however, no survey data of marijuana cultivation in Mexico; the State Department relied on random reports from Mexico which were higher than the NNICC figures, which is an extrapolation of seizure data." General Accounting Office, *Control: Drug Interdiction and Related Activities along the Southwestern US Border,* fact sheet, GAO/GGD-88-124FS, Washington, September 1988: 53; and Peter Reuter, "The Organization and Measurement of the International Drug Trade," Economics of the Narcotics Industry, Conference Report, November 21–22, 1994 (www.druglibrary.org/schaffer/MISC/economic.htm [February 18, 2003]).

2. U.S. Department of State, *International Narcotics Control Strategy Report,* March 2004 (www.state.gov/p/inl/rls/nrcrpt/2003/index.htm [March 18, 2004]).

3. For critiques of the estimation method, see, for example, Reuter, "The Organization and Measurement of the International Drug Trade"; Francisco Thoumi, "The Numbers Game: Let's All Guess the Size of the Illegal Drug Industry," TNI Crime and Globalization Paper (www.tni.org/crime-docs/numbers.pdf [October 2, 2005]); C. Peter Rydell and Susan S. Everingham, *Controlling Cocaine: Supply versus Demand Programs* (Santa Monica: Rand, 1994); Washington Office on Latin America, "U.S. Wholesale and Retail Prices of Heroin" (www.wola.org/ddhr/ddhr_data_measures.htm [November 17, 2005]).

4. The lack of systematic data also bears directly on the difficulty of constructing the universe of cases of the nexus between drugs and insurgencies. Most analysts of the drug issue, in fact, complain that no systematic data exist prior to the mid-1980s. Indeed, only in 1986 did the CIA start reporting on narcotics activities around in the world in its *World Factbook.* My expectation, therefore, is that the "universe" of cases of the drug-insurgency nexus presented in Appendix A, which I constructed from various sources, is imperfect.

INDEX